Powers of the Press

For Yasmin Ali

Powers of the Press

Newspapers, Power and the Public
in Nineteenth-Century England

ALED JONES

SCOLAR PRESS

Published by
SCOLAR PRESS
Gower House
Croft Road
Aldershot
Hants GU11 3HR
England

Ashgate Publishing Company
Old Post Road
Brookfield
Vermont 05036-9704
USA

British Library Cataloguing in Publication Data

Jones, Aled
    Powers of the Press: Newspapers, Power and the Public in
    Nineteenth-Century England.
    (Nineteenth Century series)
    1. Press—England—Influence—History—19th century.
    2. Press—England—History—19th century.   3. English
    newspapers—History—19th century.   4. Mass media and public
    opinion—England—History—19th century.
    I. Title
    072

        ISBN 1–85928–132–X

Library of Congress Cataloging-in-Publication Data

Jones Aled
    Powers of the press: newspapers, power and the public in
    nineteenth-century England/Aled Jones.
        p.   cm.
    Includes bibliographical references and index.
    ISBN 1–85928–132–X
        1. English newspapers—Great Britain—History—19th century.
    2. Press and politics—Great Britain.   3. e–uk.   I. Title.
    PN5117.J66   1996
    072'.09034—dc20   95–53260
                                                                            CIP

ISBN 1 85928 132 X

Typeset in Sabon by Bournemouth Colour Press and printed in Great Britain by the University Press, Cambridge

Contents

The Nineteenth Century
General Editors' Preface

The aim of this series is to reflect, develop and extend the great burgeoning of interest in the nineteenth century that has been an inevitable feature of recent decades, as that former epoch has come more sharply into focus as a locus for our understanding, not only of the past but of the contours of our modernity. Though it is dedicated principally to the publication of original monographs and symposia in literature, history, cultural analysis, and associated fields, there will be a salient role for reprints of significant texts from, or about, the period. Our overarching policy is to address the widest scope in chronology, approach and range of concern. This, we believe, distinguishes our project from comparable ones, and means, for example, that in the relevant areas of scholarship we both recognise and cut innovatively across such parameters as those suggested by the designations 'Romantic' and 'Victorian'. We welcome new ideas, while valuing tradition. It is hoped that the world which predates yet so forcibly predicts and engages our own will emerge in parts, as a whole, and in the lively currents of debate and change that are so manifest an aspect of its intellectual, artistic and social landscape.

Vincent Newey
Joanne Shattock

University of Leicester

List of figures and tables

Preface

E.S. Dallas in 1859 evocatively described the newspapers of his time as
a 'fugitive literature'. Newspapers were cheap, flimsy, ephemeral and
often criticised for being disreputable and unreliable, yet the possibility
that they could influence the human mind and shape social behaviour
was a matter of disquiet and fascination. For much of the nineteenth
century, newspapers remained under the anxious surveillance of
governments, and the work of editors and journalists continued to be
impaired by physical difficulties in news-gathering and distribution.
Nevertheless, the image of the newspaper as a harbinger, or indeed the
active agent, of change exerted a powerful hold over the contemporary
imagination. This book explores the combination of expectation and
apprehension that greeted this new medium of communication as it
emerged from relative obscurity and rose to occupy a dominant position,
commercially at least, in the market for popular print in England. The
idea for this book crystallised at the point at which an earlier historical
study of newspaper journalism was nearing completion. It became
evident to me, in retrospect, that the newspaper was something that was
imagined and theorised, written and spoken about, as much as a thing in
itself. The contexts within which I had endeavoured to locate the
emergence of the early newspaper press – pre-eminently the 'social'
institutions of industry, commerce, politics and religion – were also texts
which required a very different kind of historical reading. In the broader
search which I subsequently undertook for other critical and self-
reflective pieces of contemporary writing on the power and influence of
journalism, I discovered that evaluations of the newspaper as a form of
communication were present in an unexpectedly wide range of private
correspondence, articles, essays, books, ballads, cartoons and records of
speeches and public discussions throughout the nineteenth century.
Newspapers, then, not only grew in numbers and circulation in this
period, but they were also embedded in the culture. The aim of this book
is to uncover some at least of that rich and complex cultural activity, and,
in so doing, to contend that the long argument over the appropriate
social roles of journalism helped to shape not only the newspaper press
itself, but also the idea of the public – its readers – in nineteenth-century
England.

Research for this study led me to printed and manuscript collections in a number of record offices and libraries, and I am grateful for the generous assistance of archivists in Newcastle upon Tyne, Leeds, Bradford, Preston, Manchester, Liverpool, Stoke-on-Trent, Birmingham, Bristol and London. I particulary wish to thank the following for their valuable advice: Mr P. Carnell, Special Collections, University of Sheffield Library; Mr Nigel A. Roche, St Bride's Printing Library, Fleet Street, London; Ms Susan Stead, Manuscripts and Rare Books, University College, London; Ms Margaret Turner, Principal Archivist with Sheffield City Council; Mr Chris J. Underwood, General Secretary of the Chartered Institute of Journalists, London; and Mr Lesley Webster of the Institute of Alcohol Studies, London. I am also grateful to the University of Birmingham for kindly permitting me to include quotations from the Chamberlain Archive. I remain deeply indebted to colleagues, too numerous to mention, from the virtual, but none the less very real, community of the Victoria Internet news-group and the Research Society for Victorian Periodicals, for their valuable references and co-operation. Thanks also to Jeremy Ali, who didn't fail me when my computer did. This book could not have been researched and written within the agreed timetable without the generous assistance of my University Department, which granted me research leave in the Spring of 1994, and the financial support of the British Academy and the Research Fund of the University of Wales, Aberystwyth. The preparation for this study led me also into less familiar literary and analytical territory, and, as always at such times, I was grateful for the counsel and companionship of Laurel Brake, John Davidson, Michael Harris, Deian Hopkin, Angela V. John, Al Rainnie and my editor, Joanne Shattock. Finally, I wish to thank Yasmin Ali, who has travelled with me through these and other fugitive literatures, and to whom this book is gratefully dedicated.

Aled Jones,
Aberystwyth, 1995

Introduction

Driven by a sudden downpour to take shelter in the doorway of an inn at Southampton docks on the evening of 8 September 1844, the social investigator Hugh Seymour Tremenheere was unexpectedly pitched into an unfamilar world. Unsure as to how he ought to conduct himself in a public house, he nervously stepped inside only to be pleasantly surprised by the 'very *respectable*' appearance of the customers. Growing tired of standing in the draughty passage, he then asked whether he could sit in the landlord's parlour until the rain had stopped. There he was joined by the landlord, his brother and their two wives, each of whom, he was astonished to learn, 'expressed themselves well . . . in their conversations with each other'. He began to feel uneasy only when the landlord's brother picked up a newspaper, the *Weekly Dispatch*, which he then read 'for some time'. When he had finished with it, and had left the room, Tremenheere ventured to ask the landlady whether many of her customers read that particular paper. 'A great many', she confirmed, 'they never ask for any other'. Asked whether she herself approved of the paper, she thought it 'a very good paper indeed'. Some moments later, Tremenheere asked the landlord the same questions, and received similar replies. Most of the customers read it, and he himself thought it 'an excellent paper'. The exasperated Tremenheere then put it to the landlord that, surely, he must realise that the *Weekly Dispatch* attacked 'Religion in every form', and sought 'to bring all the institutions of society, as at present existing, into contempt', to which the landlord retorted that 'if a man *wants to get enlightened* he had better read the *Dispatch*. It has enlightened *me*, and it is the best paper *I* know'.

The following morning, safe in his own home, Tremenheere reflected on his experience and on the meaning of his argument with the landlord. 'Now how did this man come by *his opinions*?', Tremenheere wondered. 'And how did the Southampton shopkeepers *get theirs*?' The circulation of dangerous opinions 'on Religion, and Government, & the organization of society' among '*educated* (as the term goes) *shopkeepers*, with their wives dressed in Satin, and children with the Ostrich feathers in their bonnets', he attributed above all to their uncontrolled access to cheap newspapers.[1] Opinions were transmitted from print to reader in a

---

[1] Hugh Seymour Tremenheere to Harriet Martineau, 9 Sept. 1844, Harriet Martineau Papers, Heslop Room, Birmingham University Library (BUL) MS HM902. Tremenheere

wholly arbitrary fashion, literally picked up from the tables of public houses. Yet those opinions related to 'matters of the highest moment, religious and secular, a wrong judgement on which, prevailing in even a comparatively few minds, might seriously affect the general interests'.[2] Tremenheere was alarmed not simply by the ease with which newspapers were available in public houses, but by the seriousness with which they were read and defended by their readers. This accidental and unhappy discovery on his part on that wet evening in Southampton signified for him the existence of a pervasive form of communication which, unseen by the eyes of polite society, threatened to unravel the very fabric of his world. Even among the 'respectable' portion of the public, Tremenheere conjectured, the reading of a newspaper could affect an individual's predisposition towards loyalty or sedition, and thus tip the already precarious balance between order and disorder in the society at large.

Tremenheere was not alone among his contemporaries in attempting to disentangle the threads that connected newspapers, power and public opinion. The aim of this book is to retrace his and others' attempts to understand how a new form of communication affected the society in which it took root and grew. The book does this in two ways. At one level it describes the widely divergent range of critical responses that greeted the emergence of a popular newspaper press in nineteenth-century England. By means of that 'long argument', the newspaper was repositioned from a marginal to a central place within English print culture. Not only had the newspaper been transformed into the most dynamic and profitable of all products of the printing press by the end of the century, but it had also been securely implanted into the cultural landscape as an essential reference point in the daily lives of millions of people. That was not accomplished without considerable effort or resistance. At another level, the book considers how this process shaped both the newspaper press itself and the emerging idea of a public. The participation of individuals and groups in a multitude of forms in the 'long argument' about the role of cheap newspapers in English society itself constituted a form of public activity, a process that sought in a variety of ways to press a commercial industry to the public service. That the newspaper was a political agency in the narrow sense of helping politicians to win elections was in no doubt at the time. But the newspaper was also an agent of change in a number of much broader

---

(1804–1893) had been sent to Newport, Monmouthshire, in 1840 to investigate the violence which had erupted there in November 1839, and in 1843 had been appointed a Commissioner to inquire into social conditions in Britain's mining districts, on the subject of which he published 15 reports between 1844 and 1850.

[2] Tremenheere to Martineau, 15 Sept. 1844, Harriet Martineau Papers, Heslop Room, BUL MS HM902.

senses, prominent among them being its role in disseminating information and ideas along a wide front to large populations of readers. The readership, or the self-selected segments of it to which we have access through the historical record, read and responded to the knowledge provided by the news and to the ideas that informed it. These responses in turn conditioned the ways in which journalism was organised and professionalised, and the extent to which market mechanisms were allowed to regulate an industry which until the middle decade of the nineteenth century had been subjected to rigorous legal and fiscal controls. The account that follows is not a history of English journalism. Rather, it will seek to address the ways in which newspaper reading was perceived by contemporaries both as a social practice and as a cultural problem. The Southampton innkeepers, their clientele of shopkeepers and Tremenheere himself were all enmeshed in what Michel Foucault termed the 'technologies of power', a web of discourses which defined social and personal relations. This book contends, however, that in the course of the nineteenth century the means by which the social world was represented, and thus the way in which power was exercised at all levels of the social and the personal, was believed by contemporaries to have been transformed by the coming of cheap printed news. It follows, therefore, that the manner in which news was read, reflected upon and argued about provides an important means of mapping a hitherto neglected area of the cultural history of the nineteenth century. At the very least, the fact that an innkeeper in 1844 could conceive of enlightenment as the outcome of reading a newspaper may be rendered more comprehensible were his and others' assumptions about the powers of the press to be placed within a broader contemporary critical context.

Much of the argument about the power of news journalism to influence patterns of thought and behaviour rested on the notion that the newspaper was a separate and distinct form of printed text, one whose autonomy from other forms of print was explained primarily in terms of its economy, the regularity of its production and the fragmentary nature of its content. The social meanings ascribed to newspapers by contemporaries, though diverse, were extrapolated from this underlying belief in its distinctive identity as a form of communication. In January 1859, Eneas Sweetland Dallas, a correspondent to *Blackwood's Edinburgh Magazine*, characterised newspaper journalism as a 'fugitive literature', one whose essence consisted of endless movement rather than still contemplation, and which, instead of being displayed and consumed in the libraries of polite society, lurked in such unedifying places as inns and street corners. In this sense, the cheap newspaper was unlike any other form of media, printed or otherwise. Not only was it 'the expression of public opinion and the index of contemporary history' but, in its dialectic with the public, was itself 'a great force that reacts on the life which it represents, half creating what it professes only to reflect'. Like the Parthian bowmen, newspapers shot their 'most effective arrows' as they flew, without pausing for either forethought or reflection.[3] The following month, the same journal discerned in the newspaper 'the elemental form of modern literature',[4] a view amply confirmed some 40 eventful years later by the journalist Arthur Shadwell, who confidently declared that '"The Press" is the newspaper, and nothing else'.[5] This was precisely what the French Liberal poet and politician Alphonse de Lamartine (1790–1869) had predicted in the 1840s. However constrained by fiscal and libel legislation the press may have been in his own time, he was certain that before the end of the nineteenth century newspaper journalism would 'be the whole press', and that newspapers would be mankind's book, written 'day by day, hour by hour, page by page'. The inevitable consequence of such activity would be that 'thought [would] spread abroad in the world with the rapidity of light; instantly conceived, instantly written, instantly understood'. In this wildly optimistic account of the medium, which in many respects embodies the liberal press tradition in western Europe, the newspaper was not only the most technologically advanced form of communication but was also the summation of all other, older, more 'primitive' forms of print, including the book. 'The only book possible from today', Lamartine had sweepingly announced 'is a Newspaper'. These sentiments were strongly endorsed in England from *circa* 1850 by, among others, Frederick Knight Hunt, the first major English newspaper historian.[6]

How then did it come about that, in the course of the nineteenth century, a medium considered by many, including some literary journalists, to be a fugitive ostracised by 'reflective' literature, had come to dominate, indeed to *be*, 'the Press', capitalised and with an aggressive and self-assured collective identity? This study will not dispute that technology, wealth, political connection, frequency and the vast increase in the amount of newsprint produced and distributed daily had each played their part in effecting that transformation. Rather, it will seek to demonstrate that the rise to dominance of newspapers within print

---

[3] 'Popular Literature – the Periodical Press', *Blackwood's Edinburgh Magazine*, Jan. 1859, p. 97.

[4] Ibid., Feb. 1859, p. 181.

[5] A. Shadwell, 'Proprietors and Editors', *National Review*, Mar.–Aug. 1900, p. 594.

[6] F. Knight Hunt, *The Fourth Estate: Contributions Towards a History of Newspapers, and the Liberty of the Press* (1850), p. 1. All books published in London, unless otherwise stated.

culture was also the consequence of a process of acculturation, of a society learning, often disputatiously, that mass journalism in the form of the newspaper was an essential if problematic part of a 'speeded up' society. Often, the social debate turned on rival definitions of what constituted good and bad journalistic practices, but it was also an argument about the medium itself, its intrinsic merits or demerits and its potential for social improvement or harm. This 'long argument', conducted in books, journals, newspapers, political parties and voluntary societies, orally as well as in writing, forms the basis of this study.

The fundamental problem with the cheap newspaper in the early decades of the nineteenth century was its novelty. It was universally regarded as a new and untested form of communication, and to appreciate the importance of that fact we need not only to be reminded of the freshness of the form, but also of the changing social world into which it entered. The chronology of the newspaper itself, punctuated by technological improvement, physical growth and legislative reform, should be placed firmly in the contexts of other chronologies. These include the political (principally the electoral Reform Acts of 1832, 1867 and 1884), the demographic and infrastructural (which outline the growth of urban centres connected by improved road and rail communications), and the economic and financial (which increased disposable incomes and provided new sources of investment in news-gathering and printing). News-sheets and newspapers had been in circulation in England since the early seventeenth century, but the steam-driven expansion of the press which began in the early 1800s brought with it new possibilities and dangers. John Bright could look forward in 1860 to the day, which was 'not far distant when a daily paper [would] be found in the cottage of every poor man in the country'.[7] The significance of such general dissemination of a cheap and informative news journalism lay in what it expressed about modernity. Thus Lord Palmerston, speaking at Romsey in December 1859, could praise newspapers, the information highways of his time, for their 'quantity of information, . . . talent for dissertation [and] amount of news of every kind', seeing in them 'one of the most striking proofs of the progress which the human intellect has made in the days in which we live'.[8] The impact of such expansion, moreover, was such that it had influenced

---

[7] Saunders, Otley and Co., *The Newspaper Press Census for 1860 Showing the Newspaper Population of the United Kingdom, and Its Expansion Since 1665, Including the Births and Deaths in 1860, Together with a Statistical and General Account of Its Present Politics and Position* (1860), p. 27. Speech delivered at a Reform meeting in Birmingham, 30 May 1860.

[8] *The Times*, 22 Dec. 1859.

'every wheel in the complicated machinery of national life'.[9] It was clear to many contemporary observers that an enormous shift had occurred in the organisation and representation of social knowledge, and that a new information order had come into being which, to be rendered governable, needed to be understood. The debate about newspapers thus generated speculations that traversed the nascent disciplines of history, politics, sociology and psychology as well as engaging with the older discourses of religious and literary scholarship, and moral philosophy.

The approach adopted in this book is deeply indebted to three currents within the contemporary study of culture and communication. The first debt is to those historical studies of print culture, from Roger Chartier's work on reading practices in early modern France to David Vincent's study of literacy in the popular culture of modern England, which have explored new ways of historicising printed texts. The second is to that expanding body of research into the economic, political and literary history of the nineteenth-century newspaper, which has done so much to advance our understanding of journalism as a social practice. And the third is to twentieth-century media sociology, which has continued to address the problem of the newspaper's ideal and actual social roles. But while media sociology has provided historians with the grounds upon which to mount fresh and challenging forms of cultural criticism, its own historical myopia has all too often vitiated their utility.[10] For while studies of the impact of new forms of communications on human societies increased dramatically on both sides of the Atlantic after the end of the First World War, in a number of important respects the halting, often unsophisticated, endeavours of nineteenth-century critics to make sense of the social possibilities of cheap newspapers were responsible for laying down the conceptual foundations for much of twentieth-century media theory and practice. Historical research, as James Curran has perceptively observed, is 'the neglected grandparent of media studies'.[11] One of the objectives of this book is to aid the rehabilitation of that overlooked grandparent by giving the contemporary study of media theory a gentle but necessary nudge backwards in time.[12]

---

[9] *Dial*, 11 May 1860.

[10] For example, Denis McQuail, in an otherwise thoughtful and lucid article, locates 'the first phase' of the study of the effects of mass communication in the period 'from the turn of the [twentieth] century to the late nineteen thirties', Denis McQuail, 'The Influence and Effects of Mass Media', in J. Curran, M. Gurevitch and J. Woolacott (eds), *Mass Communication and Society* (1977), p. 72.

[11] James Curran, 'Rethinking the media as a public sphere', in Peter Dahlgren and Colin Sparks, *Communication and Citizenship* (1993), p. 27.

[12] Renewed interest in the 'neglected grandparent' is leading to the publication of

The historian Roger Chartier has argued, in relation to the early impact of print in sixteenth- and seventeenth-century France, that 'representations of the social world themselves are the constituents of social reality'.[13] Critics of newspapers in nineteenth-century England would have accepted with few reservations the validity of that view. It was precisely because so many of them held the opinion that cheap newspapers, as new forms of print communication, were capable of exerting a material, even a transforming influence on social relations that the emergence of the cheap news press became an issue of such grave concern, and the subject of so much polemic and debate, in both polite and popular culture. In the nineteenth century, however, it was not the novelty of the newspaper alone that caused anxiety, but the rapid extension of its availability to readers. Thanks to improvements in roads and the growth of railways, the newspaper market extended geographically across urban and, increasingly, rural areas of Britain. Price reductions and improvements in literacy also ensured that newspapers percolated through the middle and lower-middle classes to reach the vast and previously untapped market of the working class. The initial process of constructing 'mass' cultural forms may be discerned in the eighteenth century, when Alexander Pope, for example, by attacking the 'low' taste of the 'Political Newspaper',[14] prefigured the radical scepticism of those who saw in nineteenth-century technological change little more than the submersion of the individual into a 'mass society' dominated and directed by a 'mass media'.[15] The exponential growth of newspaper titles and circulations between the Napoleonic and the First

---

important new work on media history in a number of centres. For a notable recent example, see Julio Montero Díaz, *La Aventura Revolucionaria de un Diario Conservador. Prensa y partidos políticos en la primera España democrática (1868–1874)* (Madrid, 1994). The prologue by Jesús Timoteo Álvarez neatly situates the history of Spanish newspaper journalism within both the Spanish and the Annales schools of historiography, ibid., pp. 11–14.

[13] Roger Chartier, 'Intellectual History or Sociocultural History? The French Trajectories', in Dominic LaCara and Steven L. Kaplan (eds), *Modern European Intellectual History: Reappraisals and New Perspectives* (Ithaca, NY, 1982), p. 30. See also Roger Chartier, 'Texts, Printing, Readings', in Lynn Hunt (ed.), *The New Cultural History* (University of California, 1989), pp. 154–75. For an exemplary explication of the reading of printed *placards* in late sixteenth- and early seventeenth-century France, see Christian Jouhaud, 'Readabilty and Persuasion: Political Handbills', in Roger Chartier *The Culture of Print. Power and the Uses of Print in Early Modern Europe* (Princeton, NJ, 1989), trans. Lydia G. Cochrane, pp. 235–60.

[14] Alexander Pope, *The Dunciad* (1953 edn), book III, 1, p. 16.

[15] 'If one takes the term "mass" media to mean marketable cultural goods produced for a substantial buying public, eighteenth-century England is the first period in history where it can meaningfully be applied', Leo Lowenthal and Marjorie Fiske, 'Reaction to Mass Media Growth in 18th-Century England', *Journalism Quarterly*, Fall 1956, p. 442.

World Wars, which realised, or, as some would no doubt have argued, exceeded, some of the more pessimistic predictions of the eighteenth century, has been described and explained from a number of perspectives by twentieth-century historians including Arthur Aspinall, Joel H. Wiener, Patricia Hollis, Alan J. Lee, Stephen Koss, Virginia Berridge, Lucy Brown and James Curran. This study of contemporary responses to the extension of newspapers in nineteenth-century England is heavily reliant both on their empirical research and their insights into the place occupied by journalism in that century's literature and society.

Finally, contemporary media sociology has raised in sharp relief the problem of the media's manipulation of its audience, and, reciprocally, the uses made of the media by that same audience. The capacity of media, and in particular of television, to construct 'real' environments and to influence even those who are not directly subjected to their messages, has long preoccupied cultural critics from Theodor Adorno to Raymond Williams.[16] But, as Tom Burns has reminded us, the controversy generated by the notion that television is sufficiently powerful to determine public opinion rests on 'a set of beliefs much older than broadcasting'.[17] The distinctive paradigms of de Tocqueville and Marx are normally cited as representations of the twin polarities of nineteenth-century media theory, the former ascribing to the newspaper the liberating role of being the essential facilitator of representative democracy, while the latter, in contrast, warned of its tendency towards commodification and of its subservience to the ideological needs of capital. But, in general, speculation on the social influence of the cheap press during the nineteenth century was too complicated, contradictory and intuitively inventive to be reduced to these two paradigms alone, however formative their influences may undoubtedly have been upon twentieth-century media theory.

The book is structured around a series of related studies of the diverse ways in which cheap newspapers, as new forms of communication, were understood and received. One addresses the identity within print culture that was invented specifically for and by the newspaper. Another describes the efforts of nineteenth-century scholarship, and the increasingly professionalised occupation of news journalism itself, to impose order upon an inherently disorganised new phenomenon, and to explain what were its possibilities and limitations. A third focuses on the ways in which moral reformers and political activists sought to rationalise their attempts to harness the dynamism of the commercial

---

[16] See Kurt Lang and G.E. Lang, *Politics and Television* (1968), p. 305.

[17] Tom Burns, 'The Organization of Public Opinion', in J. Curran, M. Gurevitch and J. Woollacott, *Mass Communication and Society* (1977), pp. 2–3.

press for their own defined purposes. The final section, which owes a particular debt to the instrumental approach to media research adopted by Elihu Katz, addresses not so much the question of what newspapers did to readers, as what readers did with newspapers.[18] News supplied by journalists evidently fed into public discussion, but newspapers were themselves also the subjects of discussion. Riven by tensions between the memory of persecution and the desire for respectability, between a yearning for 'liberty' and a pious regard for 'responsibility', and caught between the moral and commercial implications of their adherence to concepts of tradition and modernity, the nineteenth-century newspaper was a fascinating but elusive topic for contemporary comment, not only in the books, journals and salons of polite society but, largely as a consequence of advances in popular literacy, also in such institutions as reading rooms, debating clubs and public houses. As the rainsoaked Tremenheere realised to his dismay in 1844, the newspaper was a fugitive only from those who policed the boundaries of a particular definition of high literature. While those boundaries were certainly not eradicated during the ensuing 50 years, they were substantially redrawn. That particular shift within print culture, which enabled the fugitive newspaper to enter and to dominate the print market, was the outcome of an extended process of cultural negotiation, the principal outlines of which the following chapters will seek to uncover.

---

[18] See especially Elihu Katz, 'Mass Communications Research and the Study of Popular Culture', *Studies in Public Communication*, vol. 2, 1959.

CHAPTER ONE

The liberty of the press

The press has been, for the most part, the unwilling slave of error, and the instruments of kings, priests, aristocrats, and imbeciles, in carrying out their irrational, ambitious, uncivilised, and uncivilising designs.

The Compositors' Chronicle, 1 Oct. 1842, p. 213.

The expansion of the press, as part of the process which Raymond Williams identified as the cultural 'long revolution', was not universally agreed to be one of its natural or legal liberties. The liberty of the press had been contested territory since the sixteenth century, and the meaning of press freedom specifically as applied to newspapers was an issue of particular concern to government, printers, journalists and sections of the reading public. The first attempt to use legislation to define news as a taxable commodity was made in 1819, and was further amended by Act of Parliament in 1836, both pieces of legislation, coincidentally, being framed during periods of severe social and political unrest. This chapter considers a range of critical responses to the changing framework of state regulation of the newspaper press by focusing on two aspects of the problem of press freedom as they were manifested before and during the nineteenth century. First, it is important to recall that the struggle waged against restrictive legislation in the first half of the nineteenth century was rooted in much older traditions, and definitions, of press freedom, whose vocabulary and terms of reference were carried over into the language of politics and newspaper journalism after 1815. Secondly, a necessarily abbreviated outline of the development of such concepts of press freedom will provide the background for an account of the emergence of a new regulatory framework, and a fresh political policy, that culminated in the repeal of the Advertisement Duty in 1853, the Stamp Duty in 1855 and the Paper Duty in 1861.

Inherited narratives

The identification of a free press with just government, and of censorship with tyranny, has, since the sixteenth century, lain close to the core of political thinking in England as elsewhere. The Leveller petition to

Parliament of September 1648, submitted in protest against Lord Fairfax's Warrant for suppressing unlicensed books and pamphlets, characteristically expressed what would become the widely held view that such restrictions on the press would 'usher in a tyrannie; mens mouths being to be kept from making noise, whilst they are robd of their liberties'. The suppression of information under the monarchy, which had deliberately kept the people ignorant of the 'truth', was 'fitted only to serve the unjust ends of Tyrants and Oppressers, whereby the Nation was enslaved . . . '.[1] During the Restoration, Charles Blount's *Reasons humbly offered for the liberty of unlicensed printing* of 1693 signalled the continuation of the agitation that led to the Press Licensing Act, and with it the *imprimatur*, the license to print, being allowed to lapse in 1695.[2] A century later, the liberty of the press, closely linked to the issues of the freedom of speech and of association, remained the subject of urgent public debate. The ban on the reporting of parliamentary affairs was successfully defied by journalists in 1771, and the activities of such metropolitan groups as The Friends of the Freedom of the Press maintained the impetus for further change during the dangerous years of the French Wars.[3] Outside London, too, the issue was held to be an important one, and a meeting of artisans in Warrington in November 1792, for example, drew up a ten-point reform programme that extolled the value of good morals and citizenship, and which demanded that 'the liberty of the press ought to be held involable (*sic*) in all nations'.[4] But the close association between newspapers and government, established principally through the granting of state subsidies to favoured titles, continued to disturb the advocates of a free press. William Godwin in November 1795 considered that the attacks made upon him and other 'republicans and levellers' by the 'treasury prints', most notoriously the *Sun* and the *True Briton*, founded in October 1792 with the support of George Rose, Secretary to the Treasury, amounted to a form of Crown prosecution.[5] The press, which Godwin described as 'that great engine

---

[1] *To the Commons. The Petition of Firm Friends of the Parliament, Presenters of the Late Large Petition of 11 September, 1648*, in *The Thomason Tracts*, British Library MS 669, f. 13, (75) [NB listed as (74) in Catalogue].

[2] Charles Blount, *A Just Vindication of Learning and of the Liberties of the Press, by Philopatris* (1693); see also Daniel Defoe, *An essay on the Regulation of the Press* (1704), and *A Vindication of the Press* (1718).

[3] See P.D.G. Thomas, 'John Wilkes and the Freedom of the Press', *Bulletin of the Institute of Historical Research*, 33 (1969), and Jeremy Black, *The English Press in the Eighteenth Century* (1987).

[4] *Minutes of a Meeting of Mechanics and other Inhabitants of Warrington and Its Vicinity, Held on Saturday Nov. 3rd 1792*, Reeves MS 942.073.A.11, 1792–93, Manchester City Library.

[5] William Godwin, *Considerations on Lord Grenville's and Mr Pitt's Bill, Concerning*

for raising men to the dignity of gods'[6] was also, as he knew to his cost, a mechanism of repression. Tom Paine agreed. Writing in the *American Citizen* in October 1806, Paine warned that in America the concept of the liberty of the press had been grievously misunderstood. It was, in Paine's corrective, emphatically not a slogan which sought special privileges for printers. Rather, it referred to a specific historical moment, the removal in 1695 of the *imprimatur* from British law, which established for printing freedom from prior restraint. For Paine, it was the public, not printers or journalists, who were to be the judges of whether or not the content of a periodical was socially acceptable.[7] Print for him was essentially a publicly accessible and accountable medium of communication, not a tool under the monopolistic control of government, journalists or printers.

The connection between the freedom of the press and civil liberty, established in the seventeenth and eighteenth centuries, had by the turn of the nineteenth century become a firmly rooted tradition in English political culture. The producers of cheap newspapers, whether they regarded themselves primarily as forces of radical opposition, or as pioneers of a new commercial medium, or both, not unjustly regarded themselves as the most direct heirs to that tradition. The *Sunday Times*, for example, carried beneath its title a masthead that crystallised the belief that 'The LIBERTY OF THE PRESS is the PALLADIUM of all the Civil, Political and RELIGIOUS RIGHTS of an ENGLISHMAN'.[8] It would be a mistake to dismiss such remarks purely as expressions of pious self-regard on the part of journalists and printers. The theory that a press free from direct state control was the foundation on which constitutional rights were based, and from which stemmed the associated and much abused notion of the 'fourth estate', was a powerful organising principle, to which a history of conflict between journalists and the legislature had provided added impetus. In particular, the prosecution of John Wilkes following the publication of the forty-fifth number of the *North Briton* on 23 April 1763, and the trials of Robert Hardy and Horne Tooke in 1794, of William Cobbett and Henry Hunt in the years between 1804 and 1811, and of Watson and Hone in 1817, retained a powerful legitimating role within journalism throughout the

---

Reasonable and Seditious Practices and Unlawful Assemblies, by a Lover of Order (1795), repr. in M. Philp (ed.), *Political and Philosophical Writings of William Godwin*, vol. 2 (1993), p. 136.

   [6] Ibid., p. 155.

   [7] Thomas Paine, 'The Liberty of the Press', *American Citizen*, 20 Oct. 1806, repr. in Moncure Daniel Conway (ed.), *The Writings of Thomas Paine*, vol. 4 (New York, 1969), p. 475.

   [8] *Sunday Times*, 20 Oct. 1822.

nineteenth century.[9] However, two landmark judgements in the courts helped reverse this process. In 1829, the Duke of Wellington failed to prosecute the *Morning Journal* for libel following the paper's attacks upon him for consenting to Catholic Emancipation. Although the King was found to have been libelled, the jury recommended leniency amidst strong cross-party disapproval of Wellington's action.[10] Two years later, Cobbett was similarly acquitted of a libel charge against government ministers, and was instead prosecuted on the lesser offence of incitement. As a result of these judgements, Erskine May argued that the freedom of the press in Britain had been assured, and that journalists had won the 'utmost latitude of criticism and invective' in their treatment of public figures and political affairs.[11] Demands for press freedom, however, did not end there, and the continuation of what were regarded to be forms of prior restraint imposed by taxation rather than by prosecutions for libel fuelled much of the campaign for a free newspaper press after 1831.

But the inherited narrative of press freedom, which had been largely responsible for propelling so many early nineteenth-century newspaper publishers onto a collision course with the law, was not simply accepted as an indisputable truth. It was also interpreted, elaborated upon, re-fashioned, even rejected by nineteenth-century journalists and critics. The role of printers in the production of newspapers was a case in point. Edward Baines, founder of the *Leeds Mercury*, fully understood the duality of his trade when in *circa* 1820 he defined newspaper journalism as a mechanical industry tied to a moral purpose. For the joint sway of 'Chaos & old Night' to be ended, Baines argued, it was not only state interference that needed to be challenged. All those who opposed mechanical improvements in newspaper publishing were also guilty of '[daring] to limit knowledge to the classes which at present enjoy it'.[12] The power of printers, as well as that of governments, increasingly came to be regarded by journalists as a danger to press freedom. The growth of printers' trade unions, which were charged with being 'as violently opposed to any change as the most conservative of landowners were to

---

[9] A series of articles on state prosecutions of journalists and printers, including Wilkes, was published in *Sell's Directory of the World's Press* in the 1880s.

[10] R. Fox Bourne, 'London Newspapers', *Progress of British Newspapers in the Nineteenth Century, Illustrated* (1900), p. 12.

[11] Sir Thomas Erskine May, *The Constitutional History of England Since the Accession of George the Third* (1861), p. 95.

[12] Edward Baines, 'On the Origin and History of Printing', draft copy, n.d. (*c.* 1820), Leeds Archives MS 89, pp. 3, 77–81. Intended as a lecture for the Leeds Philosophical and Literary Society, of which Baines Jr. was a founding member in 1819, no report of it being delivered is recorded in the minutes of the Society. Baines was quoting Milton: 'the universal host up sent/A shout that tore hell's concave, and beyond/Frighted the reign of Chaos and old Night', John Milton, *Paradise Lost*, book 1, (NY, 1968 edn), p. 26.

the repeal of the Corn Laws',[13] was a cause of particular concern. When John Walter introduced steam machinery into the print offices of *The Times* on 29 November 1814, he did so secretly and under cover of darkness, thus ensuring a *fait accompli* to which the printers were reluctantly obliged to submit. But elsewhere, the autonomy of printers as a skilled and self-regulating segment of the labour market was not to be so easily undermined. The world of the early nineteenth-century printer, working a trade dominated by the tramping artisan, was necessarily close and interdependent.[14] In 1842, for example, the *Bristol Gazette* chapel of the Bristol Typographical Society voted to ban the use of anti-Semitic language at the workplace following a complaint made by one of its members.[15] Such instances of internal discipline and solidarity helped printers to survive the restructuring of the industry that followed the introduction of Applegarth's cylinder machine, exhibited as state-of-the-art printing technology at the Great Exhibition of 1851, the new Hoe machine that followed it, which increased production from 5,000 to 20,000 copies per hour with fewer compositors, and further developments in reproducible metal facsimile stereotyping.[16] Printers also established for themselves an effective lobbying system, principally in the 1840s and 1850s by means of such publications as the *Compositors' Chronicle*, the *Typographical Gazette* and the *Typographical Circular*. These represented printers as a group that had developed its own discourses of press freedom. In an article praising the 'moral engine' of the printing press, which they alone were able to drive, a printer attributed the outbreak of the French revolution of 1830 to 'the forcible entry of the police into the printing-offices, the presses in which they rendered unfit for use'. Any actions that interfered with the liberty of the printers to use their presses in their own ways, the *Compositors' Chronicle* warned in 1842, could lead to similar scenes of 'bloodshed and horror',[17] a threat which for Baines and other newspaper owners and editors was a challenge to, rather than a reinforcement of, their notions of what comprised the liberty of the press. The narrative of press freedom was thus complicated by the question of who, within as well as outside the press, should have the greater control over its future shape.

---

[13] *Meliora*, vol. 5, no. 19, 1863, p. 216.

[14] For a later insight into printers' attitudes and work practices, see J.W. Rounsfell, *On the Road. Journeys of a Tramping Printer*, by Andrew Whitehead (ed.), (Horsham, 1982).

[15] Minutes, Bristol Typographical Society, 25 Sept. 1842, Bristol R.O. 34463/66.

[16] See articles written in opposition to the 'much-dreaded novelty' of the composing machine, *Compositors' Chronicle*, 1 Feb. 1842, p. 141.

[17] Ibid., 1 Nov. 1841, p. 118. Some printers opposed the repeal of the Stamp Duty in 1855 due to fears that wages would be cut by the 'influx of small capitalists as will flood the market with new hands', *Typographical Circular*, 2 Apr. 1855, p. 97.

The proliferation of different types of periodical publication also led contemporaries to question the relevance of the traditional notion of the liberty of the press. What, it was asked, *was* 'the press' in this new industrialised market-place? Even the newspaper itself seemed to evade all rational attempts at definition. In 1896, Sir Hugh Gilzean-Reid and P.J. Macdonell dated 'the modern press' from the joint occurrence in 1861 of the removal of the paper duty and the outbreak of the American Civil War, but conceded that the many-sidedness of the newspaper rendered it a most difficult commodity to describe with any degree of precision. What possible connection, the authors speculated, linked such titles as the *Licensed Victuallers' Mirror* with the *Spectator*, or the *Daily Chronicle* with the *Sporting Times* ? Yet , 'all these discordant elements make up THE PRESS, and to the careful inquirer certain things will be found common to all'.[18] It is, perhaps, significant, that nowhere in their survey do they suggest what those 'certain things' were. Furthermore, each of the newspaper historians, whose work will be considered in greater detail in a later chapter, proffered different definitions of what a newspaper actually was. Knight Hunt, for example, was satisfied with a broad definition of material published at fixed intervals and sequentially numbered, whereas Alexander Andrews included 'newes' books and ballads within his definition of newspaper journalism. In France, Eugene Hatin wrote only of 'The Periodical Press',[19] whilst in the United States, Horace Greely included anything printed as often as once a week, or had 'the appearance of a newspaper'. Exasperated, Greely eventually left it to the postmaster to decide what was and was not a newspaper by defining it as any publication that was subject to the newspaper rate of postage. British law was equally imprecise. In 1819, 60 George III had for the first time distinguished 'public news' as a category of text quite distinct from material that was 'newly published', and introduced also the classification of news commentary as a taxable item. But apart from the attempt to define news, for the purposes of controlling its flow, the 1819 Act left the law in a state of considerable confusion.[20] Royal assent was given to 6 & 7 William IV, c. 76, on 13 August 1836, which muddied the

---

[18] Sir Hugh Gilzean-Reid and P.J. Macdonell, 'The Press', in John Samuelson (ed.), *The Civilisation of Our Day. A Series of Original Essays on Some of Its More Important Phases at the Close of the Nineteenth Century, by Expert Writers* (1896), p. 276.

[19] Eugene Hatin, *Histoire du Journal en France* (Paris, 1846), and *Bibliographie historique et critique de la presse periodique Francaise* (Paris, 1866).

[20] 60 Geo. III., c. 9, in force from 1819 until 1836, had defined a newspaper thus: 'All pamphlets and papers containing any public news, intelligence, or occurrences, or any remarks or observations thereon, or upon any matters in church and state, printed in any part of the United Kingdom for sale, and published periodically, or in parts and numbers, at intervals not exceeding twenty-six days between the publication of any two such

waters even further. By defining a newspaper as 'any paper containing news, intelligence or occurrences, printed in any part of the United Kingdom . . . weekly or oftener',[21] it effectively empowered the Inland Revenue alone to judge which publications should and should not be included under this rubric.

In addition to its ill-defined character, the transience of the newspaper also presented difficulties for those who sought in it the promise of the free press. Recalling the origins of the *Bradford Observer* 50 years after its founding in February 1834, the editor noted that

> newspapers were so modern an invention that few of them can . . . impress us, even if they were permanent like books, instead of fleeting into oblivion every twenty-four hours. . . . Each day's issue abolishes and effaces its predecessor . . . the news ceases to be news when the succeeding section of events gets into print; the newspaper of yesterday has only the title by courtesy; and *the* newspaper is to-day's. Few readers keep a newspaper file; fewer can be concerned in the continuous individuality of a journal, when it has one; and to the vast majority the continuity implied in the title is an abstraction – a title and nothing more.[22]

Yet it was increasingly clear that the growth of the newspaper press, in terms of numbers of titles, aggregate circulations, advertising revenues, the widening geographical area of the market and its apparent capacity to impose its will on society, rendered it one of the more startling cultural phenomena of the Victorian period. Returning to the conflicts of the 1640s in search of an albeit shaky historical analogy, a commentator in 1857 remarked that 'The Press is to us what the militia was to Charles I. If we were to lose all our other liberties, it would ultimately bring them all back again'.[23] That faith in the redeeming powers of the industrialised newspaper press was echoed a decade later by 'An Old Journalist', who in 1867 perfectly caught the prevailing mood of mid-Victorian optimism:

> The newspaper press has attained its present wonderful position within the last twenty years. Next to the rapid increase of population, wealth, and intelligence, invention of machinery, railway communication, colonisation, and the removal of fiscal

---

pamphlets or papers, parts or numbers, where any such pamphlets or papers, parts or numbers respectively shall not exceed two sheets, and shall be published for sale for a less sum than sixpence, exclusive of the duty by this Act enforced thereon, shall be deemed and taken to be newspapers'.

[21] *The Newspaper Press. The Press Organ: A Medium of Intercommunication Between All Parties Associated with Newspapers and a Record of Journalistic Lore*, 1 July 1867, p. 145 (henceforth *Newspaper Press*). For a full text of this Act, see C.D Collett, *History of the Taxes on Knowledge. Their Origin and Repeal* (1896), pp. 225–26.

[22] *Fifty Years Ago, Being Some Account of the Jubilee of the 'Bradford Observer'*, Feb 6th, 1884, West Yorkshire Archive Service (WYAS), Bradford, MS 9D77/47, p. 1.

[23] A Distinguished Writer, *The Press and the Public Service* (1857), p. 4.

restrictions, I may say running parallel with these things, the main cause of its power having so rapidly grown is, that it has itself aimed at a higher and more exalted purpose, which has added the establishment of principles to the diffusion of intelligence. As a gossip it was interesting *to our grandsires*, but as an enunciator of enlarged views of morality and civilisation, it is instructive *to us*. It has changed its character entirely; it no longer waits to receive the reflection of public opinion, but gives the impress to it; and, speaking generally, it has become the monitor rather than the representative of the people.[24]

Thus by the middle of the Victorian period, the democratisation of knowledge through the liberty of the press had, for more than two centuries, been a deeply embedded element, principally if not solely, in the more liberal and oppositional aspects of English political culture. Moreover, theories regarding the ideological possibilities of the printing machine were perfectly attuned to a society increasingly fascinated by both mechanical invention and moral and political reform. But from the beginning of our period, there existed more complex, even contradictory, means of understanding the ways in which the press in general operated on society. For alongside the optimistic notion that the free press was a prerequisite of political freedom ran a series of less comforting arguments. In 1807 William Cobbett, himself an innovative and successful journalist, had warned that the power of the press, as then configured, led not to political emancipation but to subjection. Most insidiously of all, Cobbett sensed that the very notion of the liberty of the press was being used to mask a new form of repression.

If there ever was in the world a thing completely perverted from its original design and tendency, it is the press of England; which instead of enlightening does, as far as it has any power, keep the people in ignorance; which, instead of cherishing notions of liberty, tends to the making of the people slaves; and which instead of being their guardian, is the most efficient instrument in the hands of all those who oppress, or who wish to oppress them . . . . It is by the semblance of freedom that men are most effectually enslaved. [25]

James Routledge was later to describe Cobbett as 'standing alone . . . virtually a Fifth Estate in the Realm',[26] but his belief that the press possessed a dangerous as well as a potentially liberating power was to be echoed by other radicals. G.W.M. Reynolds, for instance, was equally cynical in 1872 when he announced that 'the newspaper Press is the

---

[24] *Newspaper Press*, 1 Jan. 1867, p. 26.

[25] *The Weekly Political Register*, 11 Apr. 1807.

[26] James Routledge, *Chapters on the History of Popular Progress, Chiefly in Relation to The Freedom of the Press and Trial by Jury 1660–1820, With an Application to Later Years* (1876), p. 511.

press of royalty and aristocracy, ready to lie and libel through thick and thin in order to maintain the supremacy of those it serves' and called its conductors 'one-eyed partisans'.[27] James Mill agreed, remarking that 'the liberty of the press *does not exist*, nor ever did exist in England, but by connivance', before qualifying his criticism, via a reading of Burke's *Thoughts on the Cause of the Present Discontents* and Hume's *Essays*, by attributing the stability of the Protestant states of northern Europe to the freedoms enjoyed by the press in those countries. France, he noted with some disdain, was the exception, where 'it was not the abuse of a *free* press which was witnessed during the French revolution; it was an abuse of an enslaved press'.[28] In 1857, a review of a recent survey of British newspapers was contemptuous of the commonplace eulogies to the newspaper press. Descriptions of newspapers as a 'grand institution', the 'great sentinel of the state' or 'the grand detector of public imposture', were manifestations of 'a pompous theory' which wrongly placed the press at 'the centre of England's might and morality'. Newspapers were not, and could not be, the 'magic centre' around which the values of civilised society might cluster. 'The unity which was to have shed its rays from this centre, and the influence which was thence to have directed our national destiny' was a delusion, the real influence of the press being to 'scatter discordant sentiments' rather than to unify the public mind. Particular venom was directed against 'the insects of literature . . . the ephemeral prints swarming in the sunshine of the "liberty of the Press" boasted of in England'. These '"things" called papers, were bred to grow up and pester society, flitting about for the time with a borrowed brilliancy, and cased like the beetle in the brittle armour of a grub capable of depositing a poison, insidious and fatal'.[29] James Routledge, too, in 1876, was insistent that the freedom of the press involved the responsibilty of the press. Freedom, if it was to have any meaning, should involve freedom from political party and from advertisers 'who pay for place in one column of a paper that they may have improper and misleading support in another'. All too often, Routledge argued, the liberty of the press was merely a freedom 'to hold

---

[27] *Reynolds's Newspaper*, 1 Apr. 1872, p. 98.

[28] James Mill, 'Liberty of the Press', *Edinburgh Review*, May 1811, p. 98, a review of Emmanuel Ralph's *Memoires de Candide*. Also p. 118 for Mill's observations on Edmund Burke, 'who, though his lights were not very steady, saw by glances a great way into the structure and play of the machine of society, has well described those turbulent spirits who, by means of the press, or by any other means, are in danger of becoming the authors of mischief in a revolution'. See Edmund Burke, *Thoughts on the Present Discontents, and Speeches*, (1886 edn), a pamphlet began in *c*. May 1769 and published in 1770, directed primarily against Court influence in politics.

[29] *The Newspaper Press Reviewed, by a Quarterly Reviewer* (1857), pp. 5–8.

a chastising rod over the heads of peaceful and retiring people'.[30]

Thus, even at the height of its period of 'liberation', the much proclaimed 'golden age' of the popular press between the 1850s and the 1880s, discordant voices continued to be heard from a range of political and cultural positions. These provide evidence of a number of alternative readings of the Victorian notion of the liberty of the press. The more hegemonic tended to confirm the centrality of the press in the liberal transformation of society, but others considered the social influence of the ever-expanding press with a more sceptical and critical eye. The tensions between these perspectives, and the social anxieties which each of them in their different ways articulated, provided the necessary contexts within which theories were devised to explain the influences exerted by newspapers on individual readers and on society at large.

State regulation and its opponents

As was noted earlier, state regulation of the press continued long after the ending of the Gagging Act in 1695, and the state prosecutions of the eighteenth and early nineteenth centuries. Emergency legislation passed during the Napoleonic Wars, and continued by other means by the Six Acts of 1819, had increased taxation on newspapers to four pence per copy. The resulting torrent of unstamped publications, and the political campaign to remove taxation on newspapers, seriously questioned the state's right and capacity to control the popular press by fiscal means and thereby created a particular form of radical politics.[31] Moreover, because they did so at a time of acute social unrest, they helped place demands for far-reaching reform on a public agenda. In the early 1830s, forces were concentrated on the single issue of the repeal of the newspaper stamp in part because it was expected that victory would open the way for parliamentary reform and the repeal of the Corn Laws. The symbolic and political consequences of a 'shackled' press, on the other hand, were believed by some to further deepen social conflict. One writer in January 1831 went so far as to argue that

---

[30] Routledge, *History of Popular Progress*, p. 525.

[31] Excellent accounts of these developments may be found in Joel H. Weiner, *The War of the Unstamped; a History of the Movement to Repeal the British Newspaper Tax, 1830–36* (Ithaca, NY, 1969); Joel H. Wiener, *Radicalism and Freethought in Nineteenth-Century Britain: the Life of Richard Carlile* (Westport, 1983); E.A. Royle, *The Infidel Tradition: from Paine to Bradlaugh* (1976); and Patricia L. Hollis, *The Pauper Press: a Study in Working-Class Radicalism of the 1830s* (1970). For an annotated list of unstamped papers, see Joel H. Wiener, *A Descriptive Finding List of Unstamped British Periodicals, 1830–1836* (1970).

had there been no stamps on newspapers, no obstruction to the free use of the press, there would have been no riotous assemblages of husbandry labourers, no destruction of agricultural machines, no burnings, no expensive proceedings, no trials, no transportations, no hangings, and consequently none of the terrible evils which ignorance and the administration of the law have occasioned. I consider these as the forerunners of others . . . I am by no means sanguine that any measures which can be adopted will prevent a revolution; but of this I am certain, that every man who has property to be injured, and a life to lose, is bound to do all he can to avert it; and sure I am, that if it can be averted, a free press must be the main instrument to be used.[32]

Had the press been free of taxation, the argument ran, socially useful knowledge would have percolated through 'the schools, the reading clubs, the local libraries', tending to reduce passions and cultivate a more orderly spirit of opposition. The reason why taxation had not been removed, however, was to be found in the connection which property owners had made between 'the perpetuation of ignorance' and 'the perpetuation of power, of power not only in the hands of those who governed, but of every rich man over his domestics and his neighbours'.[33] The freedom of the press was thus regarded not only as the essential safeguard of all constitutional freedoms, but also of the equitable distribution of power at the level of the estate, the parish and the home. The potential social reach of the demand for the repeal of newspaper taxation was evidently great, but arguably the means by which it was achieved was not an analysis, but a slogan. The succinct and brilliantly evocative description of newspaper duties as 'taxes on knowledge' placed the defenders of the 1819 and 1836 Acts at a rhetorical disadvantage. By imposing their own terms on the debate in this way, radical journalists were using the power *of* their medium to extract from government greater freedoms *for* their medium. The tactic of designating newspaper taxes as 'taxes on knowledge', which undermined 'the liberty of the press' and prevented the freedom to publicise, was itself a devastatingly effective publicity device.

The public argument against newspaper taxation in the early 1830s took a number of forms. Some, such as Bulwer Lytton, had sought to argue in 1831 that parliamentary reform would be flawed and incomplete unless further legislation were framed that would challenge 'the present monopoly of the five or six newspapers, which now concentrate the power of the press'. 'Why exchange an oligarchy of

---

[32] *A Letter to the Minister of State Respecting Taxes on Knowledge* (29 Jan. 1831), p. 3–4.

[33] Ibid., p. 5.

boroughs' he asked in the Commons, 'for an oligarchy of journals?'.[34] Others were more concerned with challenging the Treasury argument that repeal·would seriously reduce its revenue.[35] Underlying both, however, was the calculation that, given a free choice of titles in a free market-place, most people would reject the bad and adopt the good. 'Repeal the tax' M.D. Hill MP had argued in 1834, 'and you will find that sound political journals will soon reduce the sale of all others to insignificance'.[36] Despite the risks, the market was seen as the only reliable arbiter of public taste. In that respect, paradoxically, the unstamped papers had in the opinion of Charles Knight been legally wrong, but commercially right, a conclusion which their stimulation of a 'desire amongst the mass of the people for the species of knowledge which a newspaper supplies' had amply justified.[37]

The passing of 6 & 7 William IV in 1836, which reduced the four pence tax imposed in 1819 to one penny per copy, brought one phase of the conflict to an end as repeal activists were drawn into the Anti-Corn Law League or the Chartist associations. It was not until 1848, at a meeting of the People's Charter Union held at Farringdon Hall in London on 10 April, immediately after the Chartist rally at Kennington Common, that a nucleus of repealers which included Collet Dobson Collet, Henry Hetherington, George Jacob Holyoake and James Watson were drawn together in what would shortly become the Association for the Repeal of the Taxes on Knowledge.[38] Their renewed agitation was enormously strengthened by the support given by Richard Cobden in the Commons, but Collet in particular was eager to extend the campaign more widely in the country. In a conscious re-enactment of the unstamped strategy of the 1820s and early 1830s, he established the *Potteries Free Press* in February 1853, an unstamped penny weekly newspaper published in Hanley, Staffordshire, and deliberately challenged the Stamp Office to prosecute. When they did so, petitions were organised to defend the 'working man's newspaper' both in Hanley and in London, and the inconclusive court action taken against Collet further revealed the confusions of the law.[39] Finally, in 1855, a bill was

---

[34] National Political Union, *Taxes on Knowledge* (Southwark, 1832), pp. 10–11.

[35] *Speech of M.D. Hill, Esq., MP, on Mr Bulwer's Motion for a repeal of the Stamp Duty on Newspapers in the House of Commons, on Thursday May 22, 1834* (1834), p. 5.

[36] Ibid., p. 10.

[37] *The Newspaper Stamp and the Duty on Paper Viewed in Relation to Their Effects Upon the Diffusion of Knowledge, by the Author of The Results of Machinery* (published by Charles Knight, 1836), p. 12.

[38] Collett, *History*, p. 43.

[39] For a fuller account see ibid., pp. 96–101. See also the *Potteries Free Press*, 12 Feb. 1853 (four issues were published before it was stopped by court action), and the *Potteries*

presented to Parliament to abolish the remaining duty on newspapers. The discussions that took place at the time of the second reading of the Newspaper Stamp Bill in March 1855 revealed the nature of the few remaining arguments against repeal, and by extension against a cheap, popular newspaper press. The editors of some well-established newspapers were known to resent the repeal out of the fear both of competition from new titles, and from a more deep-seated anxiety that the proliferation of provincial and local newspapers would ultimately trivialise news and the calling of journalism. Some MPs opposed the measure both on grounds of loss of revenue to the Treasury and because they 'looked with apprehension on a measure which would allow any person to excite the minds of those who, being ignorant and uneducated, were not able to distinguish between right and wrong'.[40] Other residual oppositional voices regarded journalists as 'the most awful men alive', and complained that the press was 'open to bribery, was insolent and oppressive'. These, however, were finally silenced by Lord Palmerston's declaration that 'he had confidence in the people of the country, and had no fears that the anticipated evils from the existence of a cheap press would be realised'. The second reading was thus carried by 215 votes to 161. By 1855, therefore, most Whigs and many Conservatives had reached the conclusion that, with the passing of the unstamped and Chartist emergencies, and the growth of a commercial press rooted in the principles of the free market, the popular press could now be assumed to be sufficiently safe from radical intent to warrant a legal status unfettered by taxation.

Newspapers, however, were to remain a live political issue as long as the Paper Duties remained on the statute book. T. Milner Gibson, president of the Newspaper and Periodical Press Association for Obtaining the Repeal of the Paper Duty, adopted a somewhat different approach to this issue when, in a speech to the Commons on 21 June 1858, he argued that not only were the duties on paper a tax on knowledge but, more pertinently, that they were also a tax on industry and commerce. Capitalism and social progress were synonymous in this concerted attack on the consequences of this particular form of indirect taxation, which was blamed for interfering with the process of manufacture, impeding commerce and, given that 'the education of the present day consists, whether for good or for evil, almost entirely in impressing on the mind something that is printed' also of obstructing social improvement. The continuation of the Paper Duties also contributed to poverty by impeding investment in labour. Were it not for

---

Times, 18 Nov. 1854, a monthly penny newspaper issued 'in compliance with the law'.
   [40] *The Press*, 31 Mar. 1855, p. 298.

the tax, Milner Gibson argued, 'paper mills in country districts would employ a large number of people, particularly women'.[41] Outside the Commons, the campaign won widespread cross-class support. The editor of the *Manchester Examiner and Times* informed Joseph Cowen in May 1860 that 'the Manchester people have set our hearts on the repeal of the paper duty',[42] and in the same week, Collet feared that the campaign might go beyond what was sanctioned by the law.[43] He need not have worried. Despite opposition in the Lords, Gladstone's Budget of 15 April 1861 finally repealed the Paper Duties from 1 October of that year, thus removing the last of the Treasury controls on the production of newspapers.

Even before the Paper Duties had been repealed, the newspaper industry in England had noticeably started to grow (Table 1.1). John Francis in 1861 calculated that the number of master printers in London had increased by a factor of four in the previous 30 years, and by an average of 3.5 in the major English cities.[44] In the six years between 1855 and 1861, the increase in the number of newspapers marked a further dramatic rise in an ever upward curve.

Table 1.1 Increases in the number of newspaper titles established in the United Kingdom, 1665–1861

Period	No. of newspapers established
1665–1800	88
1800–1830	126
1830–1855	415
1855–1861	492

Source: Saunders, Otley and Co., *Newspaper Press Census for 1861* (1861).

In the same six year period between 1855 and 1861, 137 newspapers were established in 123 towns in England where there had previously been no local newspaper.[45] In 1861 itself, it was calculated that the

---

[41] The Newspaper and Periodical Press Association for Obtaining the Repeal of the Paper Duty, *The Tax Upon Paper: The Case Stated for Its Immediate Repeal* (1858), pp. 7–24. See also Palmerston's speech on the press in *The Times*, 22 Dec. 1859.

[42] George Barker to Joseph Cowen, 11 May 1860, Tyne and Wear Archive Service, Newcastle upon Tyne (TWAS) 634/C1388.

[43] C.D. Collet to R.B. Reed, 16 May 1860, TWAS 634/C1391.

[44] 'Some particulars relating to Newspapers, Class Journals, and Periodical Literature compiled by Mr John Francis . . . April 3, 1861', Edward Baines Coll, Leeds Arch., MS 60/4. For Holyoake's tribute to Francis, publisher of the *Athenaeum* and treasurer of the Taxes on Knowledge Abolition Committee, see Collet, *History*, p. x.

[45] Saunders, Otley and Co., *Newspaper Press Census for 1861* (1861), pp. 5–6.

number of newspapers had virtually doubled from 562 to 1,102, although it was conceded that a substantial proportion of these titles were very short-lived.[46] The political campaign to free newspapers from the 'taxes on knowledge' had evidently been well organised and ultimately successful, but it is worth noting also that a wide variety of other factors contributed to changing the system of state regulation in journalism. The abolition of the Advertisement Duty in 1853 had boosted commercial revenues, and conflicts in the Crimea, India and the United States in the following decade had intensified public demand for foreign news. The security system, which had stipulated that publishers submit £300 to cover possible libel convictions, was repealed in 1869, and reductions in the price of paper following the introduction of esparto grass in paper manufacture, and cheap imported newsprint, further encouraged enterprise. Telegraphy eased the transmission of news, 'cold' stereotyping and web-fed machinery increased productivity and railways, the penny post and new outlet chains such as W.H. Smith's bookstalls hugely facilitated distribution.[47]

Government policy towards the production of newspapers in nineteenth-century Britain was thus shaped not only by agitation, but also by changing perceptions of the needs of the economy and of the political and moral condition of society. But legislators did not extend the same measure of liberalisation to newspapers produced elsewhere in the British Empire. The history of state regulation of the press in India is particularly instructive. The Prince of Oudh, on a visit to London in 1839, had expressed his admiration for British newspapers, and had hoped that similar developments in his own country might 'give light to his fellow-subjects of India'.[48] Policy in India prior to that date, however, had taken a very different course to that pursued in Britain. The Marquis of Hastings had abolished censorship in August 1819, but had instead imposed strict new penalties for criticisms made by journalists of the public authorities, and the introduction of the first of the Bengal Regulations in 1823 introduced a rigid licensing system for newspapers

---

[46] James Paterson, *The Liberty of the Press, Speech and Public Worship, Being Commentaries on the Liberty of the Subject and the Laws of England* (1880).

[47] For a late-Victorian perspective on newspaper development see William Hunt, *Then and Now; or, Fifty Years of Newspaper Work* (1887). Hunt was a West Country journalist, manager of the *Eastern Morning News* in Hull and ex-President of the Provincial Newspaper Society. See also the increases in circulation experienced by individual titles, for example the *Sheffield Independent* which sold c.500 a week in 1831, a figure which rose to a weekly average of c.2000 in 1839 and c.12,000 in 1857, J.D. Leader, *Seventy-Three Years of Progress. A History of the Sheffield Independent from 1819 to 1892* (Sheffield, 1892), p. 37.

[48] *Report of the Second Anniversary Meeting of the Newspaper Press Benevolent Association, Held at the Freemason's Tavern on Saturday, 13 July, 1839* (1839), p. 25.

in the territories governed by the East India Company. These were repealed by Sir Charles Metcalfe in 1835 in an attempt to increase in India a knowledge of the West. The liberal press laws introduced by Metcalfe remained in force for some 40 years, interrupted only by Lord Canning's repressive but mercifully brief vengeance on the press following the Mutiny in 1857.[49] These developments were followed with interest by journalists in Britain, who saw in Indian policy a shadow of the thinking behind government policy at home. Rejecting the notion that the spread of knowledge through the press might undermine the stability of British rule, one commentator in 1848 insisted that, to the contrary, a free press was an essential means of informing government of the effects of its own legislation and, as utilitarian theory would have it, functioned as a 'safety-valve' for dissent which increased the stability of the Empire.[50] Alexander Andrews agreed, emphasising in 1867 his view that the Imperial government's encouragement of the vernacular press in India following the Mutiny would lead to social peace. Taking his cue from his reading of the enlightening experience of the Welsh-language press in Wales, he explained how 'religious sects and political parties throw down the weapons of physical force so soon as they can avail themselves of the pen or the printing-press, the engines of thought and moral force, to give vent to their feelings, and to make known their desires and their grievances'. The British government could not

> deny to an entire nation the privilege, the right of expressing its own feelings in its own language. . . . An almost clandestine, half suppressed, wholly ignored native Press existed in India previously to the Mutiny – an out-spoken, free native press comes out in the broad daylight now; it *may* (or some portions of it *may*) express feelings of antagonism to the British rule, but it speaks in public; it is not forced to plot in the dark. And both sides will be the gainers, while indirectly it will assimilate and reconcile the races, and by a natural process, without doing violence to native feelings of independence, smooth off rough surfaces and ugly angles that brought them into threatening contact. Anglo-Indians will tell us

---

[49] Leicester Stanhope, *Sketch of the History and Influence of the Press in British India* (1823) (Stanhope later became Lord Harrington); Sandford Arnot, *A Sketch of the History of the Indian Press During the Last Ten Years, With A Disclosure of the True Causes of Its Present Degredation . . . With a Biographical Notice of the Indian Cobbett, Alias 'Peter the Hermit'* (1829); *Papers Relating to the Public Press in India* (House of Commons, 1858); S.M. Mitra, 'The Press in India, 1780–1908', *Nineteenth Century and After*, Aug. 1908, 64: 186–206. For more recent accounts see S. Natarajan, *A History of the Press in India* (1962); R.C.S. Sarkar, *The Press in India* (New Delhi, 1984); and M. Israel, *Communication and Power: Propaganda and the Indian Nationalist Struggle* (Cambridge, 1994).

[50] *Notes and Opinions of a Native on the Present State of India and the Feelings of Its People* (Ryde, Isle of Wight, 1848), pp. 105–106.

that we are wrong, that we know nothing of the native character, that we are indulging in mere theory, &c; but tradition, influences, and prejudices may have had too long hold upon their minds to admit of their forming *quite* impartial conclusions.[51]

The 'mere theory' expressed by Andrews that a free newspaper press was an inherently stabilising force in all societies, however, came under increased scrutiny in the 1870s. In 1872 Garçin de Tassy's glowing commendations of Indian vernacular journalism were sceptically received by Andrews himself, who began to wonder whether the latitude granted to 'Oriental languages' was entirely safe. The 'encouragement of native literature is one thing', he mused, 'the perpetuation of national prejudices another'.[52] Six years later, Lord Lytton's Oriental Languages Act imposed severe restrictions on non-English language journalism and, though repealed by Ripon in 1882, was to prove to be only the first of a series of Vernacular Press Acts that sought to dampen nationalist and anti-British sentiment on the sub-continent. James Routledge, who reported the Bengal famine for *The Times*, was appalled by the return of repressive legislation, and in 1878 urged Indian journalists to lobby the British people to have them reversed. He advised them to 'shift the venue to the great life of England' by sending copies of their newspapers, not to the London clubs, 'which always run in ruts', but to the reading-rooms of London, Birmingham, Manchester, Leeds, Bradford and Newcastle.[53] Gladstonian radicals in the English provinces, however, could do little against the power of the Imperial government in this matter, not least because of the support for repressive policies that emanated from such key metropolitan titles as *The Times*. The paper's Calcutta correspondent in July 1891, for example, was sharply critical of the 'safety-valve' thesis, preferring to describe the Indian newspapers as 'symptoms of a disease' which it was necessary to check,[54] and this despite the fact that literacy levels in British India as late as 1911 were only 11.3 per cent for men and 1.1 per cent for women.[55] On a visit to India in 1897, a year after he had launched the *Daily Mail*, Alfred C. Harmsworth, too, thought the Indian press was 'full of everything . . . that is vile'.[56] Such attitudes helped legitimise the passing by the British state of further controls on the Indian newspapers in 1908 and 1910.

---

[51] *Newspaper Press*, 1 Aug. 1867, p. 162.

[52] Ibid., 1 Mar. 1872, p. 74.

[53] James Routledge, *English Rule and Native Opinion in India, From Notes Taken 1870–74* (1878), p. 298.

[54] *The Times*, 5 Jul. 1891.

[55] Judith M. Brown, *Modern India. The Origins of an Asian Democracy* (Oxford, 1985), p. 120.

[56] *Journalist and Newspaper Proprietor*, 27 Feb. 1897, p. 73.

British press policy in India was designed to meet the needs of a particular ruling class positioned in a particular context, but it was also rooted in the nexus of critical responses to the growth of newspapers that had evolved *in Britain* during the nineteenth century. While the circumstances in which legislation was enacted were very different, the thinking that shaped policy in both Britain and India was drawn from the same set of cultural assumptions, to which the incomplete and contradictory narrative of the 'liberty of the press' had contributed one cluster of ideas. The case of India suggests, at least, that the course of market liberalisation pursued in Britain was not the only option open to the state in any portion of the Empire, including its centre. In any case, it is evident that arguments which may have been lost at home in the 1850s continued to prevail elsewhere in the British Empire well into the twentieth century.

Having sketched the historical and regulatory structures within which newspaper journalism developed in Britain, and considered some of the immediate responses to them and the thinking behind them, we now turn to some of those underlying assumptions about newspaper journalism and its effects. In particular, we will consider the ways in which relationships between cultural formations, social relations and the emergence of a newspaper press were perceived and understood in the nineteenth century, beginning with a discussion of some of the symbolic and imaginative representations of the newspaper in popular iconography and fiction.

CHAPTER TWO

The newspaper imagined

'By the bye, Miss Lord, are you aware that the Chinese Empire, with four *hundred* MILLION inhabitants, has only *ten* daily papers? Positively; only ten.'

'How do you know?' asked Nancy.

'I saw it stated in a paper. That helps one to *grasp* the difference between civilisation and barbarism. One doesn't think clearly enough of common things.'

George Gissing, *In the Year of Jubilee* (1894, 1976 edn), p. 58.

Mr Samuel Bennett Barmby, Gissing's newspaper devotee, is both a comic and an ironic figure. His celebration of the Age of Progress, characterised in particular by an enlightened newspaper press 'packed with thought and information', is crowned by a 'laugh of triumphant optimism'.[1] For the reader, however, the comedy lies in the irony. Whereas Barmby considers newspapers to be a source of useful knowledge, which in turn provides the foundations for civilised life, his petulant young acquaintances, in collusion with the knowing reader, are irritated by the tedium of a conversation that rests exclusively on trivia obtained from the news columns. What for Barmby are 'common things' are for others 'atrocious commonplaces'.[2] Making matters worse for himself, Barmby mistakes their sarcasm for approbation. By 1894, the year in which Gissing's *The Year of Jubilee* was first published, newspapers signified different things to different people. The unreconstructed faith in the power of the popular press to improve society had for many individuals been clouded by doubt and distrust, and passages from the novel comprise, in fictional form, reflections on the changing cultural values placed upon newspaper journalism at a given, late-Victorian moment. Such imaginative representations of nineteenth-century newspapers took many forms, of which only the fictional remains readily accessible to readers at the end of the present century. But for contemporaries, imaginative representations of

---

[1] George Gissing, *In the Year of Jubilee* (1894, 1976 edn), p. 57.

[2] Ibid., p. 63. Samuel Barmby's father, a solemn middle-aged insurance clerk, was in the habit of writing serious anonymous letters to newspapers, which 'if collected, would have made an entertaining and instructive volume, so admirably did they represent one phase of the popular mind', ibid., pp. 212–13.

newspapers were experienced in numerous and simultaneous ways; as well as being read in novels, they were also looked at in cartoons, listened to in verses and sung in ballads. These representations did not simply mirror a debate that was taking place in the courts or in Parliament on the changing values of journalism: they were themselves constituent parts of a broader cultural process in which the social utility of news, and of newspapers as communication media, was being thought through and re-evaluated. This chapter considers two aspects of this process. The first addresses the ways in which newspapers popularised the notion that life without them would be barbaric, and that their contribution to society was an overwhelmingly positive one in both educational and recreational senses. As far as public relations went, newspapers were superlatively successful in generating public interest and enthusiasm, not so much for social or political causes as for newspapers themselves. And the commodity for which newspapers were by far the best advertisers was their own. The nineteenth-century newspaper's self-image, deeply indebted as it was to the inherited narratives of press freedom, was skilfully codified into the conventions of its visual imagery and language. Beyond this barrage of self-publicity, however, a range of different accents could be heard. In poems, ballads and novels, newspapers and their journalists were ridiculed, parodied, criticised, or praised. Some decried the trite insubstantiality of the news-sheet, while others relished the visual and tactile pleasures of the page and the smell of the ink. Poetic and fictional representations of newspaper journalism thus provided necessary alternatives to, and illuminating commentaries upon, the elaborate iconography and stylised language of the newspaper. They also indicate the ways in which social attitudes towards newspapers may have changed over time. But, most importantly, they remind us that in the debate over where news journalism ought to be situated in the culture, the nineteenth-century newspaper was as much a product of the imagination as an actually existing entity, an idea as much as a thing.

Emblems and mottoes

Gissing's Samuel Barmby, in measuring civilisation by the proportion of daily newspapers published in a given population, was articulating a set of assumptions that had long been promoted by the press itself. Most notably, the printing press was able to reinforce notions of its own 'liberty' by projecting strong symbolic representations of itself, some of which were grotesquely and terrifyingly anthropomorphic in nature. Cartoons and woodcuts from eighteenth-century Germany, for example,

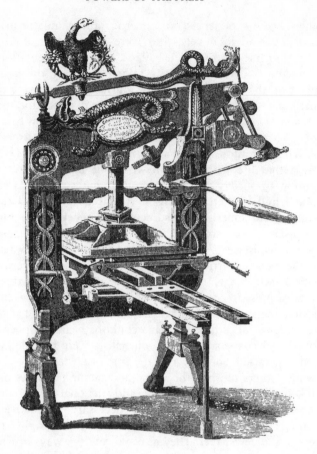

2.1 Clymer's Columbian Press, 1821

Source: James Moran, *Printing Presses. History and Development From the Fifteenth Century to Modern Times* (1973), p. 58.

commonly depicted the printing-press as a robotic, metal-clad warrior engaged in battle against ignorance and tyranny, while those from France in the nineteenth century showed Marianne being brutalised by armed mobs of priests, aristocrats, generals and politicians while defending the independence of the press.[3] The application of steam technology to the hand press was attributed further symbolic meaning, and for Charles Knight (1791–1873), the printing *machine* was the early nineteenth-

---

[3] See for example, Grandville and Desperet's *Caricature* of the promulgation in Paris of the law of 9 Sept. 1835 restricting printing, in *Histoire de l'édition Français*, vol. 3, (Paris, 1985), p. 51.

century's most powerful symbol of modernity. In March 1834, grasping the potential of the steam-driven press to mass manufacture print, he announced his belief that the accomplishments of the printing-machine in the nineteenth century were comparable to those achieved by the printing-press in the fifteenth. Both represented distinctive periods in recent history, and each symbolised the 'intellectual character' of its age.[4] Some printing-presses were designed in such a way that no operator could mistake the meanings of that symbolism. The Columbian Press (Figure 2.1), invented by George Clymer of Philadelphia (1754–1834), and the first to be manufactured in large numbers for more than a century, was so richly decorated with such icons as to prompt in 1825 the following awed commentary from T.C. Hansard.

> If the merits of a machine were to be appreciated wholly by its ornamental appearance, certainly no other press could enter into competition with 'The Columbian'. No British-made machine was ever so lavishly embellished. We have a somewhat highly-sounding title to begin with; and then, which way soever our eyes are turned, from head to foot, or foot to head, some extraordinary features present themselves – on each pillar of the staple a caduceus of the universal messenger, Hermes – alligators, and other draconic serpents, emblematize, on the levers, the power of wisdom – then, for the *balance of power* (we rude barbarians of the old world make mere cast-iron *lumps* serve our notions of the *balance of power*) we see, surmounting the Columbian press, the American eagle with extended wings, and grasping in his talons Jove's thunderbolts, combined with the olive-branch of Peace, and cornucopia of Plenty, all handsomely bronzed and gilt, *resisting and bearing down* ALL OTHER POWER![5]

Hermes, the messenger of the gods, representing 'the news-distributing function of the printing press',[6] remained a familiar figure among newspaper journalists from *Bell's Weekly Dispatch* (see Figure 2.3 below) until well into the twentieth century. The use of the symbol as frontispiece for *Mitchell's Newspaper Press Directory*, for example, was discontinued only in 1963. The all-seeing eye (*nunquam dormio*) of the early masthead of the *Observer*, a powerful masonic emblem that was also to be found situated between the classical-republican figures of liberty and justice (*invidia cum auctoritate*), was, incidentally, reintroduced into that paper in 1995.

Printers, publishers and journalists alike were fascinated by the new technology of steam printing, and for Knight and others the introduction

---

[4] *The Printing Machine: A Review for the Many*, 15 Mar. 1834.

[5] T.C. Hansard, *Typographia: an Historical Sketch of the Origin and Progress of the Art of Printing* (1825), pp. 655–57.

[6] James Moran, *Printing Presses. History and Development From the Fifteenth Century to Modern Times* (1973), pp. 59–61

THE

PRINTING MACHINE:

A REVIEW FOR THE MANY.

No. 2.

SATURDAY,

MARCH 15, 1834.

Price 4*d*.

TO BE

CONTINUED

MONTHLY

What the PRINTING-PRESS did for the instruction of the masses in the fifteenth century, the PRINTING-MACHINE is doing in the nineteenth. Each represents an era in the diffusion of knowledge; and each may be taken as a *symbol* of the intellectual character of the age of its employment."—*Penny Magazine.*

Table 2.2 Masthead of Charles Knight's *The Printing Machine*

on the morning of 28 November 1814 into *The Times* office of the Koenig cylinder was a key moment in the transformation of the modern press. Full-page illustrations of the Applegarth and Cowper printing machine, with explanations of its functions, appeared in Knight's *Penny Magazine* on 31 December 1833,[7] and in the following year the same illustration, reduced in size, also appeared as the masthead logo on the title page of Knight's new monthly 'review for the many', significantly entitled *The Printing Machine* (Figure 2.2).[8]

Part of the fascination with printing technology as iconography lay in the relative speed of production and the labour-saving potential of the press. Contrasting the press to manual writing, Edward Baines (1774–1848), proprietor and editor of the *Leeds Mercury*, whose son of the same name was depicted in *Punch* in a winged cap as Mercury instructing Cupid, his young reader,[9] calculated in 1820 that to write out the contents of one number of *The Times* with a pen would take one person 121 days. Almost 2 million scribes would be needed to write 40,000 copies of this number in one day, compressed to the same amount of newsprint. The steam press, however, completed this task in about six hours. If the same press were to be kept in motion for 24 hours, it would do the work of 7,680,000 scribes. Yet, as Baines acknowledged, all the manual operations which produced this result were performed by 150 printers.[10] The advent of the printing-machine not only accelerated this process, but vastly improved the quality of the product. Charles Knight, referring enthusiastically to his *Penny Magazine* in 1832, explained that

---

[7] *The Penny Magazine*, 31 Dec. 1833, Monthly Supplement, p. 509.

[8] *Printing Machine*, 15 Feb. 1834, (1).

[9] *Punch*, **12**, 1847, p. 210.

[10] Edward Baines, 'Origin and History of Printing', pp. 74–76.

whereas a manual printing-press would take five months to produce 160,000 copies, a machine could accomplish the same task from two sets of plates in ten days. Baines and Knight shared this fascination with the speeded up potential of printing machinery with a host of other printers and journalists, as if calculations of this kind could confer a mathematical value to the rate of 'progress', or measure in precise detail the distance between the present and the past. For improvements in the speed and quality of production were seen not only as striking proof of technical supremacy, but also as symptoms of deeper changes that were taking place in English society. For Baines, Knight and others, scientific and technological advances were, across a broad front, effecting a moral and social transformation. As Knight reasoned, the 'conditions for the production' of a penny paper were many, and included chemical developments in paper-making, improved road and rail communications, and increasing levels of literacy. The success of his penny weekly paper could thus not exist without 'large accumulations of Knowledge', and was an unmistakable sign that the society of his own time had reached 'a high state of civilization'.[11] Knight's teleology, resting as it did on the unquestioned assumption that improvement, technological and moral, was indivisible, proved to be an enormously influential current in the critical reception of Victorian newspaper journalism.

Similar preoccupations with the iconography of myth and technology were focused on newspaper titles and masthead design. A study of the nomenclature of titles undertaken in 1900 is, in a limited way, instructive. The majority of titles were found to express the commercial values that underpinned the industry, hence the predominance of *Advertisers*. The second most popular title emulated *The Times*, the paradigmatic Victorian newspaper and the most alluring name in journalism. Then followed the *Gazettes*, *Chronicles*, *Heralds* and *Journals*. At the lower end appeared the *Mercuries*, *Free Presses*, *Examiners* and *Mails*. The naming of newspapers reflected the publishers' initial intent, although the limited range from which titles were drawn also suggests that convention played a large part in title choice. The notion of a newpaper as a luminary, a light-giving source, led to the *Suns*, *Comets*, *Stars* and *Lanterns*. Some referred to the 'guiding' functions of journalism, hence the *Champion*, *Moderators*, *Vindicators*, *Leaders*, *Pilots*, *Pioneers*, *Watchmen*, *Sentinels*, *Wardens* and *Monitors*,[12]

---

[11] *Penny Magazine*, 18 Dec. 1832. Preface to the first annual volume.

[12] A survey of the most common UK titles in 1900 revealed the following statistics of frequency: *Advertiser* (160), *Times* (150), *News* (149), *Gazette* (128), *Chronicle* (120), *Herald* (119), *Journal* (104), *Express* (95), *Guardian* (70), *Observer* (68) (both 'doubtless

WEEKLY   DISPATCH.

·)l.. 22.—No. 1171.]   SUNDAY,   FEBRUARY 8, 1824.   [PRICE 8½d.

Printed, Published, and Conducted by the Original Editor, *ROBERT BELL*, at the Office, No 7, Wine-Office-Court, Fleet-street.

| *HISTORY AND POLITICS.*

THE MEETING OF PARLIAMENT. | among the numberless other splendid as well as beneficial efforts, that entitle this gentleman to the gratitude of his country. Mr. Hobhouse also deserves the thanks of the public for the spirited manner in which he took up the subject of our rela- | to secure the welfare and happiness of that part of the United Kingdom.
"His Majesty had commanded us further to inform you, that he has every reason to believe, that the progress of our internal prosperity and improvement will not be disturbed by any interruption of tranquillity abroad. |

2.3 *Bell's Weekly Dispatch*, 8 February 1824

while others revealed the underlying notion of the newspaper as a mirror reflecting the world around it, such as the evocatively entitled *The Looking Glass. A Reflex of the Times*, published in Manchester from 1877 to 1878. John B. Mackie, in his handbook for young journalists published in 1894, asserted that such titles as *Mercury* were deliberately employed in order to convey the idea that the modern newspaper embodied the functions of a 'living oracle' sent by God 'into the world to teach His final will', and as such was one of the custodians of the 'keys of power'.[13]

The combination of classical mythology with hard-headed marketing in the choice of titles also extended to the design of mastheads, where, again, appropriate messages were projected on to the public eye. Emblems and mottoes crystallised a title's identity, and provided the reader with immediate identifiers. *Bell's Weekly Dispatch* depicted itself conventionally as a blast from the winged messenger's trumpet, with the implied emphasis on accuracy and speed of transmission (Figure 2.3).

John Bull (Figure 2.4), on the other hand, is characteristic of an equally simple and direct approach to masthead design, which is none the less more self-consciously political in its appeal. Appropriately for a Tory weekly, its professed loyalty to the triple signifiers of the Constitution – the Crown, the sceptre and the Bible – is unmistakable, but is further reinforced by a monarchist motto. It is perhaps worth

---

exercise an unsleeping vigilance in the public interest'), *Standard* (48), *Mercury* (42), *Free Press* (40), *Telegraph* (38), *Post* (30), *Independent* (29), *Courier* (23), *Examiner* (23), *Echo* (22), *Mail* (31) (*Progress of British Newspapers in the Nineteenth Century, Illustrated*, (1900), p. 208). The gender of a newspaper title remained uncertain. Rachel Beer, 'Editress' of the *Sunday Times*, sent instructions to her staff that the newspaper was to be referred to as 'she'. *The Observer*, however, also edited by Beer, was to be known as 'he', *The Journalist and Newspaper Proprietor*, 8 Jun. 1895, p. 178. An editorial message could even be inserted into the date, printed immediately below the title. The temperance journal *Atlas*, for example, deliberately employed the old puritan dating method, '2 Mo. 4. 1854' for 4 Feb. 1854 (*Atlas*, 4 Feb. 1854, p. 91).

[13] John B. Mackie, *Modern Journalism. A Handbook of Instruction and Counsel for the Young Journalist* (1894), p. 114.

JOHN BULL.

" FOR GOD, THE KING, AND THE PEOPLE!"

No. 91. MONDAY, SEPTEMBER 9, 1822. Price 7d.

LONDON MARKETS. | CURRENT PRICES OF SPIRITS AND WINES | COAL EXCHANGE—Friday, Sept. 6.

2.4 *John Bull*, 9 September 1822

noting that the formula was neatly inverted, and thus subverted, in Julian Harney's post-Chartist monthly of 1851, the *Red Republican*, where the symbols of the French revolutionary constitution exactly mirror those of *John Bull's* Tory trinity (Figure 2.5). Instead of the Crown we see a Phrygian cap, the republican javelin replaces the sceptre, and the *fasces* figures in place of the Holy Bible as the symbolic basis of social order. The triadic motto of loyalism, with its incantation of God, King and People, is supplanted by its opposite, the republican battle cry of liberty, equality and fraternity. French displaces English, republican symbols usurp those of monarchy, but in all other respects the emblematic convention is respected. In terms of their marketing, if not of their political ambitions, both *John Bull* and the *Red Republican* spoke the same rhetorical language.

EQUALITY, LIBERTY, FRATERNITY.

EDITED BY G. JULIAN HARNEY.

No. 1.—Vol. I.] SATURDAY, JUNE 22, 1850. [Price One Penny.

Letters of L'Ami du Peuple.

How has this come to pass ? Whence has come this melancholy conclusion, this disheartening consummation of the heroic efforts

universal sufferage, freedom of the press, trial by jury, and the usual order of " Reforms," advocated by mere political agitators,

2.5 *The Red Republican*, 22 June 1850

No. 1.]   SATURDAY, MAY 6, 1848.   [Price THREEPENCE.

2.6 *Illustrated Weekly Newspaper*, 6 May 1848

The *Illustrated Weekly Newspaper* in May 1848 provided yet another model of masthead design. A densely packed though not unattractive cityscape, extending from St Paul's Cathedral to London Bridge, frames the busy traffic of the river (Figure 2.6). The allusions to finance and commerce, the twin motors of London's prosperity, are only too evident: the financial power of the City of London provides the solid background to the swift commerce of the Thames. Totemic significance is here applied to economic rather than to political power, at least in the direct, visual sense. The Houses of Parliament, located a mile upstream, do not figure in this representation of London. Rebuilding work, which followed the fire of 17 October 1834, was entering a critical phase in 1848. The Lords had been completed in March 1847, but continuing work on the remainder of the New Palace was a matter of controversy in 1848, due in part to the the the perceived architectural inadequacies of the Commons chamber and the spiralling building costs. The river terrace was by this time in an advanced state, but work on the great landmark of the Clock Tower remained unfinished.[14] The depiction of Parliament on the masthead of the first number of the *Illustrated Weekly Newspaper* was thus scarcely possible in 1848. But it is also conceivable that the decision to foreground the City may have been prompted by the paper's intention, expressed in the introductory address to the readers, to 'be in the real and true sense of the much-abused word, *respectable*'. Wishing to remain independent of political intrigues, the paper insists that its main concern is to raise sufficient funds to attract the best artistic talent available to illustrate the most important developments of 'a rapidly progressing age'.[15]

---

[14] M.H. Port, *The Houses of Parliament* (1976), pp. 122–41.
[15] *Illustrated Weekly Newspaper*, 6 May, 1848.

This scene differs substantially from the skyline silhouette of London printed on the masthead of T.P. O'Connor's weekly, the *Star*, launched 40 years later on 17 January 1888. Seen from the north rather than the south, and extending from St Paul's on the left to the completed Clock Tower of the New Palace on the right, this segment of London crucially includes Fleet Street, which not only connected Ludgate Circus with Temple Bar, but also, by the late 1880s, had come to represent 'the World of Journalism . . . the Centre of the World's Press'.[16] But by devoting so much space on the front page to an engraving, the *Illustrated Weekly Newspaper* was also signalling the illustrated nature of the newspaper as a whole. The masthead thus provided the potential reader with a foretaste of the visual pleasures contained within. This was evidently not the case with either the *Star* or *England*, which contained no other sizeable illustrations. In the latter (Figure 2.7), the objective appears to have been to squeeze as many allusions as possible to the national identity and imperial power of England into the smallest available amount of space. In addition to the fortress walls of the chalk cliffs of Dover in the background, and Brittania in the foreground, there are references to Britain's naval power, her imperial past and, to avoid any conceivable misunderstanding, a complete map of the modern Empire.

In view of the elaborate lengths to which so many nineteenth-century publishers were prepared to travel to secure effective and attractive front pages, it is significant that the *Pall Mall Gazette*, at the forefront of the New Journalism in the 1880s and 1890s, did not carry a symbolic

2.7 *England*, 22 September 1880

---

[16] *Sell's Dictionary of the World's Press* (1890), p. 17.

masthead at all. Its title typography was unadorned, and its initial visual impact was one of matter-of-fact simplicity. This plainness of presentation was continued in the interior of the paper. W.T. Stead's invention of the cross-head in 1881 had, at a stroke, changed the way newspapers looked and the ways in which they were read. By unpacking the closely printed columns of newsprint in this way, Stead enabled readers to scan the page far more rapidly and effectively, thus ensuring a greater versatility in reading practices. Newspapers could more easily be read whilst 'on the move', and the format was eventually emulated in one way or another by all newspapers, including *The Times* in 1890.[17] In the same vein, illustrations were tightly connected to the stories, and consisted principally of portraits, diagrams and maps, with fewer of the imaginative interpretations of news scenes that had been the stock-in-trade of the earlier illustrated newspapers.[18] The writing also tended to consist of plainer language, which prefigured in part the increasing importance of sub-editors whose task it was to ensure the even application of house styles. Arguably, this cleaner, simpler format did not require elaborate masthead illustrations to attract the attention of readers. The newspaper, in its entirety, spoke of itself.

Verse and fiction

Though adept at publicising positive representations of themselves in the public domain, newspapers were also represented in other forms of print media. Here, however, the image that was projected of news journalism was seldom so creditable. An eighteenth-century tradition of scepticism, embodied in such ballads as *The Journalists Displayed*, printed *circa* 1750, had set the tone for much of the critical and satirical literature of the Victorian period:

> Dear Friend, have you heard the fantastical Chimes,
>   Ribbledum, Scribbledum, Fribbledum, Flash,
> As sung by the *Journalists*, all of our Times ?
>   Satyrum, Traytorum, Treasondum, Trash,
> Popery, Slavery, Bribery, Knavery,
> Irruptions, Corruptions, and Some body's Fall;
>   Pensions and Places, Removes and Disgraces,
>   And something and nothing, the Devil and all.

---

[17] Cross-heads first appeared in *The Times* in the text of a report of a speech by Joseph Chamberlain on 20 Apr. 1890; see also Stanley Morison, *The English Newspaper* (Cambridge, 1932), p. 284

[18] Keith Williams, *The English Newspaper: an Illustrated History to 1900* (1977), p. 98.

'When you've read One of them,' the verse continued, 'then you've read All'. But the capacity of such newspapers to 'frighten the Mob' was in no doubt, a view with which a satirical poem of 1822 readily agreed. Reflecting that so much contemporary magazine journalism was fit more for Billingsgate than Parnassus, John Hamilton Reynolds intimated that despite the effects of the repressíve legislation of 1819, the radical press continued to exercise a baneful influence on the social order:

> The age of reason is at hand no doubt,
> Carlile and Hone will bring the change about;
> Soon, doubtless, Cobbett will our senate rule . . .[19]

Verses and songs that took the newspaper press as their subject-matter had become so numerous by the mid-1840s that Charles Henry Timperley in 1845 devoted an entire volume to the genre, complete with a glossary of printing terms. Some of the verses included in the collection described vividly, if derisively, the reading of newspapers in, for example, barbers' shops.

> A BARBER'S shop adorn'd we see
> With monster's *news* and poverty;
> While some are shaving, others bleed,
> And those that wait, the *papers* read;
> The master, full of Whig and Tory,
> Combs out your hair, and tells a story.[20]

Others were scornful of the low expectations and lower tastes of newspaper readers, who, tired of 'too much morality', hungered after 'some witch and wizzard tales/Of slip-shod ghosts, with fins and scales'. Above all, readers demanded of their newspapers

> A jumbled-up variety:
>   Variety in all things –
> A miscellaneous hodge-podge print,
> Composed, I only give the hint,
>   Of multifarious small things.[21]

A more sustained and complex literary treatment of the newspaper, however, may be found in Victorian fiction. Journalists emerge most graphically and problematically in the narrative structures and character development of novels, often written by authors who themselves had some experience of newspaper work. Rigby in Benjamin Disraeli's

---

[19] John Hamilton Reynolds, *The Press, or Literary Chit-chat. A Satire* (1822), pp. 52, 121.

[20] Charles Henry Timperley, *Songs of the Press and Other Poems Relative to the Art of Printers and Printing; also of Authors, Books, Booksellers, Bookbinders, Editors, Critics, Newspapers etc.* (1845), p. 68.

[21] Ibid., p. 69.

Coningsby (1844), for example, was recognised by critics as a reference to J.W. Croker, the Tory party's 'chief hack' in the London newspapers.[22] Disraeli's *Sybil*, published in the following year, also introduced the character of Stephen Morley, editor of the Mowbray *Phalanx*.[23] Charles Dickens, whose Blue *Eatanswill Gazette* and Buff *Eatanswill Independent* had clashed so memorably in *The Pickwick Papers* (1836–37), would a decade later act as the first editor of the *Daily News*, a post which he relinquished, exhausted, after only three weeks. J.M. Barrie went on to describe his experiences as a leader writer for the *Nottingham Journal* in 1883 and 1884 in his novel *When a Man's Single: a Tale of Literary Life*, published in 1888, and Arnold Bennett, again both a novelist and a journalist, drew on his memories of newspaper life in the Potteries in such vignettes as 'The Great Newspaper War' in *The Card* (1911). The symbiotic relationship that existed between journalism and literature, and specifically between news and the novel, which these and other writers embodied, provided further outlets for the construction and popularisation of contemporary representations of the newspaper. Newspapers were not only read, they were also read about in popular fiction. The following necessarily brief discussion of journalism as a feature of Victorian novels, however, is limited by two important constraints. First, it considers, as far as it is possible to do so, only the nature of the representation, rather than the newspaper's function in the narrative or its utility as a literary device. Secondly, it focuses only on four Victorian novelists, Thackeray, Trollope, George Eliot and Meredith, in whose work the newspaper was represented in a striking variety of ways.

William Makepeace Thackeray (1811–63) had acquired his experience of newspaper work as Paris correspondent of the 'ultra-liberal' *Constitutional*, owned by his stepfather and started on 15 September 1836, the day the Stamp Duty was lowered from four pence to a penny. Like a great many radical titles that struggled to survive in the new market, it lasted less than a year. Thackeray then went on to write for the *Morning Chronicle* and *Punch*, and may also have contributed articles to *The Times*. His *History of Pendennis*, published in monthly numbers during 1849 and 1850, describes the setting up of a fictional newspaper, the *Pall Mall Gazette*, after which Frederick Greenwood's literary evening newspaper of 1865 was named. But the fictional title was deliberately deceptive: '"why *Pall Mall Gazette*?", asked Wagg. "Because the editor was born in Dublin, the sub-editor at Cork, because the

---

[22] Benjamin Disraeli, *Coningsby* (1844). See also H.R. Fox Bourne, 'Inspired Journalism', *Sell's Dictionary* (1891), p. 44.

[23] Benjamin Disraeli, *Sybil, or The Two Nations* (1845, 1950 edn), p. 163.

proprietor lives in Pasternoster Row, and the paper is published in Catherine Street, Strand. . . . Everything must have a name. My dog Panto has got a name . . . "'.[24] The dishonesty of newspaper reporting is a recurring theme in the novel, which reveals that an article on foreign policy, attributed 'to a noble Lord, whose connection with the Foreign Office is very well known', was actually written in 'the parlour of the Bear and Staff public house' by Captain Shandon, a character based on Dr William Maginn (1794–1842), the brilliant, hard-drinking, Cork-born star writer of the London *Standard*.[25] Journalists, Thackeray remarked in another novel, largely drawn from his experience as a correspondent in Paris in 1836, 'worked for very moderate fees: but paid themselves by impertinence and the satisfaction of assailing their betters'.[26] Disturbed by their arrogance, and anxious about their effect on the public, one of his characters decried 'the crude daily speculations, and frivolous ephemeral news' supplied by journalists, and regretted the fact that readers gave up 'a lamentable portion of [their] time to fleeting literature'.[27]

Anthony Trollope (1815–82) shared Thackeray's low regard for newspapers. *The Warden*, the first sustained howl against the power of the press and its intimidating intrusion into individual privacy, was published in 1855, the year in which the explosive growth of modern journalism began. The story turns around the tragic consequences of the printing, in the daily newspaper *Jupiter*, of an unfounded allegation of mismanagement of Barchester almshouse against its warden, Septimus Harding. With a circulation of 40,000, each copy of which was read 'by at least five persons', the newspaper's revelations ensured that against the stricken Harding were ranged 'two hundred thousand readers . . . two hundred thousand hearts' that swelled 'with indignation at the gripping injustice, the bare-faced robbery of the warden of Barchester Hospital! And how was he to answer this?'[28] The Olympian doctrine of freedom espoused by its editor, Tom Towers, is unmasked as a new form of autocracy against which Parliament itself offered no adequate defence: 'Britons have but to read, to obey, and be blessed . . .'.[29] Towers, who 'loved to sit silent in a corner of his club and listen to the loud chattering

---

[24] W.M. Thackeray, *The History of Pendennis* (1850, 1959 edn), p. 354

[25] Ibid., p. 355.

[26] W.M. Thackeray, *The Adventures of Philip on His Way Through the World* (1862, 1901 edn), p. 319.

[27] W.M. Thackeray, *A Brother of the Press on the History of a Literary Man, Laman Blanchard, and the Chances of the Literary Profession*, first published in *Fraser's Magazine*, Mar. 1846, quoted in W.M. Thackeray, *Essays, Reviews Etc., Etc.* (1906), p. 96.

[28] Anthony Trollope, *The Warden* (1855, 1859 edn), pp. 71–72.

[29] Ibid., p. 141.

of politicians' relished the knowledge that 'they all were in his power'.
But unlike those politicians, he was responsible to no electorate, 'no one
could insult him; no one could inquire into him. He could speak out
withering words, and no one could answer him . . .'.[30] The theme was
continued in the person of the oleaginous but irrepressible Quintus Slide,
editor of the *People's Banner*, in Trollope's *Phineas Finn. The Irish
Member*, first published in *St Paul's Magazine* between October 1867
and May 1869. An 'advanced reformer', if an inconsistent one, Slide
sought to persuade Finn, the ambitious young politician, of the value of
a supportive newspaper. 'In public life', he insinuated, 'there's nothing
like having a horgan to back you. What is the most you can do in the
'Ouse? Nothing, if you're not reported. You're speaking to the country;
– ain't you? And you can't do that without a horgan . . .'.[31] Slide recurrs
as an important character in Trollope's later novels, *Phineas Redux* and
The Prime Minister. In the former, published in 1874, Slide, walking
defiantly up to the lobby of the House of Commons, reflects on his trade
and the nature of his political influence, and justifies his aggressive style
of journalism by insisting that this was what the market – his readers, the
'People' – both needed and desired.

> Everything done at the office of the People's Banner was done
> in the interest of the People, – and, even though individuals
> might occasionally be made to suffer by the severity with
> which their names were handled in its columns, the general
> result was good. What are the sufferings of the few to the
> advantage of the many? If there be fault in high places, it is
> proper that it be exposed. If there be fraud, adulteries,
> gambling, and lasciviousness, – or even quarrels and
> indiscretions among those whose names are known, let every
> detail be laid open to the light, so that the people may have a
> warning. That such details will make a paper 'pay' Mr Slide
> knew also; but it is not only in Mr Slide's path of life that the
> bias of a man's mind may lead him to find that virtue and
> profit are compatible. An unprofitable newspaper cannot long
> continue its existence, and, while existing, cannot be widely
> beneficial. It is the circulation, the profitable circulation, – of
> forty, fifty, sixty, or a hundred thousand copies through all the
> arteries and veins of the public body which is beneficient. And
> how can such circulation be effected unless the taste of the
> public be consulted ?[32]

Trollope's contempt for the democratic journalistic ethos of Towers and
Slide, which placed the interests of an abstracted notion of 'the People'

---

[30] Ibid., p. 148.

[31] Anthony Trollope, *Phineas Finn. The Irish Member* (1869, 1944 edn), vol. i, pp.
294–97.

[32] Anthony Trollope, *Phineas Redux* (1874, 1983 edn), vol. i, p. 238.

over and above the needs of individuals, was further elaborated in *Cousin Henry* in 1879, in which the libellous *Carmarthen Herald* again wreaks havoc with innocent and defenceless lives. For the critic John Halperin, these journalists in Trollope's fiction represent the 'pollution' of the times. The debility of the nation's journalism, however, signifies a deeper malaise, namely the perceived degeneration of the entire mid-Victorian political process.[33] In this bleak and bitter vision of modernity, the high-blown rhetoric of press freedom is represented as little more than a veil concealing the dishonourable actions of vindictive mediocrities.

George Eliot (1819–80), however, drew a much more sympathetic image of the struggling, artistic newspaper journalist in *Middlemarch*, a novel written between 1869 and 1871 and set in an English provincial community *circa* 1830–32. In this pre-Reform age, when there prevailed a 'clearer distinction of ranks and a dimmer distinction of parties',[34] contempt for 'those newspaper fellows' was a deeply entrenched social habit.[35] Into this changing world stepped Will Ladislaw as editor of the Middlemarch *Pioneer*, a local newspaper 'in the van of progress' which carried as its motto a quotation from the Liberal politician Charles James Fox.[36] Though among the least convincing of the novel's characters, and a socially ambivalent individual working at a dubious trade, a 'sort of gypsy, rather enjoying the sense of belonging to no class',[37] Ladislaw is nevertheless a man of high political and moral principle, 'a kind of Shelley' in his 'enthusiasm for liberty, freedom, emancipation'.[38] Intent on furthering the cause of Reform by making 'a new thing of opinion' through his journalism, he skilfully outmanoeuvres his politically timid employer, the newspaper's owner, and is eventually returned as a Radical MP.[39] Eliot, a humanist who was familiar with the work of Spinoza, Feuerbach, Comte and Herbert Spencer, was preoccupied by the relationship between individual self-interest and the wider social good, and in Ladislaw found a device which combined ethical behaviour at the personal level with the altruism of a liberal reformer who expressed his broader social concern through his newspaper writing. The newspaper thus emerges from the confusion and ill-discipline of an older politics to be refashioned, albeit briefly, in

---

[33] John Halperin, *Trollope and Politics. A Study of the Pallisers and Others* (1977), p. 190.

[34] George Eliot, *Middlemarch* (1872, Harmondsworth, 1994 edn), p. 88.

[35] Ibid., p. 380; see also p. 436.

[36] Ibid., p. 357.

[37] Ibid., p. 461.

[38] Ibid., p. 359.

[39] Ibid., p. 836.

Ladislaw's hands as an instrument of progress.

The progressive possibilities of newspaper journalism were taken further by George Meredith (1828–1909). A contributor to *Chambers's Journal* and *Household Words* in the late 1840s, Meredith had a decade later been employed by the Conservative *Ipswich Journal* to supply two leading articles and two columns of news each week. This, for £200 a year, he regarded as a form of 'Egyptian bondage' to the Tory party. He moved to the *Morning Post* in the early 1860s, acting as its special correspondent in Italy in 1866. His novel, *Beauchamp's Career*, published in instalments in the *Fortnightly Review* from August 1874, opens with an extended meditation on the capacities of newspapers to influence both the public mind and political power. Writing of the immediate post-1815 period, Meredith noted how newspaper correspondents had deliberately set out to panic readers by reviving the 'ancient nightmare of Invasion' by reiterating the notion that defence spending was too low. When, as a result of the ensuing panic, stock markets began to fall, 'the formidable engines called leading articles' moved to calm the troubled waters by stressing the patriotism of the press and its belief that it could easily mobilise volunteers should such an invasion occur. Having created the anxiety in the first place, the same newspapers were then responsible for minimising its impact. Government defence policy, however, was formed in reaction not to one, but to two conflicting directions in newspaper opinion. Little wonder then that both public thinking and political policy-making were muddled.[40] Beauchamp's own critique of journalism focused on the hidden pressures that were brought to bear on editorial independence by financial imperatives and the corrosive influence of the ideology of Conservatism.

> The covert Toryism . . . of the relapsing middle-class, which is now England before mankind, because it fills the sails of the Press, must be exposed. It supports the Press in its own interests, affecting to speak for the people. It belies the people. And this Press, declaring itself independent, can hardly walk for fear of treading on an interest here, an interest there. It cannot have a conscience. It is a bad guide, a false guardian; its abject claim to be our national and popular interpreter – even that is hollow and a mockery! It is powerful only while subservient. An engine of money, appealing to the sensitivities of money, it has no connection with the mind of the nation.[41]

The failure of the press to connect with 'the mind of the nation' amounts, for Beauchamp, to a conspiracy to subject the British people to a new form of social control. The liberty of the press is for him a 'delusive mask . . . a trumpet that deafened and terrorized the people; a mere engine of

---

[40] George Meredith, *Beauchamp's Career* (1874, 1922 edn), pp. 2–4.
[41] Ibid., p. 500.

leaguers banded to keep a smooth face upon affairs, quite soullessly'. The only adequate response to this hegemony is to challenge the leading newspapers on their own ground. As he walks, angry and disillusioned, out of London, Beauchamp pauses to rest and turns to gaze at the receding city. What he sees is not an unredeemable Great Wen, but rather, if only a new and radical daily newspaper could be established there, 'a place conquerable yet'. The novel ends with his dream of launching such a liberated and liberating newspaper, symbolically entitled *The Dawn*.[42]

Meredith, like Eliot, thus saw in newspaper journalism a heroic and counter-hegemonic potential, although both authors recognised that the contribution made by the actually existing press to the improvement of English society was less than helpful, and in some respects was positively damaging. For their part, both Thackeray and Trollope had projected overwhelmingly negative images of the newspaper journalist in their fiction, and were equally pessimistic about the capacity of the press ever adequately to reform itself into a socially useful and responsible medium. Gissing, too, had pictured the avid newspaper reader and amateur correspondent as faintly ridiculous figures. There is perhaps in each of these constructions an element of the novelist's disdain for the inferior, 'miscellaneous and *bric-à-brac*' nature of newspaper writing.[43] Yet, as a reviewer for the *Athenaeum* observed in 1884, the public's fascination with the lifestyles of 'ingenuous young men who desire an easy and independent career' had ensured that newspaper journalism had become a 'stock subject' with Victorian novelists.[44] This ambivalence testifies to the extent to which newspaper journalism had impinged upon public consciousness by the later-Victorian period, whilst simultaneously signalling public uncertainty regarding the social status of journalists and the social value of their work. This brief study of fictional representations of journalism does, however, suggest that fresh possibilities for a revived, non-partisan newspaper press were being seriously proposed by some novelists towards the end of the nineteenth century. What cannot adequately be measured is the way in which working journalists themselves read and responded to this *genre*. Some clearly relished the Bohemian mythology of independence and eccentricity popularised by these novels, whilst others complained that their trade was being grossly misrepresented. One editor in 1897, for

---

[42] Ibid., pp. 501–502. Beauchamp considered weekly newspapers to be of of little value, 'an echo, not a voice . . . [i]t has no steady continuous pressure of influence. It is the organ of sleepers' (ibid., p. 502).

[43] Eliot, *Middlemarch*, p. 436.

[44] Review of Anon., *My Ducats and My Daughter*, *Athenaeum* 17 May 1884. I am indebted to Professor E. Casey, of the University of Scranton, for this reference.

example, argued that readers of novels in which journalists figured 'were generally given to understand that a footing in one or two newspaper offices as leader-writers or what not is as good as a fortune. It is rarely anything like that . . . ',[45] but such attempts to correct the distortions of contemporary fiction were rare. In conclusion, it can be seen that while the self-image of the free press was challenged in Victorian fiction, it does not appear to have been seriously damaged by the encounter. This may be explained in part by the ambivalence of the representation, but it should also be borne in mind that fiction was only one of many forms of text that sought to characterise and explain the newspaper in Victorian England. The formation of a new corpus of historical literature, and its attempt not only to provide the newspaper with a past but also with a position within polite society, is a subject to which we now turn.

---

[45] Frederick Greenwood, 'Forty Years of Journalism', *The English Illustrated Magazine*, vol. xvii, Jul. 1897, p. 498.

CHAPTER THREE

Imposing order: historians and indexers

'The Journalists are now the true Kings and Clergy: henceforth Historians, unless they are fools, must write not of Bourbon Dynasties, and Tudors and Hapsburgs; but of Stamped Broad-sheet Dynasties, and quite new successive Names, according as this or the other Able Editor, or Combination of Able Editors, gains the world's ear. Of the British Newspaper Press, perhaps the most important of all, and wonderful enough in its secret constitution and procedure, a valuable descriptive History already exists, in that language, under the title of *Satan's Invisible World Displayed*'. . . . Thus does Teufelsdröckh . . . stumble on perhaps the most egregious blunder in Modern Literature!

Thomas Carlyle, *Sartor Resartus.*
The Life and Opinions of Herr Teufelsdröckh
(1834, 1920 edn), book i, pp. 48–49.

The sudden physical expansion of the weekly and daily newspaper press, and its more pronounced presence in the culture, required new forms of order to be imposed on the ensuing chaos. Not only did contemporaries not know what the social consequences of expansion might be, but, beyond what might be gleaned from local impressions, they were also in ignorance of the most basic information about its historical development, geographical diversity, management, circulation, content and political orientation. Ordering the new medium took two forms. The first sought to construct for it a historical narrative, which rendered its multitudinous and multivocal character comprehensible within particular readings of the social and political history of the British Isles. The second endeavoured to classify and conserve the teeming ephemera of newspapers in indexes, directories and collections. Both forms of ordering further defined newspapers as a distinct typology within Victorian print media.

Until 1850, accounts of newspapers and their development had generally been subordinated to studies of printing or outlines of the campaigns against the 'taxes on knowledge'. Such studies included those by the historian and critic John Oldmixon in 1742[1] and John Crawfurd

---

[1] John Oldmixon, *Memoirs of the Press, Historical and Political, for Thirty Years Past, From 1710 to 1740* (1742).

in 1836.[2] The 966 pages of C.H. Timperley's hugely ambitious
Dictionary of Printers and Printing, which began its account with the
pre-Christian era and the chapters of which were grouped into centuries,
appeared in 1839. The origins of the book lay in a series of two lectures
read by Timperley before the Warwick and Leamington Literary and
Scientific Institution in April 1828 'and the very flattering
commendations then bestowed' had induced him 'to pursue the subject
further, as a means both of self instruction and amusement for my leisure
hours'. In this leisurely pursuit of his enthusiasm, Timperley noted with
approval the progress made by newspapers despite restrictive legislation,
yet was alarmed to find that what ought to have been the 'glory of a free
country' was in fact far from 'being a free and independent record of the
vicissitudes of politics and power'. Whereas he expected newspapers to
record 'the moral and physical career of nations, . . . all accidents by
flood and field, aiding the cause and dissemination of knowledge, which,
while it amuses, ought also to instruct', what he discovered was a press
that had 'become the vehicle of party strife and petty feuds, in the hands
of designing men, who make no shame of being bought and sold like
common ware'. His many allusions to the liberty of the press, he assured
his readers, referred to his ideal of 'what the press should be, not what it
is'.[3] None the less, the assumption underlying Timperley's work was that
newspapers comprised an enlightening power, which liberated
knowledge from being 'bound up' in books, 'and kept in libraries and
retirement'. When 'distinct sheets' were to be found in 'every assembly,
and exposed on every table . . . the mechanic may equal in science,
however inferior in genius, the friar, whom his contemporaries feared as
a magician'.[4] A lecture by Edward Baines, proprietor of the *Leeds
Mercury,* on the origins of printing, however, conceded that while it
'would be very curious and interesting to form a computation of the
increased power' given by newspapers to increase 'the circulation of
knowledge', it was impossible for him to do so with any accuracy.[5]

Both Timperley and Baines, despite the graver reservations of the former,
had extrapolated from their histories of printing the thesis that newspapers
represented the most recent phase, and in some respects the culmination,
of the process of social transformation begun by the printing-press in the
sixteenth century.[6] Some 40 years after Baines drafted his lecture in Leeds,

---

[2] John Crawfurd, *The Taxes on Knowledge* (1836).

[3] C.H. Timperley, *A Dictionary of Printers and Printing, with the Progress of Literature,
Ancient and Modern* (1839), p. iv.

[4] Ibid., p. 807.

[5] Edward Baines, 'On the Origin and History of Printing', draft copy, n.d. (*c.* 1820),
Leeds Archives MS 89, p. 80.

[6] Ibid., p. 81.

Joseph Cowen, another Liberal journalist and editor of the *Newcastle Chronicle*, addressed his own local Eclectic Debating Society on the marvels of newspaper journalism. He presciently conceded that 'the new power . . . is very far yet from having developed either its extent or its energy, or the benignity of its influence upon man'. It remained too soon to know how best to work 'this great machinery', and mankind was still only serving its apprenticeship to it. A long apprenticeship, Cowen suggested, rather like his own as a printer, was 'the best mode of ascertaining the duties of those to whom this engine is entrusted and the benefits to be derived by those who are the recipients of its influence'. Cowen then surveyed the uses made of the press in politics, religion and literary culture over the previous three centuries, culminating in the most recent period of newspaper journalism. Only in the most recent times had the press come to minister to the services of the people, its 'long neglected but most important function'. Like Baines, Cowen regarded books as inaccessible reservoirs of knowledge. Quarterly and monthly periodicals too were narrow in scope and preoccupied with the 'toilsome labour of the literary and the learned'. The newspaper, in relation to the book and the periodical, was, admittedly, at first 'a poor and imperfect thing'. Gradually, however, its growth in size, range of content and circulation had led to the creation of a stimulating and entirely new kind of medium of communication, with 'its wondrous aggregate of matter and information; its universality and freedom of communication'.

The power of newspapers stemmed from their changed relationship with their society. Unlike books or periodicals, newspapers allowed 'the most distant classes of society' to communicate with each other, 'as if the penny post sent letters open that all might be read by all'. It identified with the interests of millions, not hundreds or thousands, and 'around it the high and low, the rich and poor may gather together all being represented'. Cowen believed that this tendency, if it did not serve to 'make all men one great family', then at least made them into 'one great society' in which 'obstinate inveterate prejudices' would be removed by 'reiterated attacks of reason until they give way'. Thus the function of newspapers was not to provide news and entertainment alone, but to challenge established practices, popular assumptions and political power. For Cowen, it would be the newspapers, by organising and concentrating public pressure, that would 'ultimately bring to a successful conclusion the noble struggles for Temperance, Voluntarism and Radicalism' as well as secure the abolition of the death penalty and slavery. The reduction of newspaper journalism to 'a sordid trade' that dealt in 'polluting trash' was an unwelcome and reactionary development that undermined the social mission of the press, and which required vigilant monitoring by both liberal journalists and the public alike. Only a journalism committed to the ideals of public service, Cowen insisted, could adequately address the pressing social needs of early-Victorian England.[7] Contemporary and modern readers could, perhaps, discern a self-justificatory tone to these self-reflective, though rarely self-critical, meditations by Baines and Cowen on the nature of their occupations. But both appear to have held with similar conviction the view that it was necessary to invoke a historical theory in order to explain and legitimate the business of newspaper publishing.

As Baines had acknowledged, however, the task of constructing historical accounts of the press on which such theories could be tested was hamstrung by a paucity of knowledge. In particular, the absence of any systematic attempt to impose bibliographic control over the many thousands of titles and editions of newspapers thus far published in the United Kingdom comprised a serious obstacle to research. The first consistent attempt to provide such an index began in 1846, when Charles Mitchell (1807–59) published his first volume of the *Newspaper Press Directory*, aimed primarily at advertisers but dedicated 'to the conductors and proprietors of the Public Press, the true and enlightened promoters of knowledge'. This annual listing of the newspapers of Britain, signifying price and date established, with titles grouped regionally and classified politically,[8] also included essays on the origin and progress of the newspaper press, including a debunking of the fraudulent claims made for the *English Mercurie* to be the earliest English newspaper produced during the Armada alarm of 1588. Advice was also provided for newspaper proprietors respecting the libel laws, and items of other news were gathered from various newspaper offices across the United Kingdom. Mitchell's ambitions for his *Directory* were founded on his conviction that newspapers had by that time become major publications, as he explained in his initial publisher's address:

> the newspaper press has obtained, and maintains, so prominent a station in the literature of the country; it is such a distinguishing feature of our social scheme; and forms so necessary an adjunct to every pursuit . . . that it requires a more dignified and permanent record of its statistics . . . than the mere sheet lists are calculated to afford.

He hoped that the *Directory* would swiftly become the 'standard book

---

[7] Joseph Cowen, 'An Essay on the Press, Read Before the Eclectic Debating Society, 1846', TWAS MS MF825/F17.

[8] For example, the entry for the *Morning Herald* read as follows: 'Daily, Price 5d, Established 1781. Advocacy – Conservative – Ministerial – Moderately Protectionist – Episcopal', followed by a general descriptive paragraph and name and address of the publisher.

of reference', and that it would also 'be valuable . . . as showing the origin and progress, also existing state of the most powerful engine in directing public opinion . . . '. In the following year, a second introductory essay spelt out the objectives in even grander terms, insisting that it was 'in the interest of the public . . . if they wish to continue to breathe the air of freedom' that they should 'hold high in honour and estimation the public journalist'. This was a point to which Mitchell returned in 1851 in an essay on 'The Power and Character of the Press', in which he denied that journalists in England, unlike those in France, lacked the social status associated with access to positions of political power. Such a separation of the journalist and the politician, he announced, like that of Church and State, should rather be a matter of national pride. Mitchell thus not only provided the first intelligible index of extant newspapers in Britain, but he simultaneously provided a platform for new histories of the newspaper press and boosted the morale of journalists with his sympathetic descriptions of their work. It could be argued also that by enabling journalists and editors to learn of each other's activities, and to communicate with each other as a particular interest group, Mitchell's *Directory* marks the beginning of the long and uneven process of professionalising the editorial segment of the newspaper industry.[9] The following section draws together the major endeavours by nineteenth-century historians and cataloguers to subject the products of the newspaper press to some semblance of order, and thus to offer a young and dynamic form of communication a higher commercial and political profile in the present by providing for it a better documented and more distinguished past.

Newspaper history

Cataloguing and systematising the products of an expanding newspaper industry, though essential for future historians, did not solve the problem of how contemporaries could write about newspapers in the past. The

---

[9] Charles Mitchell, *The Newspaper Press Directory* (1846), *passim*. See also Walter Wellsman, 'The *Newspaper Press Directory*, Its History and Progress, 1846–1895', *Newspaper Press Directory*, Golden Jubilee edition, 1895; David Linton, 'A Classic Among Directories', *The Media Reporter*, vols i, iii, 1977; David Linton, 'Mr Mitchell's National Work', *Journal of Advertising History*, vol. ii, 1979. No issues of the *Newspaper Press Directory* appeared in the following years: 1848, 1849, 1850, 1852, 1853, 1854, 1855. From 1848, *Eyre's Guide* listed newspapers and periodicals in the United Kingdom and her colonies, now continued as *Benn's Media Directory*. Mitchell's stepson, Walter Wellsman, succeeded him as editor of the *Directory* from 1859 to 1905, and was responsible for introducing in 1860 the first newspaper map of the United Kingdom.

first major attempt to do so was by Frederick Knight Hunt (1814–54), whose *The Fourth Estate: Contributions Towards a History of Newspapers, and the Liberty of the Press* appeared in 1850. Initially a physician, Knight Hunt's professional life as a journalist was principally associated with the *Daily News*, for which he served as assistant editor from its inception in 1846, and as full editor from 1852 until his death of typhus in 1854. Harriet Martineau, who wrote several hundred articles for his newspaper, remembered him as 'a man of sensitive conscience'.[10] Dedicated 'to the Journalists of England, and to their "constant readers"', Knight Hunt's two-volume work was, he confessed, in a curious echo of Timperley, 'written during disjointed odds and ends of time, before or between, or after, real work'. He was also aware that he was venturing down 'an almost untrodden path'. The first volume traces the history of the newspaper from its origins to 1800, but in it he also outlined his general approach. The newspaper for Knight Hunt was 'a great mental camera, which throws a picture of the whole world upon a single sheet of paper', but 'if it teaches, it teaches imperceptibly'. In a world that has grown 'tired of orators, and weary of the mimic stage, it should be more and more faithful in its reference to the intellectual familiar . . . the friendly broadsheet'. The purpose of the study was thus to discover how the newspaper had become 'a necessity of modern life'. He found it curious that, although so many talents had been drawn to the writing of newspapers, few had thought it sufficiently important to devote time to its history. One explanation for this was that only journalists had access to the necessary information, and, almost by definition, journalists were too busy meeting their deadlines to write such histories. However, it is significant that most of the historians of the newspaper press who were to follow Knight Hunt were either editors, working reporters or individuals engaged in some other capacity directly in the production of newspapers.

The first chapter of *The Fourth Estate* begins with a series of interleaved quotations from an impressive raft of commentators, including Dr. Johnson, Lord Lyndhurst, Canning, Thiers, Macaulay, Bulwer and Thomas de Quincey. Each in turn were drawn upon to attest to the beneficial powers of a free newspaper press. The stage was thus set to begin the historical argument, pursued in a series of chronologically ordered chapters, that sought to establish the truth of the assertion that the newspaper press 'wields the power of a FOURTH ESTATE'.[11] The second volume adopts a more thematic approach, with

---

[10] Harriet Martineau, *Harriet Martineau's Autobiography* (1855, 1983 edn), p. 413.

[11] Frederick Knight Hunt, *The Fourth Estate: Contributions Towards a History of Newspapers, and the Liberty of the Press* (1850), vol. i, pp. 1-8.

chapters on the press in the nineteenth century, the London dailies, the morning and evening papers, and reporting methods. At the end, the author warns his readers of the inevitability of factual errors in such an enterprise. 'This . . . is a first attempt', he reminds them, and they must 'understand the great difficulty of avoiding faults, both of omission and commission'.[12] In conclusion, he suggests that there existed a direct connection between the level of sophistication attained by newspapers and the general condition of society. Moreover, a truly popular press liberated the people from the more oppressive aspects of the state.

> The prevalence or scarcity of Newspapers in a country affords a sort of index to its social state. Where Journals are numerous, the people have power, intelligence, and wealth; where Journals are few, the many are in reality mere slaves. . . . The moral of the history of the press seems to be, that when any large proportion of a people have been taught to read, and when upon this possession of the tools of knowledge, there has grown up a habit of perusing public prints, the state is virtually powerless if it attempts to check the press.[13]

The relationship between the press, government and a liberal polity thus lie at the core of Knight Hunt's thesis concerning the significance of newspaper history. One reviewer of these volumes took this argument one step further, stating that there was no value associated with the history of newspapers in themselves, other than in its capacity to illustrate the course of social and political progress:

> The only history of the press in which the world at large is interested, or which, indeed, conveys a moral worth gathering, is the history of public opinion illustrated by the progress of the liberty of printing. The mere chronicle of the rise and expansion of newspapers is of no further value, beyond any curiosity that may attach to its personal details and anecdotes, than as it bears upon the larger question of personal liberty.[14]

Such prejudices about the medium, and about the past, were not uncommon in the 1850s. A lecture on the *Manchester Magazine* of 1743 delivered at the Liverpool Literary and Philosophical Society on 1 December 1856 noted disdainfully that the paper contained 'no theatrical notices, and very few advertisements; no public meetings; no reviews of books, or literary extracts; no leading articles; no notices of sermons, lectures &c'.[15] Congratulating themselves on the sophistication

---

[12] Ibid., p. 289. See also pp. 292–302, especially the reproduction of 16 Nov. 1839 by Thomas Watts, of the British Museum, on the *English Mercurie* forgery, ostensibly produced during the Armada alarm of 1588.

[13] Ibid., p. 292.

[14] Robert Bell, 'Review of F. Knight Hunt, "The Fourth Estate"', *Bentley's Miscellany*, June 1850, p. 596.

[15] *Minutes of the Liverpool Literary and Philosophical Society*, Liverpool Record Office, Liverpool City Libraries, MS D 060 Lit/1/6, 1 Dec. 1856.

of the more recent northern newspapers, contemporaries considered that the press of the previous century contained little that was of any intrinsic interest.

The next important texts to appear dealt not so much with personal liberty as with the relationship between journalism and political parties. For example, Benjamin Disraeli's brief period of ownership of the *Press* newspaper was chronicled in 1856, the year of the paper's dissolution.[16] Meanwhile, in France, a fuller history of the British press, in association with developments in the United States, was published in Paris by Philippe Athanase Cucheval Clarigny, formerly editor in chief of the *Constitutionnel* in Paris.[17] Whilst known in Britain, this important book was not to be translated into English for a further 11 years. It was followed in 1859 by a minor history by Charles A. Mackintosh,[18] a book whose significance was overshadowed by the publication in the same year of a two-volume history by Alexander Andrews. This was the first full-scale historical account to follow Knight Hunt's of 1850, and its publication met with general acclaim.[19] Andrews's history of British journalism to 1855 was the result of 14 years of research, and claimed an accuracy to which Knight Hunt could only have aspired. The first volume covered the period from the seventeenth to the end of the eighteenth century, but in a rare note of self-criticism he also reflected upon the peculiar difficulties of writing a chronological history of newspapers.[20] He explained that during his research he had organised his material in more thematic terms, gathering evidence on legislation, reporting methods, editors and so forth. Only when he began to write did he take the decision to coerce his material into a chronological structure, leaving the completed text as a 'puzzle' for which the index alone could provide the key. In relation to his sources, Andrews was also keenly aware of the importance of secrecy to the internal structures of

---

[16] The Press, *A Sketch of the Political History of the Last Three Years in Connection With The Press Newspaper, and the Part It Has Taken On the Leading Questions of the Time* (1856), founded by Disraeli in 1853 'for progressive Toryism', see also p. 126 below.

[17] Philippe Athanse Cucheval Clarigny, *Histoire de la Presse en Angleterre et aux Etats-Unis* (Paris, 1857, trans. by Alexander Andrews in 1870).

[18] Charles A. Mackintosh, *Popular Outlines of the Press, Ancient and Modern . . . With a Notice of the Newspaper Press* (1859).

[19] Alexander Andrews, *The History of British Journalism, From the Foundation of the Newspaper Press in England, to the Repeal of the Stamp Act in 1855 With Sketches of Press Celebrities*, vol. i, (1859).

[20] J.W. Robertson-Scott would later argue that it was not possible to periodise newspaper history, insisting that 'the story of journalism is one long course of steady natural progress', J.W. Robertson-Scott, 'The New Journalism', in *Sell's Dictionary of the World's Press* (1889), p. 48; see also the series on 'Anecdotal History of Journalism' published in *Sell's Dictionary of the World's Press* in 1897 and 1898.

journalism. The 'Press of England', he explained 'being, by general consent as well as by the desire of its conductors, worked behind a screen, it would be far from our province as from etiquette, to attempt to raise the curtain for the gratification of a few inquisitive minds'. Nevertheless, wherever journalists had allowed information about their work and private lives to enter the public domain, Andrews assured his readers that he had not hesitated to make use of the available evidence. Andrews's sensitivity to his sources, his concern for his readers and his engagement with the difficulties of historical narration mark him as the most perceptive of the early historians of the press in Britain.[21]

In Andrews's analysis, we find once more the same broad interpretation being proposed of the newspaper press as an index of the sacrifices made to secure English liberties. It was small wonder that the evolution of the newspaper had been gradual and problematic given the way in which it was 'checked by the indifference of a people or the caprices of a party; suppressed by a king, persecuted by a parliament, harassed by a licenser, burnt by a hangman, and trampled by a mob'.[22] The history of the newspaper was essentially the story of its long struggle to surmount these difficulties and to construct a better society. This much was to be expected in mid-Victorian newspaper historiography. Less expected, however, was the hostility towards earlier press historians. In a brief historiographical overview in the Preface, he paid tribute to a paper delivered by P.L. Simmonds on 21 June 1841 to the Statistical Society of London, 'which was the most elaborate, if not really the first, published collection of facts relating to the subject', but no such generosity was extended to his most recent predecessor, the pioneering Frederick Knight Hunt. His facts, Andrews claims, were merely 'thrown together' in what he disdainfully referred to as Knight Hunt's 'Contributions towards a History of Newspapers' (Andrews's italics). Similarly, Andrews had scant regard for any of the other early histories. *The Periodical Press of Great Britain; or, an Inquiry into the State of the Public Journals* of 1809 was 'a wretched pamphlet', and the *Encyclopaedia Britannica* contained a 'stereotyped falsehood', though *Chambers's Journal* in 1837 was grudgingly acknowledged to be 'about the best on the subject', along with articles in the *Edinburgh Review* and the *British and Foreign Quarterly Review* in 1837.[23] Finally, with a sideways glance at Cucheval Clarigny's recent efforts, Andrews noted that it was 'quite impossible for foreigners to *understand* our press: they

---

[21] Andrews, *History*, vol. i, pp. i–viii.

[22] Ibid., vol. i, pp. 1–2.

[23] Ibid., vol. i, p. 2. Andrews had also drawn upon Nichols's *Literary Anecdotes*, Chalmers's *Life of Ruddiman*, Timperley's *Encyclopaedia of Literary and Typographical*

have nothing like it'. In any case, Clarigny, like Knight Hunt, had marched too rapidly, and thus had 'embarrassed himself'. Having thus cleared the ground for his own work, Andrews set about to write his own account of the 'mighty Mind-Engine – of this tremendous Moral Power'.[24]

In general, Andrews's own volume was well received by the critics. *The North British Review* welcomed it as 'the best as well as latest on the subject . . . almost the only history of British Journalism deserving of the name', and agreed that the rise of the newspaper press was 'the fitting accompaniment and exponent of the era of prosperity which had dawned on our country'.[25] The same anonymous reviewer also approvingly quoted Macaulay on the press as an embodiment of the notion of 'constant improvement', which could be ascribed only to the 'ever advancing intelligence of the nation'. He did not add, however, that Macaulay had tempered his enthusiasm for the progressive potential of journalism by remarking that 'the influence exerted by popular sentiment on the politics of the newspaper press' imposed an important and much welcomed restraining influence on the capacity of journalism to dictate as well as to report events. Nor did he much appreciate J.S. Mill's 'tame and chilling' treatise *On Liberty*, whose author he berated for asserting that England was 'not a place of mental freedom', and for suggesting that the *'regime* of public opinion' policed by the middle class speaking through the newspapers, amounted to an insidious form of moral repression. Mill's interpretation of the role of the press as 'an intolerance and a tyranny . . . whose yoke must be broken assunder' outraged Andrews's reviewer, who regarded newspapers as 'our highest glory, the source and security of our liberty'. 'What eccentric freaks does Mr Mill meditate?' he wondered, describing Mill's anxieties as 'the Quixotism of liberty' which actively endangered the hard-won freedoms of the press.[26]

Despite the venom generated by his book, Andrews remains one of the most important of the newspaper historians of the nineteenth century.

Anecdote, and papers read by J. Hearn, editor of *Salisbury and Wiltshire Herald* to the Salisbury Mechanics' Institute in 1836, G.F. Richardon to the Marylebone Literary and Scientific Institution, 27 Jul. 1840, and C. Kemplay, to the Leeds Philosophical Society, 2 Jan. 1855.

[24] Andrews, *History* (1859), vol. i, p. 6. Another reviewer, writing in the temperance journal *Meliora* in 1863, was saddened to encounter such hostility to Knight Hunt's earlier work. Knight Hunt, it was claimed, was 'quite alive to the imperfections of his work, and was busily engaged in bringing out a new edition when he died'.

[25] 'The British Press: Its Growth, Liberty and Power', *The North British Review*, vol. xxx, May 1859, review of Alexander Andrews, *The History of British Journalism* (1859), p. 384–86.

[26] Ibid., pp. 398–402. See also Macaulay, *History of England*, vol. iv, p. 607.

For in addition to his two-volume *History*, we find him constantly engaged with historical matters in the *Newspaper Press*, the trade periodical which he edited. Andrews was well aware of the difficulties of locating sources of evidence for newspaper history, and rejected the writing of contemporary newspaper history on the grounds that it was 'open to invidious influences and construction'. However, he found that 'the records of the Press were so scattered, and we had to seek them out from such obscure and, in many instances, incongruous collections, that we feel a great help might be given to future historians by accumulating facts as they occur'.[27] Whether or not the task of resolving such methodological difficulties as these had matured Andrews as a historian, he had become by 1870 far more sympathetic to the shortcomings of earlier press historians than he had been at the time of the first publication of his *History* in 1859. He intended in 1870 to update the history of newspapers by purchasing the copyrights to 'the standard works' of Knight Hunt, Clarigny and others 'till the *Newspaper Press* will become the general title for a complete collection of all works heretofore published on journalism . . . '. Andrews began by arranging the translation of Clarigny's history of 1857, an edited version of which appeared in instalments in the *Newspaper Press* from 1 June 1871. By this time, Andrews had come to appreciate that Clarigny 'had some wonderfully clear opinions of the gradual growth of our political power through the steady stages of the development of the freedom of the Press'.[28]

Andrews's *History*, the impact of which on the burgeoning industry of newspaper studies in mid-Victorian England can scarcely be exaggerated, led to numerous new ventures. Saunders, Otley and Co.'s index of *The Newspaper Press of the Present Day*, first published in 1860, relied

---

[27] *Newspaper Press*, 1 Dec. 1869, p. 3.

[28] *Newspaper Press*, p. 3. Among these were Clarigny's account of the abandoning of a narrow dependence on political patronage at the end of the eighteenth century, with the appearance of such newspapers as *The Globe* and the *Morning Advertiser*, 'it is at that date in fact that the birth or transformation of journals, which are still in existence in England, took place . . . not one of these papers was founded under the influence or with the support of any prominent politician, but were purely private speculations. All of them, from their commencement or soon after it, assumed the character of advertisement sheets, which united, with the news of the day, a political commentary, but which above all made it their special business to collect the kind of information which the public was most anxious for. We can even mention instances of journals being started solely with a view to advertisements,' for example, the *British Press*, *Newspaper Press*, 1 Nov. 1871, p. 224. See also Clarigny, *Histoire*, p. 67, 'C'est aux derniers jours du XVIIIe siecle que nous marquerons le commencement de cette troisième période'. It was with this 'third period' that Andrews and other Victorian newspaper historians were, understandably, most concerned.

heavily on Andrews for its material. His description of newspapers as 'an army of liberty, with a rallying point in every town . . . a police of public safety, and a sentinel of public morals' was approvingly reproduced, but in other respects it departed from Andrews's own agenda by focusing more on newspaper statistics in the period following 1855.[29] This was followed in 1861 by Arthur Hall and Co.'s, *The Newspaper Press Census for 1861*, which set itself the task of making the reviled penny papers more socially acceptable to both readers and advertisers. Though treated by many as 'an intrusive and unwelcome guest', the cheap press should nevertheless 'be acknowledged as legitimate descendants of the old newspaper family, and as possessing, though yet in their infancy, great influence on the masses, for good or evil'. Such an approach was welcomed by a correspondent to the *Quarterly Review* as a sign that 'the penny papers . . . are worthy of study, as the pioneers of public opinion for the past, and as beacons for the future'.[30]

Shorter newspaper histories by James Amphlett and Charles J. Gratton appeared in 1860,[31] but the significance of the growth of journalism was also dealt with in more general studies of law and ethics. Sir Thomas Erskine May devoted two chapters of his *Constitutional History of England* of 1861 to 'The Press and Liberty of Opinion',[32] whilst William Edward Hartpole Lecky, in his *History of European Morals* of 1869 described the 'most momentous intellectual revolution' currently taking place in England as a consequence of the development of newspapers. Lecky was struck by the notion that books and monthly and quarterly periodicals no longer monopolised good writing on literary and philosophical matters, and that a discernible shift was occurring from these venerable literary forms to the weekly and daily newspapers. Newspapers had for many years dominated the field of political writing

---

[29] Saunders, Otley and Co., *The Newspaper Press of the Present Day: Its Birth and Growth Throughout the United Kingdom and British Islands, From 1665; Including the Young Cheap Press and the Metropolitan and Suburban District Papers, 1860* (1860), pp. 1, 11. They also drew on material recently published in the *North British Review*, vol. xxx, May 1859, and the *British Quarterly Review*, Apr. 1859.

[30] Arthur Hall and Co., *The Newspaper Press Census for 1861, Showing the Newspaper Population of the United Kingdom, and Its Expansion Since 1665, Including the Births and Deaths in 1860, Together With a Statistical and General Account of Its Present Politics and Position* (1861), pp. 3–4.

[31] James Amphlett, *The Newspaper Press, in Part of the Last Century, and Up to the Present Period of 1860* (1860); Charles J. Gratton, *The Gallery: a Sketch of the History of Parliamentary Reporting and Reporters* (1860). For the classic account of parliamentary reporting in the late nineteenth century, see Michael Macdonagh, *The Reporters' Gallery* (1913).

[32] Sir Thomas Erskine May, *The Constitutional History of England Since the Accession of George the Third* (1861, 1912 edn), vol. ii, chs ix and x, pp. 1–123.

and information, but in the past decade they had also begun systematically to address a broader range of issues. Lecky was excited by the potential of such publications to transform patterns of thought and behaviour on a mass scale. As a consequence of their 'immense circulation, their incontestable ability, and the power they possess of continually reiterating their distinctive doctrines, from the impatience, too, of long and elaborate writings', Lecky calculated that newspapers exercised 'a greater influence than any other productions of the day in forming the ways of thinking of ordinary educated Englishmen', adding that 'the many consequences, good and evil, of this change . . . will be the duty of future historians to trace'. Specifically, he was impressed by the ability of lawyers, too busy to write books, to contribute shorter articles on law and ethical matters for the newspapers, and ascribed the continuing influence of utilitarian ideas to the literary activities of this professional group, writing for the public through the medium of the popular press.[33]

The next major historical study of newspaper journalism appeared with the publication in two volumes of James Grant's *The Newspaper Press: Its Origin – Progress – and Present Position*, in 1870 and 1871. Grant (1802–79) was editor of the *Morning Advertiser,* the organ of the Licensed Victuallers' Association, from 1850 to 1871, and author of more than 40 monographs. Unlike his predecessors, Grant focused almost exclusively on the London newspapers. Beginning with a reference to Macaulay's dictum that 'the only true history of a country is to be found in its newspapers', Grant began with the usual overview of the early newspapers of the *Acta Diurna*, the *Gazettas* and the *English Mercurie* forgery. The first volume focused on a chronological history of the newspaper up to the early nineteenth century, with chapters eight to ten chronicling the development of the main London newspapers. The second volume adopted a more thematic approach. Following five chapters on *The Times* and other London dailies were studies of the structure of management, Parliamentary reporting, special correspondents and penny-a-liners, the struggle of the unstamped, the telegraph, advertisements 'viewed as illustrative of human life', and births, marriages and deaths. A closing chapter compared journalism in the London, Paris and New York dailies, and, in the conclusion, Grant addressed what he characteristically termed 'The Mission and the Power

---

[33] William Edward Hartpole Lecky, *History of European Morals From Augustus to Charlemagne* (1869), vol. i, pp. 136–37. Lecky's comment on the power of the press in 'forming the ways of thinking of ordinary educated Englishmen' was noted approvingly by Alexander Andrews in the *Newspaper Press*, 1 May 1869, p. 107; see also further extracts from Lecky in *Newspaper Press*, op. cit., p. 156.

of the Press'. Wondering when and where the extension of newspaper journalism would end, Grant confided his belief that there was

> something absolutely sublime in the thought that there is at this moment so mighty a combination of intellectual, social, and moral agencies engaged, through means of newspaper journalism, in the great work of seeking to improve men's minds, to liberate them from all sorts of slavery, . . . and to transform their moral character.[34]

That the historicism is Whiggish in its optimism is hardly surprising in this liberal, free-trade account of a commercial medium emerging out of a system of state regulation. But the fact that so many newspaper historians and their reviewers were adopting this relatively unproblematic approach, often in sharp contrast to other forms of discussion on the social and intellectual consequences of popular newspapers, suggests that, professional jealousies notwithstanding, they were engaged in a joint project whose outcome was to provide for the new medium a tradition and a dignity sanctified by time which it had not hitherto possessed. And they did so not in newspapers, but in books. The 'mission and power' of popular journalism was being articulated and explained in the very medium that was ostensibly being overtaken by it.

Alexander Andrews, however, remained unimpressed by Grant's endeavours. Reviewing his two volumes in three consecutive issues of the *Newspaper Press* beginning in November 1871, Andrews remarked on a style that was 'gossipy, and occasionally discursive'. He later reflected that 'Mr Grant's researches led to no original discoveries . . . sheer trifling with his subject, which can scarcely be tolerated with patience'. 'Is this', he asked, 'the slipshod way in which Mr Grant supposes that history should be written?' Finally, he corrected Grant's errors against his own research and that of Knight Hunt and suggested somewhat condescendingly that, should Grant wish to write further volumes, he would be at perfect liberty to make free use of Andrews's personal archive of newspaper history.[35] James Routledge, in his study of the freedom of the press since 1660, which appeared in 1876, was also wary of Grant's work and was obliged to distinguish clearly between Grant's facts and his opinions. Of the latter, he would 'have no concern'. In particular, he found the profile of Edward Miall, editor of the *Nonconformist*, to be a curious and unjust caricature.[36]

---

[34] James Grant, *The Newspaper Press: Its Origin – Progress – and Present Position* (1871), vol. ii, pp. 454–56.

[35] *Newspaper Press* in Nov. 1871, pp. 227–29; 1 Dec. 1871, pp. 9–11; 1 Jan. 1872, pp. 32–34.

[36] James Routledge, *History of Popular Progress*, pp. 496–97.

Charles Pebody (1850–91) was similarly critical of Grant in his own tribute to English journalism, published in 1882. As a reporter on the *Morning Advertiser*, Pebody had worked under James Grant until his appointment as editor of the *Yorkshire Post* in 1882. Yet, he was adamant that the history of English journalism was yet to be written, and dismissed Grant's 'well-known volumes'. Whereas Andrews had stressed the poverty of evidence as the principal reason for the absence of an adequate history of newspapers, Pebody pointed to other, more methodological difficulties. In part it was because the press was of relatively recent origin, and partly because historians preferred 'if possible, to deal with accomplished facts . . . instead of dealing with one of the living forces of the moment, where everything is controversy, criticism, chaos'. Historians were singularly ill-equipped to engage with an institution which was continually in flux, and which, day by day, was 'striking out fresh developments of its enterprise and power . . . and . . . arrogating to itself some of the chief functions of Parliament – most of its functions of public criticism, most of its functions of debate, and many of its functions as a Constitutional check upon the conduct of Ministers'. Finally, Pebody expanded on what he regarded to be the broader implications of newspaper history. The history of the press in England was the history, if not of English liberty, then 'of all those popular forces and political franchises which have given strength and solidity to English institutions' and 'welded together the whole British Empire'. Not untypically for this type of study, he again began with the Roman newspapers and jumped to England in the early seventeenth century, followed by five chapters on *The Times*.[37] But his short text is revealing in that it embodies a more ambivalent approach to the liberal theory of the press, and to the connection between newspapers and individual freedom, than had so far been seen in histories of this kind. Newspapers, he acknowledged, were in themselves not literature, 'except in the sense in which playbills are literature', their purpose being to reproduce daily 'a picture of the state of the world . . . and to tell us . . . what we ought to think and feel about everything'.[38] Pebody pursued the argument to question the notion that the newspaper press constituted a Fourth Estate, describing it perceptively instead as the 'second representation of the Third Estate', a form of 'Popular Parliament' in a polity that did not yet allow for universal suffrage.[39]

The 1880s was a particularly fertile decade for historical writing on newspapers. Following Pebody came a study of the key London daily

---

[37] Charles Pebody, *English Journalism and the Men Who Have Made It* (1882), pp. ii–iv.
[38] Ibid., pp. 164–66.
[39] Ibid., p. 176.

newspapers by Joseph Hatton (1839–1907), whose *Journalistic London* of 1882 drew on his own experiences as an editor of some ten newspapers and magazines, and as a reporter for, among others, the *Observer*, the *Daily Telegraph*, the *Standard*, and the *People*.[40] Three years later, Mason Jackson brought out *The Pictorial Press: Its Origin and Progress*, in which he reminded his readers of the origin of news transmission in formats other than the written. News had preceded print and the newspaper, and had long been the subject of songs and recitations by wandering ballad-singers. With the spread of printing, however, sermons, satires and accounts of journeys had often 'assumed the character of *news* to attract readers'.[41] Beginning with the illustrated broadsides of the late sixteenth century, Jackson went on to focus principally on the history of the *Illustrated London News*, founded by Herbert Ingram on 14 May 1842, with 16 pages and 32 woodcuts. The paper's circulation rose to 66,000 within the first year, doubled in the crisis-ridden year of 1848, and saw further increases in 1851 during the Great Exhibition. These figures remained high throughout the Crimean War, though did not again reach 1851 levels, which Jackson saw as a hopeful sign that peaceful events could compete with wars and disasters for public attention.[42] But the main value of Jackson's account was the significant contribution it made to the broadening of the definition of journalism to include illustration, and to preparing the way for the innovations early in the next century of photojournalism. In the same year a shorter historical survey of newspapers also appeared in the *Printer*, the quarterly journal of the printing trade. Lacking Andrews's grasp of the evidence, and Pebody's reservations concerning the influence of the press, this article reiterated the liberal faith in an unreconstructed form. In less than two centuries since the abolition of censorship in 1695, it was argued, the press had become a power which, if impossible to measure, was also 'impossible to limit'. Its history was the 'history of progress in science, art, learning, truth, and Freedom'.[43]

The last major historical study of English newspapers to be published in the Victorian period appeared in two volumes in 1887. Its author, Henry Richard Fox Bourne (1837–1909), was, like Knight Hunt, Andrews and Grant, a working journalist. Originally a civil servant at the War Office, he had retired in 1870 after criticising Gladstone from a 'radical independent' position. He subsequently served as editor of the

---

[40] Joseph Hatton, *Journalistic London: Being a Series of Sketches of the Famous Pens and Papers of the Day* (1882), *passim*.

[41] Mason Jackson, *The Pictorial Press: Its Origin and Progress* (1885), pp. 5–6.

[42] Ibid., pp. 300–03. See also Denis Gifford, *Victorian Comics* (1976).

[43] E.J.C., 'Notes on News and Newspapers', *Printer*, May 1885, pp. 18–20.

Weekly Dispatch from 1876 to 1887, as well as being an active social reformer and secretary of the Aborigines Protection Society. After such a range of experience in public life, he felt confident in declaring that 'Newspapers are now thrones and pulpits, and journalism assumes to itself the right and power to control and reform the world', although he could wryly comment on newspaper history that 'a complete account of English Newspapers, past and present, would fill many volumes, which, when written, would probably find very few readers'. A chronological survey, the first volume of Fox Bourne's study covered the period 1621 to 1820, and the second, the years 1820 to 1887. In it, he paid homage to Knight Hunt, Andrews, Grant and Pebody, but regarded one purpose of his book as being to 'fill many gaps and correct many errors in previous works on the subject'. His real ambition, however, was to 'call attention to the ways in which newspapers have influenced the general progress of society – sometimes hindering as well as helping it, and have been used as agents for such help or hindrance'. The intention was to understand more fully the relations that had developed between newspapers and the spheres of politics and literature, 'in successive generations and under various direction'. Earlier historians had dealt inadequately with these issues. Many 'incidents and episodes in the history of journalism' had previously been touched upon by Nichols, Chalmers, 'and other antiquaries, and by writers of gossip-books and memoirs'. The only serious studies, he conceded, had been undertaken by Frederick Knight Hunt, in a work which he described as 'painstaking and instructive', and Alexander Andrews, both of which served as rich sources for Fox Bourne's own work. But diligent as these writers were, he added, 'they left many things unsaid and said many things inaccurately. Their narratives closed, moreover, at dates now somewhat remote'. Charles Pebody's 'bright little shilling volume' of 1882, had been 'mainly compiled from Grant's book, but avoiding most of its blunders and containing some fresh and welcome information'. Neither Pebody, nor Joseph Hatton's volume of the same year, occupied much of the ground which Fox Bourne had selected for his study. Henry Sampson's *History of Advertising* and Mason Jackson's work on the pictorial press were similarly tangential to his own project. The only self-criticism which he conceded was his admission that disproportionate space had been devoted to the *Examiner* and the *Weekly Dispatch*, both of which he had edited during his 20-year career as a journalist.[44]

The second volume, also published in 1887, was a tribute to a style of journalism that Fox Bourne believed was in danger of disappearing from

---

[44] Henry Richard Fox Bourne, *English Newspapers. Chapters in the History of Journalism* (1887), vol. i, pp. i–ix; see also vol, ii, p. 390.

the pages of the popular newspapers, and provided a stinging critique of some contemporary trends. 'The Modern Revolution' brought about by the fiscal reforms of the period 1855 to 1861, being the consequence of earlier struggles, was for him 'a culmination as much as starting point for a Golden Age'.[45] Of the cumulative effect of newspapers on social thought and behaviour he was in no doubt, 'even the humblest journals have done something to influence public or local opinion, not only by their bare statements of facts, but by their modes of stating them, and by their few or many comments thereon'.[46] However, this influence had been at its most benign, and at its 'highest level of real value', in the early 1870s. By this time, the technologies of printing and distribution, and methods of news-gathering, had reached their peak, while virtually all fiscal and legislative restraints had been removed. Moreover, the competition for readers between titles had sharpened, and if anything had improved the quality of British journalism, but was not yet keen enough to drive editors into 'unworthy ways of attracting and amusing readers'.[47] Fox Bourne went so far as to attribute the Conservative victory in the 1874 general election to the power wielded by the press in this unique period of its history.[48] The late 1880s, however, had brought unwelcome changes in the style and content of newspapers. Fox Bourne expressed his distaste for W.T. Stead's 'Americanisation of English journalism', and if he was sceptical of its claim to have mobilised public opinion to pressurise government to dispatch General Gordon to Khartoum, he was clearly shocked by the 'Maiden Tribute' articles which had led to Stead's imprisonment. As 'self-constituted censors of public morals and reckless pursuers of private objects', the newspapers had relied increasingly on 'insinuations and innuendoes when the scandalous details they sought for were scanty or had no existence'. Fox Bourne found 'mild precedence' for this style of journalism in the writings of Charles Dickens and Henry Mayhew, and before them in those of Defoe and Steele, but there was much that was new in the work of 'these latest travellers in the field of sensationalism'.[49] It would thus be mistaken to assume that Fox Bourne was adopting in his history the same uncritical Whig view of the progressive improvement of newspaper journalism and its increasingly beneficial effects on society which had so dominated earlier accounts. He acknowledged that the power of the press to influence opinion was probably greater in the late 1880s than it had ever

---

[45] Ibid., vol ii, p. 232.
[46] Ibid., vol. ii, p. 252.
[47] Ibid., p. 284.
[48] Ibid., p. 327.
[49] Ibid., pp. 343–44.

been, and that newspapers

> not only tell their readers what is being done in every part of the
> world, but also . . . instruct them in every imaginable line of thought
> and action. It is not easy to conceive how newspapers can make
> much more progress than they have already made, either as business
> concerns or as guides of public opinion.

Yet, the greater commercialism of the newspaper industry in the 1880s
was for him a powerful disincentive to good journalism. Fox Bourne
acknowledged that newspapers could only operate in a free, commercial
market, but he was fearful that 'the community suffers, though the
individuals connected with it might gain, when a paper is "worked" for
money-making purposes alone, like a shop, or a factory, or a patent
medicine'. To avoid this, it was essential that all those engaged in the
production of newspapers 'from the penny-a-liner to the capitalist
manager' should regard themselves as members of a profession, with its
own ethos and code of conduct, more like preachers, physicians or
soldiers than 'tradesmen'. He was certain that the battle for a liberal,
socially useful newspaper press had not been lost, but none the less the
public needed to be on its guard. Whilst fiscal reform had undermined
'sedition, blasphemy, scurrility, and immorality' in newspapers, the
freedom of the press from state controls had itself brought certain
disadvantages.[50] Quoting from the *Weekly Dispatch* of 30 January 1887,
he reminded his readers that 'the great weakness of democracy is that it
makes easy the path of demagogues'.[51]

In a follow-up survey published in 1900, Fox Bourne offered a clearer
chronology of newspaper development. A period of 'press persecution',
which began in the eighteenth century, culminated with the Duke of
Wellington's failure to prosecute the *Morning Journal* in 1829. This was
followed under the more enlightened ministries of William IV by a
period of 'press liberation', which reached its fruition in 1855. As a
consequence, aggregate newspaper circulations, calculated on the basis
of stamp returns, had increased from 39 million in 1836 to 122 million
in 1854. The third period, from 1855 to 1875, was one of 'press
cheapening', and the current fourth period of 'press widening' had
opened with W.T. Stead's innovations in the *Pall Mall Gazette* from
1883. By 1900, Fox Bourne was less reserved in his judgement than he
had been in 1887 and, on balance, the author concluded that the
progress of the newspaper press over the previous century had been
'marvellous, and in most respects altogether satisfactory'. One other
significant aspect of Fox Bourne's later writing was his re-evaluation of

---

[50] Ibid., pp. 368–70.
[51] Ibid., p. 353.

the history of the unstamped press of the early 1830s. The attack on the unstamped had provided the early free-trade reformers with a powerful lever to shift government fiscal policy, on the grounds that a level playing field in the newspaper market would remove the dangers of the unstamped far more effectively than would the persecution and imprisonment of the editors, publishers and distributors of the illegal sheets. But in 1900, Fox Bourne could 'honour them for their good work' since 'their faults were not of their making [and] the fruits of their faulty action are ours'.[52]

The 1890s saw further studies in newspaper history, beginning with the publication in 1890 of Alfred Baker's *The Newspaper World: Essays on Press History and Work, Past and Present*. H.W. Massingham's *The London Daily Press* followed in 1892, reproduced from the *Leisure Hour*, with chapters on *The Times*, the *Daily News*, the *Standard*, the *Daily Telegraph*, the *Daily Chronicle*, and the penny and halfpenny evening papers, providing brief histories of each. It also contained a series of articles on the history of the British newspaper written by Sir Edward Russell, editor of the *Liverpool Daily Post*, for the *Brooklyn Daily Eagle* in 1897, which stressed, for foreign consumption, the fact that 'the newspaper Press of the Queen's reign . . . has been revolutionized'.[53] Studies of newspaper journalism also began to appear in scholarly journals, for example William Henry Allnutt's survey of 'English provincial presses' appeared in *Bibliographica* in 1896, or the account by J. Holland Rose of 'The Unstamped Press, 1815–36' in the *English Historical Review* of October 1897. The following year A. Berkeley's 'A Sketch of Early Provincial Journalism' was published in the *Association of Archaeological Societies Reports and Papers*. As the newspaper industry matured, newspaper history was beginning to acquire a degree of scholarly respectability. Finally, in 1899, C.D. Collet published his *History of the Taxes on Knowledge: Their Origin and Repeal*, not a history of the press as much as an account of the campaign to free the press of the remaining burden of taxation. Finally, as newspapers became more acceptable as a historical source, and as the legitimate subject of research, their articles also began to be used in education, especially in the teaching of politics, history and journalism itself. Harry Findlater Bussey and Thomas Wilson Reid's *The Newspaper Reader: the Journals of the 19th Century on Events of the Day*, written in 1879 at the prompting of

---

[52] H.R. Fox Bourne, 'London Newspapers', *Progress of British Newspapers in the Nineteenth Century, Illustrated* (1900), pp. 9–18. During the previous decade or so, heroic accounts of the persecutions of Wilkes and Leigh Hunt had appeared in numerous publications, including *Sell's Dictionary of the World's Press*, (1888), pp. 63–84.

[53] 'Sir Edward Russell on the Victorian Press', *Journalist and Newspaper Proprietor*, 5 June 1897, pp. 198–99.

an educationalist, was one of the earliest of the journalism textbooks.

Individual titles also found their historians in the closing decades of the century. Jubilee editions were intended by their publishers to signal the maturity, trustworthiness and respectability of the older titles, as well as to rescue from the oblivion of the files 'valuable and interesting matter that was deemed worthy of permanent record' in a more easily accessible form.[54] In the 1890s a stream of such jubilee histories were published, among them *Berrow's Worcester Journal – the Oldest English Newspaper* in 1890, the *History of the Bath Herald, Established 1792* in 1892 and John B. Hardcastle's *History of the Wolverhampton Chronicle* in 1893. London's first halfpenny paper celebrated its thirtieth birthday with a special issue of *The Echo* on 8 December 1898, and in 1903 James Beresford Atlay saluted the centenary of the *Globe*. More substantial newspaper biographies also appeared in the 1890s, including most notably *The Daily News Jubilee: a Political and Social Retrospect of Fifty Years of the Queen's Reign* by Justin McCarthy and John Robinson.[55] Though not a jubilee history, William Shepherdon's study of the *Sheffield Daily Telegraph* of 1876 was characteristic of the hagiographical style that would in future dominate the genre. Regional studies were also a product of the last two decades of the nineteenth century, with studies appearing on the development of the press in such cities as Liverpool and Manchester, counties such as Hampshire, and the rather different trajectories taken by the press in Scotland and Wales.[56]

Finally, the story was told by means of biography and autobiography. These texts may broadly be divided into three categories. The first represented journalism as adventure, mainly of a military nature. William Howard Russell, for example, published ten volumes of memoirs of foreign wars between 1855 and 1895, the last being a retrospective account of the Crimean campaign. Others included

---

[54] *The Jubilee Chronicle of the Newcastle Exhibition*, May 1887.

[55] *Berrow's Worcester Journal – the Oldest English Newspaper* (Worcester, 1890); *History of the Bath Herald, Established 1792* (Bath, 1892); John B. Hardcastle, *History of the Wolverhampton Chronicle* (Wolverhampton, 1893); James Beresford Atlay, *The Globe Centenary: a Sketch of Its History* (1903); Justin McCarthy and John Robinson, *The Daily News Jubilee: a Political and Social Retrospect of Fifty Years of the Queen's Reign* (1896); William Shepherdson, *Reminiscences in the Career of a Newspaper: Starting a 'Daily' in the Provinces* (1876). Curiously, a full biography of Delane did not appear until Arthur Irwin Dasent, *John Thadeus Delane, Editor of 'The Times'*, vol. i, (1908).

[56] John Christopher Morley, *The Newspaper Press and Periodical Literature of Liverpool*, (Liverpool, 1887); Frederick Leary, 'The Manchester Press: a History', *Manchester Monthly*, no. 1, 1894; F.E. Edwards, *The Early Newspapers of Hampshire* (Southampton, 1889); H.A. Boswell, *About Newspapers: Chiefly English and Scottish* (Edinburgh, 1888); J.D. Cockburn, 'Beginnings of the Scottish Newspaper Press', *The Scottish Review*, vols 19, 1891 and 21, 1893.

Michael Burke Honan's history of the Austro-Italian war of 1848, and
Edmond O'Donovan's exotic account of his travels in central Asia as a
reporter for the *Daily News*.[57] The second category includes a large
number of Victorian biographies of prominent figures who were also
engaged in journalism at one stage or another of their lives, of which
George Jacob Holyoake's studies of Henry Hetherington (1849) and
Richard Carlile (1870) are prominent examples. The third type involve
studies that foreground newspaper work, and include the tribute paid by
Edward Baines Jr to his father in 1851, which he described as 'the first
full scale biography of a newspaper owner',[58] and W. Robertson Nicoll's
study of James Macdonnell, published in 1890, which, with 'scrupulous
regard for the great traditions of English journalism', sought to write 'the
life of a journalist – perhaps the only life of a journalist pure and simple
ever written'.[59] Many of the individuals who had been involved in the
refashioning of the mid-Victorian press were, by the last two decades of
the nineteenth century, either dead or had reached a reflective old age. In
either case, it was apparent that there was growing public interest in
their life histories as newspapermen, and in that generational sense at
least, modern journalism had come of age.

Directories, indexes and collections

The efforts of the London Statistical Society in 1841 and 1844 to gather
evidence on the distribution of newspapers, and of Mitchell's *Newspaper
Press Directory* from 1846 to provide an accurate list of existing titles,
were followed after 1855 by numerous other attempts to index, collect
and preserve newspapers. The *Scottish Newspaper Directory and Guide
to Advertisers* of 1855, published in anticipation of the passing of the
third reading of the bill to repeal the Stamp Act, predicted the imminence
of 'a complete revolution in the established order of things with regard
to the Fourth Estate'. Its publisher, Thomas Jack, observed that in
Glasgow large numbers of speculators were ready to start daily

---

[57] Michael Burke Honan, *The Personal Adventures of 'Our Own Correspondent' in
Italy* (1852); Edmond O'Donovan, *The Merv Oasis: Travels and Adventures East of the
Caspian During the Years 1879, 1880, and 1881* (1882), in 2 vols.
[58] George Somes Layard, *Mrs Lynn Linton: Her Life, Letters and Opinions* (1901), is a
particularly important biography of the first salaried woman journalist to be employed by
a London daily (the *Morning Chronicle*).
[59] W. Robertson Nicoll, *James Macdonnell, Journalist* (1890), p. 1. Other examples
include Thomas Frost, *Reminiscences of a Country Journalist* (1886, 1888), William Hunt,
Then and Now; or, Fifty Years of Newspaper Work (1887).
[60] Thomas C. Jack, *Scottish Newspaper Directory, and Guide to Advertisers. A*

newspapers 'at an hour's notice',[60] and he warned advertisers that since the Stamp Returns of 1854 were probably the last that would ever be issued, they would in future have no means of comparing the circulation of different newspapers other than by consulting such commercial *Directories* as his own. Once the legislative reforms of 1855 and 1861 had been secured, Thomas Jack's speculative venture in Glasgow was followed by a host of imitators. Samuel Deacon's *Newspaper Handbook and Advertiser's Guide* appeared intermittently between 1863 and 1904, while Frederick May's *London Press Directory and Advertiser's Handbook* was published for 20 years after 1871 before being transformed into *Willing's Press Guide* in 1891. *Everett's Directory of the Principal Newspapers of the World* appeared in 1881 and *The Philosophy of Advertising* of 1881 and 1882 acquired the more mundane title of *Sell's Dictionary of the World's Press* in 1883. Though essentially an index of titles, *Sell's Dictionary* contained valuable introductory essays on the history and current condition of the newspapers of the United Kingdom. Directories and histories of advertising also provided overviews of the development of newspapers, including T.B. Browne's *The Advertiser's ABC* from 1886 and Henry Sampson's *History of Advertising* of 1874. Local directories also added to the growing literature, for example *Arrowsmith's Dictionary of Bristol* of 1884 included profiles of local newspapers, whilst local lists of titles were collated by H. Wightman in his *List of Newspapers in Lancashire, Yorkshire and Cheshire*, published in 1887, and in T.B. Browne's *Geographical Arrangement of the Country Press of the United Kingdom* of 1891.[61]

Accessibility to the contents of newspapers also improved markedly as the scale of the press was enlarged after 1855. The first newspaper cuttings agency was opened in London by Romeike in 1851, and early indexes appeared shortly thereafter. These included *Giddings' Index to The Times* of 1863–64, and *Palmer's Index to The Times Newspaper*, launched in 1868. The latter, published by London bookseller Samuel Palmer, also began to issue retrospective indexes which eventually

---

Complete Manual of the Newspaper Press (Edinburgh, 1855), pp. iii–iv, 24. See also sections on 'The Position and Character of the Newspaper Press', pp. 19–28, and 'The Law of Newspapers', pp. 29–33.

[61] T.B. Browne, *The Advertiser's ABC* (1886), Henry Sampson, *History of Advertising* (1874) [see also T.R. Nevett, *Advertising in Britain, a History* (1982)]. *Arrowsmith's Dictionary of Bristol* (Bristol, 1884); H. Wightman, *List of Newspapers in Lancashire, Yorkshire and Cheshire* (1887); T.B. Browne, *Geographical Arrangement of the Country Press of the United Kingdom* (1891).

[62] For a fuller account of the indexing of *The Times*, see Colin H.J. Kyte, 'The Times Index' in *The Indexer*, Spring 1967. *The Official Index to The Times* was started in 1906.

reached back to the first issue in 1790.[62] One reviewer remarked that, with the existence of such an index 'the newspaper can hardly ever be said to be dead'.[63] William F. Poole's more comprehensive *Index to Periodical Literature* was launched in the United States in 1882, though coverage of British periodical literature was initially poor. Little work had been completed by the English librarians who had agreed in October 1877 to contribute to the venture, a failure which Poole laconically ascribed to the 'climate and social customs of England [which] are not so favourable as they are in America for night work'.[64] *Curtice's Index and Register of Periodical Literature* followed in January 1893, listing references to articles in newspapers as well as those in the weekly, monthly and quarterly publications, and expanding into an index of *The Times*, the London morning and evening newspapers, some 120 weeklies and 31 provincial newspapers between July and September 1893. The proliferation of such publications reflected a growing demand for rapid and accurate means of gaining access to material in past issues of newspapers. In short, for all manner of reasons other than the purely academic, newspapers were increasingly being regarded as valuable historical records.

But indexes of contents presupposed the ready availability of catalogued copies of old newspapers, and the provision of adequate library provision was the next essential phase in the attaining of a measure of cultural acceptability for the newspaper press. Files had long been kept in local libraries, but the most significant steps to create a systematic newspaper archive were taken by the British Museum in Bloomsbury, London, where a specially equipped newspaper reading room was opened in 1881 (Figure 3.8). Here, if nowhere else outside individual newspaper offices, bound copies of newspapers, among the most ephemeral and disposable of all forms of Victorian media, were transformed effectively into books.

News-sheets and broadsides of the Civil War period, collected in the remarkable Thomason Tracts, had been acquired by the British Museum in 1762, and in 1822 the Trustees arranged with the Commissioners of the Stamp Office in London that copies of London newspapers deposited there would, as required by law, be transferred after three years to the British Museum for permanent storage. The arrangement was extended to include English and Welsh provincial newspapers in 1832, and to Irish and Scottish newspapers in 1848. Newspapers were brought within the scope of copyright deposit legislation for the first time in 1869, and collections held since that date have been virtually complete. By the

---

[63] *Brighton Guardian*, 18 Aug. 1869.
[64] William F. Poole, Preface to *Index to Periodical Literature* (Boston, 1882), p. vi.

3.1 The Newspaper Room, British Museum, 1893

Source: *Sell's Dictionary of the World's Press* (1893), p. 109.

1880s, however, the growing numbers of newspaper acquisitions began to create storage difficulties for the museum. In 1882 1,700 titles a year were being deposited in the archive, a number which by 1896 had risen to 3,300. By 1887, some 600 tons of newsprint was deposited in the White Wing and on shelves on either side of the corridor that circumvented the Dome, yet the collection had been so effectively catalogued that obtaining a newspaper was no more difficult or time-consuming than retrieving a book.[65] The storage issue raised doubts as to whether the museum's resources were wisely spent on a collection of newspapers, but a bill was finally passed by Parliament in July 1902 that enabled the museum to purchase land in Colindale for a much enlarged newspaper repository. This building was opened to readers as a dedicated Newspaper Library in 1932.[66]

The process of imposing order on the vast and endlessly permutating

---

[65] *Sell's Dictionary of the World's Press* (1893), p. 112.

[66] Geoffrey Hamilton, 'The British Library Newspaper Library', in Denis Griffiths (ed.), *Encyclopedia of the British Press* (1993), pp. 638–40.

newspaper press was accomplished discursively by means of historical narrative and classification, and physically by providing catalogued shelf-space in the country's leading libraries. Both provided the newspaper with a distinct identity as a form of printed communication while, at the same time, forcing its pulsating, inchoate mass into explicable patterns so that its dynamics might more readily be comprehended. Outside the composed order of the history book and the quiet of the library, however, a clamorous debate was taking place on the power of newspapers to influence the minds of individuals and to transform English society as a whole.

CHAPTER FOUR

The voice of the charmer

The mission which the press then modestly assumed to itself was merely to indicate public opinion – practically, I found it created, guided, and controlled public opinion . . . I have perhaps had something to do in helping the public towards a decision on some of the highest questions of the day.

W.H. Watts, *My Private Note-Book;*
or, Recollections of an Old Reporter (1862), p. 2.

The Victorians were much agitated by the evangelical possibilities of a cheap, multi-centred newspaper press. The difficulty, however, lay in finding a language with which these possibilities might be explored and explained. Thomas Carlyle in 1834 had favoured the religious trope of the iconoclastic mendicant Friar who 'settles himself in every village, and builds a pulpit, which he calls Newspaper'.[1] Though admittedly vivid, this language inadequately conveyed the commercial imperatives involved in the growth of newspaper journalism, and failed to suggest how such paper pulpits affected the lives of those whose words and images they reached. But the assumption that journalism was fashioning a new clergy which could affect patterns of individual and social behaviour, and form and inform a 'public mind', remained powerful long after the religious paradigm had lost its salience. Yet the fabric of argument used to clothe that assumption remained a difficult one to weave, and the solution to the problem of what kind of influence the press exerted on readers, and on society generally, remained elusive. English newspapers had long been regarded as organs of a 'General Will' which reflected rather than governed public opinion,[2] much in the way that Hazlitt had regarded the book as 'a kind of public monitor, a written conscience, from which nothing is hid'.[3] But the newspaper introduced a new dimension: speed. By 1830, one insightful critic recognised that the

---

[1] Thomas Carlyle, *Sartor Resartus* (1834), book iii, p. 261.

[2] *Parliamentary Debates*, xix. 550 (28 Mar. 1811), quoted in Arthur Aspinall, *Politics and the Press, c. 1780–1850* (1949), p. 5.

[3] Hazlitt continued, 'the consciousness that this is the general language and means of communication throughout the civilized world, gives strength and boldness to it. Power, interest could at one time easily overawe and stifle the scattered and imperfect expression of popular feeling; but from the moment that it obtained the assistance of the press as its organ, it became an over-match or a dangerous antagonist to its hated rival', William Hazlitt, 'The Influence of Books on Manner', *New Monthly Magazine*, May 1828, p. 414.

power of print depended 'upon causes in part unconnected with the ability of its conductors'. Rather, its strength lay in its capacity to spread its opinions

> whatever they are, from its means of rapid communication and perpetual transmission. A sentence though feeble in itself gains a momentum merely by its being sent before ten thousand individuals at the same instant; just as in theatres, the expression that would but faintly affect a single individual falling upon the ears of a large assemblage simultaneously acquires a vast additional force, and will move to tears or laughter the same person who was not touched in solitude. Something like this occurs in newspapers. The man who can publish what he pleases in a journal habitually read by a multitude, is a man of power even though he may not be a man of ability . . . what is publishing, but permanent talking to a great number of persons at once.[4]

The technology of speed in composing, printing and distribution, allowed print to acquire a teleology, a historical trajectory that, as the political reformer, orator of genius and editor of the *Monthly Repository*, W.J. Fox (1786–1864) wistfully explained, began with priests, extended to men of letters and 'so from one grade of society to another the influence of the press passed, and spread wider and wider, till the vast reading public arose, and the reign of patronage passed away'.[5] The course and consequences of this trajectory were the subjects of relentless commentary throughout the nineteenth century, during which there was a keen awareness at many levels that society was 'permeated with an undefined sense of the power and innovating character of the common literature of the day', an uneasy recognition of change which itself expressed 'the confused and transitional state of . . . modern life'.[6] Newspapers appeared to be changing everything, from the appearance of city streets[7] to the ways in which the English language was written and spoken.[8] But however difficult it was to put forward a credible theory which might explain as well as describe this trajectory, and however imprecise might be the vocabulary available to articulate it, the search for a theory of newspaper power was well under way by the time Victoria ascended to the throne in 1837. Gibbons Merle, writing in the *Westminster Review* in 1830, had observed that the newspaper press

---

[4] Gibbons Merle, 'Journalism', a review of H. Carnot and P. Leroux, *Du Journalisme* (Paris, 1832), *Westminster Review*, Jan 1833, p. 204.

[5] W.J. Fox, 'On the Duties of the Press Towards the People', *Lectures Addressed Chiefly to the Working Classes*, vol. iv (1846), pp. 8–15.

[6] James Hannay, *Westminster Review*, Apr. 1857, pp. 534–35.

[7] F.A. Paley, *British Quarterly Review*, Apr. 1880, pp. 107–08.

[8] Robert Louis Stevenson, 'The Morality of the Profession of Letters', *Fortnightly Review*, Apr. 1881, p. 515.

was 'a new power' whose possibilities had yet to be properly understood. Nevertheless, he felt it would be socially useful to begin to ask questions about the potentially transforming nature of the medium while the newspaper press was still in its infancy, and while its future course might still be subject to control. In particular, Merle felt compelled to speculate on the influence which was exercised 'by the provincial papers on the minds of the population, and the extent to which liberal, or in other words, correct and just ideas on religion and politics, have been created by the greater diffusion of knowledge through this medium'.[9] Almost 30 years later, it was still thought to be too early to grasp the nature of the influence of newspapers on society, although it was by that time clear to some that the increase both in circulations and the number of titles had 'introduced new processes and habits', and had inaugurated a new social era.[10] The first section of this chapter outlines some of the scientific and quasi-scientific theories of the press that were developed in Victorian England, while the second pursues the ways in which those theories were brought to bear on the Victorian idea of the public.

Moral philosophy and communication

More probing than allusions to the powers of the Church in explaining the social influence of the press were those developments within moral philosophy that sought to apply scientific methods to enquiries into the operations of the human mind. George Payne, in his study of the *Elements of the Mental and Moral Sciences*, published in 1828, argued for a more rational approach to the question of how the mind was influenced by external forces. Wherever the object was to 'originate certain habits, or trains of thought, and to awaken various feelings of pleasure, transport, enthusiasm, anger, fear, sympathy, &c.', as might be the case with journalism as well as with education, poetry, eloquence and criticism, it was, he argued, best to understand scientifically the ways in which the mind worked. If

> thoughts and feelings are united in the relation of cause and effect, and, consequently, follow one another in a certain train, how can it be doubted that the teacher, the poet, the orator, &c. must be acquainted with the order of their succession, before he can cherish any rational hope of effecting the object he has in view?[11]

---

[9] Gibbons Merle, 'The Provincial Newspaper Press', *Westminster Review*, Jan. 1830, p. 69.

[10] 'Popular Literature – the Periodical Press', *Blackwood's Edinburgh Journal*, Jan. 1859, p. 97.

[11] George Payne, *Elements of the Mental and Moral Sciences* (1828), pp. 7–9.

Ignorance of these mental processes might lead the putative opinion-former to strengthen the very 'propensities and habits . . . which he desired to subdue; and rouse, into fearful and resistless energy, passions which, as he imagined, he was taking the most prudent measures to allay'. To prevent such unexpected and socially dangerous consequences, Payne advised opinion formers of all kinds to become intimately acquainted with 'the nature and powers of the mind', and thus of 'the anatomy of human nature'.[12] The free will of the individual was necessarily compromised by such skilful and scientifically based forms of mental manipulation. As J.C. Symmons observed in his treatise on *Volition and Agency* in 1833, the 'overruling power' which controlled human actions was concealed from the immediate perception of the subject, and was 'so immediately blended with the ordinary motives of humanity, and so perfectly master of the agency of circumstance' that the subject was led to mistake its influence for his or her own will.[13] This line of argument involved the transference of the religious notion of immanence into the secular public domain, where the immanent was structured less by divine will than by human agencies operating through new forms of communication.

Explanations of the causal relationships between textual stimulus and behavioural response, between the writer's motive and the reader's reaction, turned largely on recent speculations on the physical anatomy of the mind. Thomas Reid's survey of the 'new philosophy' from Descartes to Hume had concluded that 'all that we know of the body, is owing to anatomical dissection and observation, and it must be by an anatomy of the mind that we can discover its powers and principles'.[14] By the early 1820s, certain social consequences were being deduced from such theories concerning the ways in which the human mind functioned. J. Foster (Philostratus) had argued in 1823, along with Pestalozzi and Robert Owen, that early influences were the most important determinants of opinions and attitudes in adult life, stressing the need to remove children 'from all sources of groundless superstition and imaginary theories, and of storing their young minds with useful knowledge'. The 'superior power of early chains of ideas to resist the effects of time and of violence done to the brain' explained why many 'opinions and prejudices' were entertained by adults 'without knowing why'.[15] The ideological

---

[12] Ibid., pp. 7–9.

[13] J.C. Symmons, *A Few Thoughts on Volition and Agency* (1833), pp. 11–12.

[14] Thomas Reid, *An Inquiry Into the Human Mind On the Principles of Common Sense* (1785), p. 4. See also *The Mirror of Human Nature* (1775), p. 55, whose object it was to describe the 'Mental Powers' and the 'moral Anatomy of the human Mind'.

[15] Philostratus (J. Foster), *Somatopsychonoologia showing that the Proofs of Body Life*

environment of childhood, rather than the nexus of influence exerted on the individual in later life, was thus the dominant shaper of human character. Newspapers, or any other medium, affected adult behaviour only in the most marginal and contingent sense.

The burgeoning advocates of phrenology also warned of the dangers of exaggerating the impact of external stimuli on the human character. Despite the scepticism of those such as Thomas Wallace, who pointedly observed in a critique of the philosophical speculations of Henry Brougham in 1835 that psychology was one of the least dependable sources from which to 'derive matter for philosophical *induction*',[16] phrenology as an approach to psychological inquiry became enormously popular in the Victorian period. As a materialist science which claimed to be able to describe and explain the operation of the human brain, and thus of human behaviour, phrenology aroused the interest of a number of those who, like journalists, sought to exert an influence over human beliefs and actions. Richard Carlile, who studied phrenology at Dorchester Gaol in 1820,[17] was one of the earliest newspaper editors to consider the advantages of applying phrenological theory to the tasks of political persuasion. Others participated in learned discussions on the subject in local societies, and pursued their interest in popular publications. Six debates were held on phrenology at the Liverpool Literary and Philosophical Society between 1828 and 1843,[18] a pattern that was replicated in similar discussion groups across the country, and in the 31 years between 1864 and 1895, Lorenzo N. Fowler sold 100,000 copies of his illustrated *Phrenological Instructor*.[19] But the implications of phrenological teaching on the course of the debate on the

---

and Mind Considered as Distinct Essences Cannot Be Deduced From Physiology (1823), pp. 71–73.

[16] Thomas Wallace, *Observations on the Discourse of Natural Theology by Henry Lord Brougham* (1835), p. 53.

[17] Theophila Carlile Campbell, *The Battle of the Press, As Told in the Story of the Life of Richard Carlile* (1899), p. 58.

[18] See for example Revd John Grundy, 'Essay on Phrenology', 4 Jan. 1828; Ellis Sweetlove, 'Essay on Phrenology', 2 May 1834; Robert Cox, 'Phrenology and the Operations of the Human Mind', 26 Dec. 1837; Revd Henry Giles, 'Essay on Phrenology', 20 Feb. 1837; Alfred Higginson, 'Physiological Aspects of Phrenology', 17 Mar. 1838; Francis Harrison Rankin, 'Mesmeric Experiments Combined with Phrenology', 20 Mar. 1843; William Stuart Trench, 'Mesmerism', 24 Mar. 1845, *Minutes of the Liverpool Literary and Philosophical Society*, Liverpool RO, MS 060 Lit/8/1. See also, for example, James Cowles Prichard, 'Observations on the Evidence of Phrenology', and 'An Outline of the History of Animal Magnetism', papers read before the Philosophical Society annexed to the Bristol Institution, 8 Jan. 1835, Bristol RO, 32079/146.

[19] L.N. Fowler, *Fowler's New Illustrated Self-Instructor in Phrenology and Physiology* (1895), p. i.

responsiveness of individuals to external stimuli were ambivalent. On the one hand, the editor of the *People's Phrenological Journal* emphasised in 1844 the narrowness of the margin within which individuals could be changed or reformed, given the original configurations of the organs of the brain. People, he argued, 'possess no means of increasing the measure of power which nature has primarily bestowed upon them. The perfection of these senses may vary in races as well as in individuals, but this variation depends upon original formation, not upon exercise or education'.[20]

Joseph Hands and other advocates of 'libertarian phrenology', however, argued for a more open approach to the stimulation of the brain, believing that its organs might be improved, even 'perfected', by the implementation of regimes of mental exercise. The application of libertarian phrenology to criminology, for example, led to the advocacy of liberal penal reform and opposition to the death penalty on the grounds that psychology was the 'best antidote to crime' and the surest means of rehabilitating the offender.[21] If it was possible to alter aspects of personality and patterns of behaviour among a target group of convicted criminals by the implementation of these libertarian phrenological principles, it was, by extension, possible to alter and improve the 'public mind' by means of popular forms of communication that encouraged a regular habit of reading and thinking. Lorenzo Fowler went further by suggesting that newspaper editors and reporters could exert a greater influence over their readers by means of the application of these phrenological principles. Editors, he advised, ought to begin by analysing their own 'mental temperament', which ideally should consist of a

> large Individuality and Eventuality, to collect and disseminate incidents, facts, news, and give a practical cast of mind; large Comparison, to enable them to illustrate, criticise, show up errors, and the like; full or large Combativeness, to render them spirited; large Language to render them copious, free, spicy, and racy; and large Ideality, to give taste and elevated sentiments.[22]

Fowler tantalisingly concluded that 'an Editor who understands and *applies* Phrenology possesses a power which he may use with great effect'.[23]

Contrary to the phrenologist's emphasis on the limited susceptibility of

---

[20] 'On the Influence of "Education and Circumstances" in Modifying Character and Organization', *People's Phrenological Journal*, vol. ii, no. xlv (New Series no. v), 1844.

[21] Joseph Hands, *Will-Ability, or, Mind and Its Varied Conditions and Capacities* (n.d.), p. 70, see also pp. 33, 48–49, 60 and 76.

[22] Fowler, *New Illustrated Self-Instructor in Phrenology*, p. 181.

[23] Ibid.

the human mind to external attempts to change or improve it, the mesmerists believed that the brain was intrinsically vulnerable to external influence and manipulation. Mesmerism, which flourished in Europe following the death of its founder, F.A. Mesmer, in 1815, considered that the brain could 'be played upon like a musical instrument',[24] and in their study of *Animal Magnetism* of 1887, Alfred Binet and Charles Féré drew attention to their belief that the number of persons liable to hypnotic suggestion was immense, not only in cases of hypnosis or intoxication but also 'in the waking state'.[25] Furthermore, they affirmed that although there were legitimate objections to the 'malicious mesmerism' practised for purposes of popular entertainment or criminal deception, mesmerism defined as a form of hypnotism operating on fully conscious individuals was an important means of communicating knowledge and morals by enabling both to seep 'naturally' through the 'mental pores' of the people.[26] Thus when A. Shadwell observed in 1900 that the newspapers 'fairly hypnotizes' the public, he was using a metaphor that had long since acquired a particular, and an increasingly sinister, kind of resonance in relation to the subliminal impact of the press on nineteenth-century English society. He complained that it had become impossible for any individual to ignore the press, whose messages were seeping inexorably through the public's 'mental pores' despite the entreaties of such sceptics as himself against the 'almost superstitious reverence' with which the public regarded their newspapers.[27]

General speculations of this nature on the susceptibility of the human mind to external forms of influence framed much of the discussion on the capacity of newspapers to affect patterns of public belief and behaviour. However, explorations of psychology and the paranormal also impinged on Victorian journalism in a more direct if less plausible way. Journalists were not isolated from trends in intellectual and popular culture, and some actively sought to apply their knowledge of the mental sciences, however esoteric, to the practice of their craft. Harriet Martineau's enthusiasm for hypnotism, for example, overcame Charles Knight's initial fear of not seeing his way 'through delusions and perhaps impostures', and her articles on mesmerism in 1844 opened for him 'a

---

[24] Dr Andrew Boardman to George Combe on Mesmeric-Phrenology, *People's Phrenological Journal*, vol i, no. xi, 1843. See also *The Phreno-Magnet*, edited by Spencer Hall.

[25] Alfred Binet and Charles Féré, *Animal Magnetism* (1887), pp. 172–78. See also Alfred Binet, *Alterations of Personality* (trans. Helen Green Baldwin) (1896), pp. 247–48.

[26] W.J. Colville, *Old and New Psychology* (Boston, 1900), p. 190.

[27] Arthur Shadwell, 'Proprietors and Editors', *National Review*, June 1900, pp. 592–93. See also Shadwell's article on 'Mesmerism and Hypnotism' in *Quarterly Review*, July 1900.

new chapter . . . in the history of man' that he avowed to read 'with wonder and reverence'.[28] Half a century later, spiritualists such as Alex Duguid, editor of *The New Age: a Magazine of Spiritual Knowledge and Psychical Research*, outlined their intention to persuade news journalists and the conductors of 'vehicles of public opinion' of the 'educational power of spiritualism', and thereby assist in bringing about a genuinely 'liberal and religious feeling [into] the elementary structure of social life'.[29]

By this time a number of leading journalists had dabbled with the occult.[30] W.T. Stead, for example, had attended his first séance in 1881, during which his qualities as a medium – 'the St. Paul of Spiritualism' – had been lauded. The séance involved communicating with a sorcerer, 'a squat little man whose tripod was a substantial armchair at one end of a square table' housed within a 'nineteenth century substitute for the Cave of Delphi'. The oracle replied at length to Stead's enquiries about future Government policy in Ireland, and explained how Gladstone would attempt to navigate the Coercion Bill through Parliament against both Irish and internal Liberal opposition. In retrospect, Stead wryly remarked that his time in the séance 'was spent at least as profitably as if I had passed the weary hours at the House of Commons listening to the oratory of Mr Biggar, Mr Finnegan, and Mr Healy'. More seriously, Stead also claimed to have forseen the mental breakdown which he suffered in January 1904, just as the first numbers of his *Daily Paper* came off the press (the newspaper was a failure, and was discontinued the following month).[31] He was also preoccupied by the possibilities of automatic writing, where, supposedly, the words of a spirit would be transmitted onto paper through the involuntary actions of Stead's own hand. Stead's biographer, Frederic Whyte, was sceptical of the authenticity of Stead's *Letters From Julia, or Light From the Borderland, Received by Automatic Writing From One Who Has Gone Before* (1897), an account of his communication with his dead mentor which Stead claimed had been for him 'for fifteen years a source of constant inspiration, consolation and encouragement'. Messages from Julia

---

[28] Charles Knight to Harriet Martineau, 7 October 1844, University of Birmingham, Heslop Room, Harriet Martineau Papers, MS HM1109. See also *Harriet Martineau's Autobiography* (1983 edn), vol. ii, pp. 191–204, and John B. Newman, *Fascination, or the Philosophy of Charming* (New York, 1871), in *Library of Mesmerism*, vol. i (New York, n.d.).

[29] *The New Age: a Magazine of Spritual Knowledge of Psychical Research*, no. i, Sept. 1894.

[30] Charles Bray, *On Force. Its Mental and Moral and Correlates* (1866), p. iii.

[31] Estelle W. Stead, *My Father. Personal and Spritual Reminiscences* (1913), p. 103; see also pp. 170, 254.

included useful references to the private lives of Queen Victoria, Parnell and Tennyson, and prophecies regarding election results. Automatic writing informed him, for example, that John Morley, his predecessor as editor of the *Pall Mall Gazette*, would win the 1883 by-election in Newcastle upon Tyne with a majority of 1,400 votes. In the event, Morley won with a majority of 1,700. Julia's apparently unruffled explanation of the discrepancy was that a larger number of Liberals than she had anticipated had turned out to cast their votes. Darker prophecies also emerged from Stead's automatic writing, such as Julia's warnings of his imminent imprisonment and the prediction of his death in a riot. Stead openly courted the first with his audacious campaign against child prostitution, while his death by drowning on the *Titanic* in 1912, though not a riot, was violent and unexpected. Stead's involvement with spiritualism signified a conviction, held by many of his generation, that there existed forces beyond the material, and that if they were understood and engaged with they might become useful agencies for the better understanding of the physical world. Even Frederic Whyte put his rationalist doubts to one side where the significance of Stead's exploration of the paranormal were concerned, recognising that Stead's daughter Estelle had been justified 'in regarding her father's interest in Spiritualism as fundamental to an understanding of his motives and activities'. All that W.T. Stead did, Whyte acknowledged, 'had its roots in the visionary'.[32]

If the mental sciences offered forms of explanation for the workings of the human brain, the development of Victorian psychology provided new and apposite points of reference for those who sought to understand the ways in which print journalism affected its readers. In 1876, Edward Cox argued that while both phrenology and cranioscopy had failed to substantiate their claims, they had, none the less, settled the controversy surrounding the question of whether or not the brain was the organ of intelligence. Phrenology in particular had 'given to Science the most correct map of *the Mind* ever drawn, even if it has failed to construct a perfect map of *the brain*', and, even more importantly, by providing the first rational analysis of the human mind, phrenologists had been the first to adapt 'mental Science to the practical business of Society.'[33] By

---

[32] Frederic Whyte, *The Life of W.T. Stead*, vol. i, (1925), pp. 329–38. Journalists' fascination with the paranormal continued well into the twentieth century; see, for example, a description of a séance held at the offices of the *Daily Express c.* 1920 in Sydney A. Moseley, *The Truth About a Journalist* (1935), pp. 128–32.

[33] Edward W. Cox, *The Mechanism of Man: an Answer to the Question What Am I? A Popular Introduction to Mental Physiology and Psychology* (1876), vol. 1, pp. 220–21. See also R. Flint, 'Associationism and the Origin of Moral Ideas', in *Mind. A Quarterly Review of Psychology and Philosophy*, vol. 1, 1876, (ed. George Croom Robertson), pp. 321–34.

making such connections between psychological theory and the 'business of Society', speculations on the power of the press were drawn into three related areas of inquiry. These involved the nature of language, the interpretive categories of social science and the problem of 'public opinion'.

Just as the mental sciences differed in their prognostications on the potential power of the press to influence opinion, theories of language too pointed in notably different directions. In a perceptive essay read to the Literary and Philosophical Society of Newcastle upon Tyne in 1851, J.P. Dodd claimed that humans no longer reasoned 'upon the objects, but upon the symbols which denote them', that is to say, on language itself.[34] But certain speculations on the nature of language and communication were in little doubt that the capacity of books or newspapers to influence opinion was insignificantly small. This was not an observation on the autonomy of the reader as a social agent, but an assumption that readers were already trapped in a web of meaning that was beyond the capacity of authors of printed texts to affect. The problem for journalists, who communicated information and its interpretation by means of the printed language, was that it was difficult to say anything new owing to the restrictions imposed on that language by the readers' own limited response to it. In 1881, Henry William Challis proposed that the subjectivity of the reader effectively neutralised any intentions which the author may have harboured to persuade or to challenge the reader's understanding of the world. Ideas aroused by words, Challis mused, 'are those with which the words are associated, not in the speaker's or writer's mind, but in the mind of the hearer or reader'. Attempts to express new ideas in print were frustrated by the language itself, where words were merely 'the arbitrary signs by which old ideas are aroused and placed in order'. Thus the 'new ideas' which most readers imagined they were acquiring from books and newspapers were in reality 'nothing but novel collocations of old ideas', with nothing new about them except 'their order and grouping'. Forever hamstrung by the lack of real communication between the writer and reader, even the most radical journalism was doomed, at best to be ineffective, at worst functionally to reinforce the *status quo*. For Challis, the gap between the signified and the signifier was small in relation to the chasm that separated the signified from the audience. Yet he hinted at a possible course of action which might avoid the endless chain of misunderstanding which he believed characterised the late-Victorian communications media. To

---

[34] J.P. Dodd, 'Language as an Instrument of Thinking, and as a Medium of Thought', 16 Jan. 1851, minute book, MS, The Literary and Philosophical Society, Newcastle upon Tyne 3510.

break that chain, writers needed not only to accept that their impact on their readers was small but to understand the reasons why this might be so. Greater influence might be exerted were writers able to study their supposed readers in greater depth, and to address them with a greater understanding of the ways in which they thought and reacted to stimuli. It was by researching the psychology of the readership, and by adapting and fine-tuning the language used to communicate with it, that authors and journalists would begin to exert an influence. The writer, Challis advised, 'must find his meaning in the mind of his reader, as the sculptor finds the stone in the block of marble'.[35]

One means of bridging the chasm between the writer and the reader involved manipulating the reader's senses in order to trick the intellect. Thus by acting on the reader's mind at levels other than the conscious, different readings of the world might be insinuated into the brain. A dissertation on the nature and influence of taste read to the Literary and Philosophical Society of Newcastle upon Tyne in February 1815 had noted how 'by seizing upon those features which captivate the eye' the author ensured that 'the seduction of our heart is accomplished before we are aware'.[36] But before the reader could be taken unawares in this way, the writer needed to understand the world which the reader both inhabited and imagined. Specifically, the discovery of meaning 'in the mind of the reader' required an engagement with the discourses that the readers employed to structure and make sense of their lives. As has been indicated by Judith Walkowitz, Patrick Joyce and others, narrative, or the representation of actuality as a series of stories, was central to the means whereby this process of sense-making was achieved.[37] Narrative, particularly in its melodramatic form, was also evolving as the newspaper journalist's favoured method of representing knowledge as news. Theorists of the 1860s were not slow to make the connections, and to propose the narrative form of discourse as the dominant strategy of persuasion. Alexander Bain considered the search for knowledge to be 'attended with plot' and that the 'sense of difficulty to be solved, of darkness to be illuminated, awakens curiosity and search'. This 'attitude of suspense' was, for Bain, 'identical with earnest attention'. It was for this reason that sports and contests of various kinds were 'peculiarly fitted to arrest the gaze of the spectator', and could for that reason be found in public amusements

---

[35] Henry William Challis, 'Language as a vehicle of thought', *Contemporary Review*, Nov. 1881, pp. 808–09.

[36] Revd Robert Clarke, 'Essay on the Influence of Taste', 7 Feb. 1815, minute book, Literary and Philosophical Society, Newcastle upon Tyne, MS 3.

[37] Judith R. Walkowitz, *City of Dreadful Delight. Narratives of Sexual Danger in Late-Victorian London* (1992); Patrick Joyce, *Democratic Subjects. The Self and the Social in Nineteenth-Century England* (1994).

'of all times'. Turning his attention to the communication of news, Bain regarded the 'daily business of the world', including the affairs of nations, to contain 'uncertainty, and a final clearing up preceded by a state of suspense', the element of suspense having consciously been cultivated by the presentation of news in the form of the 'Literature of Plot, or Story'. By imposing narratives on the events that were occurring in the world around them, journalists could 'command the elements of the situation, and thence derive much of their power of detaining the mind'. Events thus narrated became more real than actually occurring events, which, although they might contain elements of suspense, often disappointed the expectations of the spectator. But in order to attain the hyperreality of the news story, the composer of news narratives needed to know how to work up the interest of the reader 'to the highest pitch'.[38] This was not solely a matter of literary and typographical style, but involved the repositioning of the journalist as a 'professional' social actor, a theme to which we will return in a later chapter.

The influence of news, narrativised and infused with an 'attitude of suspense', was further strengthened by the power of repetition and the social environment in which news and newspapers were read and discussed. Herbert Spencer had argued in 1855, the year in which the newspaper Stamp Tax was abolished, that the 'constant repetition' of certain messages effected deep psychic changes in the individuals to whom such messages were addressed. In much the same way, the growth of weekly, and even more pertinently of daily, newspapers by institutionalising the constant repetition of images, formats and messages within the public sphere, possessed the ability to transform private and social actions which had once been voluntary into ones which were becoming automatic.[39] The conditioning of human responses in this way acted at deep and imperfectly understood levels of consciousness, but Spencer also acknowledged that the authorial power of journalists sprang equally from the cultural and social contexts in which texts were read. Central to this discussion was the possibility of employing scientific methods to construct a cohesive national character. In 1861, Alexander Bain had embarked on a mission to form a 'national and collective character' by applying the scientific laws of Mill's ethology 'that govern the formation of character, individual and national' to the rapidly changing society of mid-Victorian England.[40] Later in the same decade, Bain developed J.S. Mill's anxieties regarding the conservatism

---

[38] Alexander Bain, *Mental and Moral Science. A Compendium of Psychology and Ethics* (1868), p. 272.

[39] Herbert Spencer, *The Principles of Psychology* (1855), p. 617.

[40] Alexander Bain, *On the Study of Character, Including an Estimate of Phrenology* (1861), p. 13.

of social majorities by searching for a socio-psychological explanation for the 'preponderance of certain sentiments, opinions, and views' which, in most societies, had the effect of compressing 'individuality into uniformity'. Few, he observed, had either the strength or the will to resist the 'feelings of a majority powerfully expressed', a propensity which explained the prevalence of social conservatism and the capacity of 'creeds, sentiments, opinions', once they had 'obtained an ascendancy' to survive through historical time. Even when individuals did form independent judgements, social pressure was sufficient to ensure that such notions remained in the private rather than the public realm for fear that, by expressing difference, those individuals might renounce 'the support that social sympathy gives to the individual'. Bain also acknowledged the significance of 'opinion' as a means both of defining an individual's sense of self and as an emblem of a shared social identity.

> The Sympathy of others lends support to our own feelings and opinions. When any feeling belonging to ourselves is echoed by the expression of another person, we are supported and strengthened by the coincidence. . . . The strength and earnestness of the language used, its expressiveness and grace, our affection, admiration, or esteem of the sympathizer, and our own susceptibility to impressions from without, are the chief circumstances that rule the effect. The sympathy of persons of commanding influence, and especially the concurring sympathies of a large number, may increase in a tenfold degree the pleasures of the original, or self-born feeling. . . . Through the infection of sympathy, each individual is a power to mould the sentiments and views of others.[41]

In this fashion a 'public' formed an 'opinion' when a cluster of ideas emerged to exert their hegemonic power over the society. In seeking to understand the complex means by which such hegemonic clusters came into existence, nineteenth-century theorists of the press did not, in the main, distinguish too clearly between what have since become discrete disciplinary discourses. Rather, they moved more or less effortlessly between spiritualism, psychology and social science. Charles Bray's 'treatise on spiritualism' of 1866, for instance, intimated that a science of psychology, based on physiology, promised 'the same command over mind, as we already have over physical force', and that the doctrine of philosophical necessity was 'only another name for "Law" or a fixed order of Nature in the department of Mind, and there can be no Social *Science* without it'.[42] A comparable degree of catholicity greeted Auguste Comte's writings in mid-Victorian England.[43] His views that 'ideas

---

[41] Alexander Bain, *Mental and Moral Science*, pp. 280–81.
[42] Charles Bray, *On Force. Its Mental and Moral and Correlates* (1866), p. iii.
[43] See Royden Harrison, *Before the Socialists* (1965), *passim*.

govern and turn the world topsy-turvy', and that 'all the machinery of
society rests at bottom upon opinion', were favourably reviewed by G.F.
Green in an article on 'Spiritualism and Positivism in relation to
Problems of Government' published in December 1879.[44] Comtian
'social physics', moreover, were understood to have liberated philosophy
from a narrow preoccupation with the state and helped to open fresh
avenues of enquiry into a myriad forms of social action, as was shown
in J.S. Mill's treatment of the psychology of crowds in his *System of
Logic*.[45] The new sociology was also visionary in the sense that it
proposed a very different system of social organisation, the advent of
which demanded new leaders and reformed institutions. Crucially, a new
moral leadership, a secular priesthood, was required to communicate
knowledge to the people, and 'to diffuse the science which centuries have
accumulated'. In so doing, the new clerisy of communicators would
accomplish in the modern age what Catholicism had achieved in
medieval Europe, namely the establishment of 'intellectual unity as the
basis of moral and social communion'.[46]

Much of the speculation regarding the power of the new popular press
was closely associated also with developments in nineteenth-century
educational theory. In particular, the Comtian notion of moral leadership
resonated with the concerns of educationalists who sought to build in
Britain a more participatory political culture. Sophie Bryant, writing in
1887, emphasised the duty of 'the stronger members of the moral
community' to improve the condition of society by utilising the
'institutions for public service', and transforming them into 'centres of
moralisation, making available to all the lessons of the community'.
Bryant here referred not only to schools, but also to forms of public
communication and debate. Polemic, even certain forms of conflict,
aided the moralising process and served further to enrich the life of the
society.

> When the contest rages round some special policy, such as the
> disestablishment of a Church, the enfranchisemant of a class, or an
> alteration in the political constitution, the reference of all thought
> and effort to a moralised conception of the common good becomes
> explicit: all argument is directed to produce the conviction that the
> community will be better or worse for the change proposed. The
> community is better for the struggle almost always, because each

---

[44] G.F. Green, 'Spiritualism and Positivism in Relation to Problems of Government', *The
Psychological Review*, Dec. 1879, p. 449.

[45] B. Bosanquet, 'The Relation of Sociology to Philosophy', *Mind*, Jan. 1897, pp. 1–4.

[46] 'The Religion of Positivism', *Westminster Review*, 1 Apr. 1858, p. 316. On spiritual
leadership and social change, see also A.A. Watt, 'Ethics of the New Age' *The
Psychological Review*, Apr. 1878, p.7.

member has been called upon, not only to think, but to act under the conviction that he is doing the public service.[47]

The mass production and dissemination of such contested readings of political affairs, pre-eminently in the form of newspaper journalism, was thus infused with a deeply moral imperative. Almost irrespective of the outcome, the 'struggle' over ideas, the cacophony of discordant voices, was a social good in and of itself. The communication of knowledge as the means of political participation had, for Bryant, become a socially useful educational end.

Newspapers and the problem of public opinion

The problem of public opinion in nineteenth-century politics has rightly been the subject of renewed attention in recent British historiography.[48] Not surprisingly, given the contemporary concerns outlined above, it was also a problem that was debated in a variety of forums throughout the Victorian period, when the cultural establishment became aware of a new, ill-defined but inescapably extant category of political life. The account that follows will consider the ways in which the newspaper press, specifically, was linked to the process of constructing public opinion in nineteenth-century England. Once scientific discourses had offered hypotheses which sought to describe and explain the influence a popular press might exert on individuals and social groups, it became possible to speculate on the consequences of that influence. Most significantly, the question was posed as to whether the press reflected or created public opinion, whether in its myriad forms it represented shifts in public mood or whether it determined the direction and extent of those discernible changes in popular attitudes. The difference between the two readings of the impact of the press on what was generally assumed to be, certainly in the context of the new electoral politics after 1867, a measureable entity, remained central to Victorian – and subsequent – debates on the press. The Revd George Robert Gleig (1796–1888), Chaplain-General to the Forces and biographer of Wellington, clearly outlined the two approaches, and the gulf that lay between them, when, in 1867, he sought to demonstrate that those who believed that 'the English people speak through the press – in other words, that the newspapers are more the expression of an educated

---

[47] Sophie Bryant, *Educational Ends. Or the Ideal of Personal Development* (1887), pp. 95–100.

[48] For a particularly pertinent example see Jonathan Parry. *The Rise and Fall of Liberal Government in Victorian Britain* (1993), p. 27.

public opinion, than vehicles made use of with a view to create a public opinion in this country – altogether mistake the real state of the case'.[49]

But the main difficulty in resolving Gleig's argument, in one way or the other, was the absence of an inherited theoretical framework and an appropriate vocabulary which could be employed to explain the operation of a technologically novel form of communication. One means of beginning the task of constructing such a framework was to draw comparisons between the new popular newspapers and older forms of public communication. In this exercise, the most important paradigm was provided by the platform, in the form of the theatre, the pulpit or the speaker's soap box. The supremacy of orally transmitted information continued to have its defenders, particularly where the immediacy of the physical presence of performers on a stage praising 'heroic deeds and noble actions' could be shown to provide morally uplifting experiences for audiences.[50] The power of the spoken word was acknowledged by James Dawson in his dissertation on 'pulpit power' of 1865. Whilst the press had 'done much to enlighten and influence mankind', and doubtless would 'in future do much to supply the place of the living instructor', Dawson regarded it as a limited form of communication which could never accomplish as much as had been achieved by the preaching of the gospel.[51]

But by the end of the century, following 30 years of press expansion, opinion had shifted decisively. Although a number of writers drew attention to the different nature of the experience of being a reader and being a listener–spectator, the power of the former was increasingly acknowledged. And while printed texts might be seen to lack the 'social feeling' and the 'accompaniment of look, gesture and intonation' that were associated with speech, the expansion of the popular press, 'in influence for civilization and enlightenment', had left the pulpit 'helplessly, hopelessly, ignominiously in the shade'.[52] In the scale of persuasive effectiveness, newspapers were increasingly seen as the most immediate and influential of media. Frank Taylor, in his Chancellor's address to the University of Oxford in 1898, chose to explore the relative importance of speech and print as agents of influence. The stage, he

---

[49] George Robert Gleig, 'The Government and the Press', *Blackwood's*, Dec. 1867, p. 763.

[50] 'The Moral Influence of the Drama', *Monthly Express*, no. 1, 30 Jan. 1847, p. 1.

[51] James Dawson, *Pulpit Power, and How to Attain It; or Thoughts on the Preparation of Sermons Required by the Age* (1865), p. iii.

[52] James Leatham, *Westminster Review*, 'The Press and the Pulpit', June 1892, pp. 602–07. See also William Ogden, 'Observations on Public Speaking and Writing for the Press', *Odds and Ends . . . a Manuscript Magazine*, vol. xl, 1894, pp. 230–38, Manchester City Library MS m38/4/2/40, on the monotonous and dull nature of public speaking.

concluded, was a stronger force than the review, but in the order of the magnitude of its influence it was 'infinitely beneath' that exerted by the newspaper press. Taylor in particular paid lavish tribute to the music-halls, where the poor had received their training in patriotism, and warned his readers not to 'despise a force which touches so many of the class most easy to move'. But although the stage, the pulpit, the platform and the pamphlet, had each in their different ways enabled individuals to intervene in social life, each, to be effective, also needed the newspaper press to amplify their messages. The role of the press as an echo chamber, however, changed the nature of social discourse in at least two ways. First, in their refusal to 'disseminate the outpourings of a nobody', the press established a hierarchy of voices. Not only did newspapers inflate the star rating of favoured individuals – Gladstone was a notable example – but Taylor also charged them with reducing the visibility of 'the little men who fume and vapour in obscure "Bethels"', who once might have swayed local audiences but who were of little concern to the journalists and editors of the national press. Secondly, as if to compensate for their own anonymity when compared to preachers and platform speakers, newspaper editors recognised the importance of acquiring for their newspapers distinctive individualities so that their arguments might be quoted and their conduct judged exactly as though they were themselves preachers or politicians of flesh and blood.[53]

By identifying the differences between print and speech in public communication, and by acknowledging the extent to which print journalism had been moulded by the oral tradition, Frank Taylor had provided the basis for a fresh interpretation of the social influence of popular newspapers at the close of the nineteenth century. Yet speculation on the peculiarities of the newspaper press as indicators of the public mood had been circulating for decades prior to 1898. What then were the antecedents of Taylor's late Victorian theories? As was suggested earlier, the search for a metaphor with which to express the complex relationship between the press and the public had commenced virtually as soon as newspapers had started to proliferate in the middle of the eighteenth century. By 1824, it had been proposed that periodicals, unlike books, were like straws in the wind, whose very lightness indicated far more accurately than could heavier 'works of a higher character' the shifts and nuances of public attitudes, however limited that early concept of the public might have been.[54] A related metaphor,

---

[53] Frank Taylor, *The Newspaper Press as a Power Both in the Expression and Formation of Public Opinion. The Chancellor's Essay, 1898*, (Oxford, 1898), pp. 19–20.
[54] William Stevenson, 'On the Reciprocal Influence of Periodical Publication', *Blackwood's*, Nov. 1824, p. 519.

and one which became increasingly common as the mid-Victorian period approached, was of the newspaper press as a mirror.[55] Especially in the years that followed the abolition of the newspaper Stamp Duty in 1855, newspapers were routinely assumed to act as faithful and continuous reflectors of public opinion, mirrors that cast 'their light back upon the public'.[56] But while the reflection theory encompassed, and in fact required, the participation of the implied readership in the formulation of editorial policy, a counter-argument proposed that the press was a means whereby élites might communicate a one-way stream of messages to a wider audience. Far from articulating the thoughts of the inarticulate, and representing the otherwise complex cross-currents of popular opinion, newspapers were active agents in the construction of such opinion. Abraham Hayward, in March 1840, quoted Benjamin Constant's belief that 'power . . . was only to be acquired or retained through opinion', and opinion was formed by means of the press, 'the mistress of intelligence'.[57] James Hannay, writing in the *Westminster Review* in April 1857 agreed that '[e]verything depends now on our attempts to form a strong, powerful, strict and conscientious *public opinion*, a result which can only be brought about by the influence of the language through the medium of the press and periodical literature'.[58] Two years later, a more nuanced thesis was advanced anonymously in *Blackwood's Edinburgh Magazine*, one that played on the ambiguities of reflection and construction in the 'fleeting literature' of the press. Although it was true that the newspaper contained 'the expression of public opinion and the index of contemporary history', it was also a force which 'reacts on the life that it represents, half creating what it professes only to reflect . . . it leads while it follows'.[59]

The notion that the press maintained a symbiotic relationship with the public complicated the concept of representation implied in the mirror theory without wholly abandoning the idea that public opinion was, in some ill-defined way, being constructed by journalism. The attempt to define more clearly the nature of the public's representation in the press drew heavily on Herbert Spencer's 'law of differentiation', noting that not only had newspapers grown in number and circulation during the nineteenth century, but that they had also been politically and socially redistributed. Whereas in the past journalists had written broadly for a

---

[55] For an early example, see 'The Stamped Press: the Mighty Organ of Good and Evil', *Tait's Edinburgh Magazine*, Mar. 1835, pp. 167–75.

[56] John William Draper, *History of the Intellectual Development of Europe*, vol. ii, (New York, 1876), p. 250.

[57] Abraham Hayward, 'Journalism in France', *Quarterly Review*, Mar. 1840, p. 424.

[58] James Hannay, 'Literature and Society', *Westminster Review*, Apr. 1857, p. 505.

[59] 'Popular Literature – the Periodical Press', *Blackwood's*, Jan. 1859, p. 97.

Whig or a Tory readership, in the changed political, social and legislative climate of the late 1850s it was becoming increasingly difficult to find newspapers that were not targeted at very specific niche markets. Where once news had been broadcast, it was now very deliberately being narrowcast. 'Our periodical literature', *Blackwood's* declared, 'is essentially a classified literature. The sphere of every new publication is more and more limited. Every class has its organ; every topic finds a journal; every interest has a friend in the press'. Moreover, this 'system of classification', or the matching of titles to interest groups, was deemed to be so complete as to provide 'a genuine system of popular representation'. Admittedly, not every individual could be represented, yet, unlike parliamentary representation, 'journalistic representation [was] of classes, interests, subjects, opinions – in one word, abstractions, things which do not exist except in thought'. Significantly, the organic linkages that were discerned between individual titles and a constellation of social groups were explained by the decline of authors as a 'distinct order', and the emergence of authorship simply as one of the many attributes of all such social groups. This was the epoch in which A.J. Lee's vividly evoked 'host of nobodies'[60] dominated the press, particularly in the provinces, but the hiatus opened up between the supposed death of the author, and the emergence of another 'distinct order' of writer, the professional reporter, was brief. None the less, in 1859, we can detect a note of satisfaction, perhaps even of complacency, in the belief that journalism was no longer a 'weapon of certain secret societies, of cliques and coteries, of cabals and leagued assassins, but ... a reflection of public feeling, a representation of popular opinion'.[61] After 30 years of continuous agitation, *Blackwood's*, at least, had conferred its authority on the view that the newspaper press had at last been converted into a safe and socially useful means of communication, one that served as both a provider of public information and an articulator of public opinion.

The nature of the connection between the two functions of informing and expressing the public mind was considered also to be the guarantee which the press offered to society that its power was being used properly and responsibly. Since its main stated objectives were to collect and disseminate news, the English newspaper grew daily both more and less powerful. Its power increased as the information which it supplied became increasingly more comprehensive, but its was also diminished to the extent that, at the same time, journalism nurtured the analytical skills of the readers that enabled them to make their own sense of the

---

[60] A.J. Lee, *The Origins of the Popular Press in England, 1855–1914* (1976).

[61] 'Popular Literature – the Periodical Press', *Blackwood's*, Feb, 1859, pp. 181–84.

fragmented world portrayed in the news-sheets. This delicately balanced argument allowed newspapers to claim that their power was being prodigiously increased, as they became essential instruments for the conduct of modern life, but that this augmentation need not cause alarm since the increase was taking place under conditions that effectively prevented them from arbitrarily exercising that power by exerting a dominant influence over society. And the more diverse the range of titles, the safer the medium. 'Let us multiply the newspapers', the *Blackwood's* article of 1859 concluded. 'The multiplication of newspapers will create a Babel of opinions which will neutralise each other. The more newspapers, the weaker each will be, the more harmless will be the aggregate result.' That result would not be chaos, as some had predicted, but a 'most startling unanimity' across the society, an informed, mature and consensual public opinion.[62]

Within a decade, however, such optimism had given way to a new scepticism. The narrativisation of the world, some believed, had resulted in social confusion. Above all, the political world described and embodied in the press was a dangerous illusion only very remotely connected to the comparatively prosaic procedures of the Houses of Parliament. In the words of one critic writing shortly before the Second Reform Act, readers no longer wished to believe that

> the commonplace, unexciting scenes which he witnesses, or hears of, in the House of Commons really constitute the process of governing a great nation. People look for something more striking, and they find it in the notion of an invisible power called 'Public Opinion', produced as we suppose by a set of unknown persons of prodigious genius, whose names are mysteriously concealed by the editors of the leading London papers.[63]

In May 1868, Leslie Stephen sounded a further warning by questioning the grounds on which newspapers claimed the right to be the voices of 'that strange abstraction, public opinion'. Vacillating and arrogant, journalism, and in particular anonymous journalism, embodied only a very narrow range of metropolitan, clubland opinion, and reflected the sensibilities primarily of the particular social group among which copies of their newspapers were intended to circulate. Thus, for Stephen, journalism was palpably

> not the power which some of its injudicious admirers are apt to imagine. . . . The power exercised by the press finds no external fulcrum from which to move the earth. It is a machinery for methodising and rendering articulate the confused utterances of what is called public opinion; but it does not dictate them. . . . The

---

[62] 'Popular Literature – the Periodical Press', *Blackwood's*, Feb. 1859, pp. 192–94.
[63] Sir James Fitzjames Stephen, 'Journalism', *Cornhill Magazine*, July 1869, p. 52.

public whisper confused guesses and opinions into a kind of ingenious acoustic machine, and mistake the echo which comes back for the utterance of independent wisdom.[64]

Yet what Stephen had underestimated here was the growing strength of the press outside the metropolis. By 1880, however, it was no longer possible to commit the same error. It had long been suspected that the political power of provincial newspapers in certain parts of the country might be more extensive than that of the London press,[65] but the failure of an overwhelmingly pro-Tory press to prevent the collapse of the Conservative Party at the polls in the 1880 general election led to some serious soul-searching. The national dailies and weeklies had utterly misrepresented the solidly Gladstonian sympathies of the borough voters beyond London, and with devastating effect. The *Fortnightly Review* noted with scarcely concealed contempt how 'these London newspapers have already during the past year mistaken the feeling of the country, and the realities of the political situation, in a manner which must seriously discredit their claim to anything beyond a local authority as organs of public opinion'.[66] The experience had thus cast doubt on the notion, succintly phrased by William Blanchard Jerrold in 1883, that public opinion on political matters might be 'manufactured on a large scale by machines of various kinds, as nicely adjusted as the Jacquard loom'.[67]

The scepticism of the late 1870s had, by the mid-1880s, deepened into cynicism and nostalgia. H.D. Traill (1842–1900), writing in the *National Review* in July 1885, fondly described the supposedly 'palmy days' of journalism in the mid-1850s, when the 'leading journal', a high-priced print addressing a middle-class public, and which included 'some diffused experience of political affairs, and some inherited traditions of political duty', had believed that its function was to create, educate and direct public opinion. In the terms of this ideology, the role of the newspaper editor, a man socially representative of his male, middle-class readers, was to co-ordinate and develop the unsystemised thoughts of those socially cohesive readers, to act as an instructor not as a mouthpiece. His successors in the mid-1880s 'in accordance with the traditions of the newspaper, but not with anything else' were content to advance the same pretensions. In the intervening 30 years, however,

---

[64] Leslie Stephen, 'Anonymous Journalism', *St Paul's Magazine*, 63, May 1868, pp. 218–23.

[65] Richard M. Bacon, 'Journals of the Provinces', *New Monthly Magazine*, Oct. 1836, pp. 142–48.

[66] T. Wemyss Reid, 'Public Opinion and Its Leaders', *Fortnightly Review*, Aug. 1880, p. 234.

[67] William Blanchard Jerrold, 'The Manufacture of Public Opinion', *Nineteenth Century*, June 1883, p. 1081.

much had changed in the newspaper industry and in the broader society. The repeal of the paper duty in 1861 had resulted in the vigorous expansion of cheap newspapers but, contrary to the confident predictions expressed by *Blackwood's* in 1859, a multitudinous press reflecting the spectrum of political opinion was now deemed to be an 'absurdity'. Each in competition with the other, newspapers were now 'instructors who had failed to instruct', and the 'people', now an electorate 'growing by the million', spoke with a striking and strident 'disharmony of voices'.[68] In the rapidly changing world of the 1890s, Frederick Greenwood, founding editor of the *Pall Mall Gazette*, also voiced his regret for the passing of the 'fortunate time' of the immediate post-Repeal period, the formative decades during which journalists emerged from penury and 'the dull years from the thirties to the fifties'.[69] In the 30 years between 1860 and the late 1880s, Greenwood confessed to have drawn 'more pleasure and reward' from journalism than he had been able to do either before or since.[70] Lasting for less than a generation, that 'very distinct period in the character and status of the newspaper press' was followed by the equally distinct but less distinguished epoch of the New Journalism, a time when there were 'so many voices that . . . they drown[ed] each other'.[71] Conjuring once more the image of the tower of Babel, and the audacity and destructiveness which it implied, Greenwood lamented the gentler age when a more limited journalism had attuned itself to the 'public' which it acknowledged as its readership. In the age of free-market journalism and franchise reform, however, public opinion as previously understood could no longer exist.

Others such as Henry Cust, Conservative MP for Stamford from 1890 to 1895 and editor of the *Pall Mall Gazette* between 1893 and 1896, also sensed Greenwood's mood that developments in the *fin de siècle* newspaper press signified deeper shifts in English society and culture. The decade that followed the Reform Act of 1884 had, for Cust, experienced both a 'complete Democratisation of life' and a thorough, though not by any means welcome, revolution in the practices of

---

[68] H.D. Traill, 'What is Public Opinion?', *National Review*, July 1885, pp. 654–57. Traill was at this time a staff reporter with the *Saturday Review*, having previously worked for the *Pall Mall Gazette* (1873–78), the *St James Gazette* (1880–82) and the *Daily Telegraph* (1882–96). He subsequently served as editor of the *Observer* from 1889 to 1891.

[69] Frederick Greenwood, 'The Newspaper Press. Half a Century's Survey', *Blackwood's* May 1897, p. 704.

[70] Frederick Greenwood, 'Forty Years of Journalism', *The English Illustrated Magazine*, vol. xvii, July 1897, p. 497.

[71] Frederick Greenwood, 'The Newspaper Press. Half a Century's Survey', *Blackwood's*, May 1897, pp. 716–17.

journalism. Where once newspaper journalism had served a double purpose of distributing news and principles, now, with the extension of education, the removal of newspaper taxes and the 'enfranchisement of class after class', it had adapted itself to 'the kindred mental habits of the many'.[72] Traill and Custs's impatience with the new ways was taken up by other writers who saw in the new dispensation a serious threat to Britain's national security. The role of this new press in wartime, and its capacity to influence public thinking and behaviour, became a cause for grave concern. The new public, educated, enfranchised and growing in prosperity, now had the sort of power of which contemporaries admitted they had 'no experience whatever'. Yet, in the emergency of war, the only available means with which to reach this public were the 'leading articles and letters in the daily and weekly Press, and by the sentiments expressed in leading magazines and reviews'. It was thus imperative that journalism reasserted its power as an instructor, as a shaper of public conduct. With this end in mind, calls were made for ever more skilful forms of news management, particularly with regard to military campaigns and imperial expansion. Such were 'the duties of those who really initiate and control public opinion [since a] wrongly directed public opinion might easily in this country lead us into a series of disasters, even to the point of real national peril'.[73]

Greenwood was equally concerned about the perceived decline in the political influence of newspapers during the last decade of the nineteenth century. Whereas in the 1860s and 1870s, 'the fresh heyday of newspaper influence', it was said (even then with a degree of 'half-humorous exaggeration') that the press had superseded Parliament as a political forum, the press had now in turn been overtaken, paradoxically, by the platform. Public meetings and public speeches, as he saw them, exerted a greater influence 'over the common mass of opinion and sentiment than any similar machinery', including the cheap daily press – a view wholly at variance with those of Frank Taylor and other end-of-century observers who had seen in the 1890s the final victory of print journalism over the oral tradition. Yet in an important sense, Greenwood was right. For he did not regard the emergence of the new platform as an atavistic return to an older, oral political culture, but rather as a sign of the decisive shift 'from plane to plane' which he sensed had occurred in British politics during the 1890s. The immediacy of the platform, and the dramatic vigour of the live human performance, could just as effectively subordinate the newspaper press to its own agendas as could the press manipulate events in its own interest. The modern contest

---

[72] Henry Cust, 'Tory Press and Tory Party', *National Review*, May 1893, p. 363.
[73] P.H. Colomb, 'The Patriotic Editor in War', *National Review*, Apr. 1897, pp. 253–63.

between politics and the media had begun.

But while newspaper editors were conscious of the loss of their power over the affairs of high politics, Greenwood detected an awareness of their growing sway over '"a new public" – an entirely new and uncultivated field for newspaper teaching and newspaper influence'.[74] It was to this 'new public' of the emerging democracy that Frank Taylor, too, turned in his Oxford address of 1898. The 'revolution in public opinion', as expressed through the ballot-box, had, he noted, irrevocably altered British political culture, yet the part played by the press in sustaining or changing that new world remained ambiguous. Taylor concluded his analysis by attempting to apply the century's most persuasive press theories – the power of repetition, its ubiquity – to the newspapers of the age of the 'new public', and found those theories to be wanting.

> The newspaper is the most potent of all the permanent forces operating on the public mind. The subtle and often undefinable process by which it acts has been several times suggested. Perhaps the most vital part of that process is its perpetuity. The daily reiteration of the same argument, the daily presentation of the same aspect, the daily contact with the same mental and moral atmosphere, these things are like the dripping of water on a rock. In shaping the raw and confirming the weak the party press is unrivalled. But there is a tendency, encouraged perhaps by the natural vanity of journalists, to exaggerate the strength of forces external to the public mind. In reality the power of all such forces is slowly declining. Education, especially the education of going to the poll, makes men more self-reliant and less subservient to the voice of the charmer. The mysterious 'majesty of print' is evaporating with every accession to the number of those who are capable of forming a judgment of their own. The newspaper is strong not only because it is permanent, but because it is almost alone in its permanence. . . . The cheap press is in every house. Whoever would compete with it must follow it thither.[75]

Whether or not the 'majesty of print' did actually evaporate with improvements in education, or even with the coming of cinema or, in less than 25 years, of radio, Taylor's judgement remains pertinent. In the course of the nineteenth century, a new information order had come into being, one that was based on science, mental and social, and a more rapid and sophisticated form of communication which had been made

---

[74] Frederick Greenwood, 'The Newspaper Press', *Nineteenth Century*, May 1890, pp. 835–41.

[75] Frank Taylor, *The Newspaper Press* (Oxford, 1898), pp. 17–19. Following the press into 'every house' was precisely what both radio and television, as future competitors of the newspaper, were to do so successfully in an age when the newspaper was no longer 'alone in its permanence'.

possible by recent developments in print technology, legislative reform and popular education. Journalists, the new idol-breaking mendicant clergy who had so insolently disrupted the quiet of Carlyle's village England had, by means of their monopoly of the means of communication, thrust knowledge and modernity if not into every home, then into a substantial proportion of them. This was the ground on which all observers and critics were obliged to stand, whether they were excited, or appalled or simply bewildered by the possibilities of an expanded newspaper press. Yet none could wholly subscribe to the view that rational human beings were the helpless victims of journalism's siren songs. A belief in the relative autonomy of the reader, who was capable of remaining critical of the new medium while engaging with it, remained strong, and it was precisely out of this tension between text and reader that the late Victorian idea of the public was born. Yet, while the voice of the charmer might be challenged, if not stilled, many remained wary of its influence, preferring instead to belive that while it may have been 'easy to exaggerate the power and possibilities of the Modern Press; it [was] easier to overlook or undervalue them'.[76]

---

[76] Sir Hugh Gilzean-Reid and P.J. Macdonell, 'The Press', in John Samuelson (ed.), *The Civilisation of Our Day. A Series of Original Essays on Some of Its More Important Phases at the Close of the Nineteenth Century, by Expert Writers* (1896), p. 288.

CHAPTER FIVE

The cultural debate

Newspapers . . . keep alive and encourage a quick and wholesome
sympathy among men. Here is one of the compensating forces of
modern life, helping to draw us all closer together, against the
counter influence of antagonism and repulsion, that tend to isolate
us and make us selfish. . . . And I think this tends to make us better,
– it is helpful, softening, humanising, christianising influence.

Revd Brook Herford, 'A Sermon on Newspapers',
Newspaper Press, 1 Dec. 1866, p. 6.

Few doubted the power of the newspaper to charm the reader or to
shape certain aspects of social life. Fewer still claimed to understand how
such influence was effected. With the decline of the relative importance
of the radical press after 1836, emphasis shifted from the danger that lay
in the diversity of the range of titles available to the reader to the
influence exerted by the few titles that came to dominate the market. In
these publications were to be found, according to one observation made
without irony in 1858, 'the greatest combination and concentration of
forces known in the intellectual world'. These newspapers, by impressing
their values and prejudices immediately and simultaneously upon many
thousands of minds, possessed a power of such unprecedented
magnitude that it was not surprising that the public generally could have
'no adequate conception of it, because it is so infinitely above and
beyond any other popular medium of intelligence with which it may be
compared'.[1] The power of this new medium, as was suggested earlier,
was discussed initially in an older language. But in a period of
accelerating technological and legislative change, the inherited frame of
reference supplied by the constitutional discourse of press freedom was
no longer adequate. The problem of newspaper power was thus drawn
into a broader debate, one that sought to connect developments in
journalism with changes in English culture, including religious
observance, popular amusement, drinking and reading habits, education
and crime. This cultural debate was conducted broadly on two levels.
One was concerned with what might be termed the macro-cultural
question of whether or how a means of communication might alter or
transform existing social and ideological formations. The different

---

[1] W.S. Robinson, 'The Press: Its Achievements and Influence', address to the Liverpool
Chatham Society, 23 Dec. 1858, Liverpool RO 374 Cha/8/2.

effects on the popular mind of reading cheap fiction and news was a central consideration in this larger, more diffuse debate. At the other level, the micro-cultural issues of newspaper language and content acquired greater prominence. Here, discussion focused on the dialectic between morality and commerce in the conduct of newspapers, and on the perceived social and moral status of the text.

Poison and antidote

The key metaphor in the cultural debate was drawn neither from Biblical texts nor from mental science, but from physiology. Depending on the perspective, newspapers were described as means whereby the individual or social body might either be nourished or poisoned. In some cases, newspapers might also inject the only effective antidote to the venom ingested through unwise reading. In this respect, the arguments connected with those employed elsewhere in the contemporary treatment of cultural issues. Although the newspaper as a specific form of communication was subjected to considerable scrutiny, newspaper journalism was also known to operate within a larger context of other media forms, each of which produced its own critical theoretical discourses. In particular, the capacity of journalism to influence individuals, and to construct and interact with a public, formed part of a wider debate on the social consequences of cheap literature. Much of this debate focused on cheap radical pamphlets, ballads, broadsides, magazines and popular fiction. At first sight, the newspaper, as a modern, cheaply accessible and strikingly illustrated publication was unlikely to be regarded as a safer alternative to these older popular forms of print. But the elasticity of newspaper formats, and the polymorphic nature of news, meant that descriptions of events were encased within particular readings of those events. This might be achieved either implicitly within the news item, or explicitly by juxtaposing the story with editorial comment. Either way, readers would be getting a message, or so James Graham hoped when in 1808 he addressed the Literary and Philosophical Society of Newcastle upon Tyne on this issue. By arguing that the extension of social knowledge through literacy provided the best safeguard against popular insurrections, he proposed that food riots and other popular disturbances were caused not by food shortages, unemployment or price rises in themselves, but by an inability of those in power to explain to 'the lower orders of the people' why these things were occurring. Social conflict was the product of poor communication between governments and people. In contrast, in those parts of the country where literacy was high, and good, cheap forms of printed communications were readily available, the labouring poor were

> contented and happy, regular in paying their attention to all the
> duties of the situation in which they are placed, clean and neat in
> their appearance, happy at home and taking the greatest pleasure in
> training their children, in the same virtuous principles, which they
> themselves are practising. . . . If such be the happy effect of
> knowledge on mankind, surely every encouragement ought to be
> given, to promote so desireable an object.[2]

By the 1820s, such views had gained greater currency. In an anonymous review of *The Periodical Press of Great Britain and Ireland; or, an Inquiry Into the State of the Public Journals, Chiefly as Regards Their Moral and Political Influence* (1824), published in the *Westminster Review* in July 1824, the reader was confidently assured that

> newspapers . . . are the best and surest civilizers of a country. They
> contain within themselves not only the elements of knowledge but
> the inducements to learn. There is no one so instructed, there is no
> one so ignorant, who cannot find in them something from which he
> can learn, something which he can understand. We take it to be
> impossible that any people, within whose reach good newspapers
> are brought, can resist the temptation to letters.

It was, above all, their 'miscellaneous character' that gave newspapers their value over publications that specialised purely in political news and comment. By scanning discrete items on the page, 'the understandings of its readers are led on by degrees from the simplest domestic occurrences to those which affect their remotest interest, or appeal to their noblest sympathies: from the overturning of a coach to the overturning of an empire'. It was hardly possible, according to the reviewer of 1824, that a newspaper reader, however narrow his own interests might be, could 'cast about in such a mass of information . . . without stumbling on something which enlarges his ideas or exercises his reason'. It was, he insisted, necessary to have 'seen a people among whom newspapers have not penetrated, to know the mass of mischievous prejudices which these productions instantly and necessarily dissipate'. Citing the belief in witchcraft, and the fury directed against bakers and other 'dealers in provisions' during periods of food shortages, the reviewer argued that

> [n]o man who is accustomed to watch the accounts of the crops, the
> state of the markets, the speculations on the adequacy of the supply
> for the wants of consumers, on the deficiency or surplus of millions
> of quarters, can for a moment suppose that scarcity or plenty
> depends upon the bakers or millers of his district, or that violence
> towards them can produce any effect but a bad one. This is an

---

[2] James Graham, 'An Essay on the Education of the Poor', June 1808, Literary and Philosophical Society, Newcastle upon Tyne, MSS 2 1794–1814.

example of the general effects of newspapers.

Much emphasis was also placed on the greater accuracy of printed information, particularly where, as in the reporting of court cases, the only alternatives were by word of mouth. The act of printing a story was, in itself, often assumed to be a sufficient guarantee of its veracity. Belief in the truthfulness that was inherent in the permanence of print, in contrast to the mutability of speech, meant moreover that newspapers had brought early nineteenth-century English society 'back from tradition to scripture'.[3] William Stevenson, writing in *Blackwood's Edinburgh Magazine* in November of the same year, agreed that the growth of 'more accurate and extensive information, spread over a larger surface of the community' could be attributed to the newspaper, which had 'insinuated itself into every nook and corner', and, 'like caloric', expanded whatever it entered into. This process could not fail to 'enlarge the capacity of the human mind, create new intellectual desires and wants and the means of satisfying them'.[4] Such socially useful and stabilising information, however, was not conveyed 'by the direct inculcation of opinions, but by the habit of looking beyond the narrow circle of one's own personal observation to the results of a more enlarged observation'. In this manner, a newspaper became the instrument which enabled the individual to make fresh connections between disparate events and experiences, and to 'avail himself of the experience of the whole community'. *Ipso facto*, by virtue of being a newspaper reader, the individual joined a larger if ill-defined and scarcely imaginable community of readers.[5] Opinions and tastes were formed in this nexus, as readers, unaware at first of the inconsistencies and 'strange mixture of truth and error in their opinions', were, by means of the information habitually supplied by the newspaper, able to 'test all that education, habit, authority, and circumstances, have led them to believe'.[6] Thus the press contributed to progress not only by publishing new ideas, but, more simply and importantly

> by facilitating their interchange between man and man . . . wits sharpen one another. . . . Our thousands of Newspapers . . . cross and jostle each other, hurrying to carry to every nook and corner of the empire a vivid picture of the thoughts, deeds, and feelings of all

---

[3] Anon., 'Newspapers', *Westminster Review*, July 1824, pp. 194–212. The author was probably Walter Coulson, utilitarian and parliamentary correspondent of the *Morning Chronicle*.

[4] William Stevenson, 'On the Reciprocal Influence of Periodical Publications', *Blackwood's*, Nov. 1824, p. 521.

[5] Anon., 'Newspapers', *Westminster Review*, July 1824, p. 211.

[6] William Stevenson, 'On the Reciprocal Influence of Periodical Publications', *Blackwood's*, Nov. 1824, p. 528.

the rest. The activity and intelligence disseminated through the land
by these means, will not of themselves, make a moral nation, but
they are the best, and indeed the only imperatives.[7]

The hypothesis that newspapers had a beneficial effect on the moral
order was ostensibly supported by the experience of developing societies,
particularly in the American West. For example, in 1837 Charles
Mackay reported approvingly of the Cherokee newspaper, the *Indian
Pheonix*, edited by native Americans in Washington, DC, to lobby for
the creation of an independent Indian state in Mexico. By drawing new
groups of people into a society whose modernity, that is to say its
structures, dynamics and political practices, were represented by the
newspaper, Mackay argued, 'the newspaper [was] not only the effect, but
the cause of civilisation – not only the work itself, but the means by
which the work [was] performed'.[8]

Closer to home, a task of equal magnitude awaited the civilising touch
of journalism. The work of two moral reformers, Joseph Livesey and
Charles Knight, exemplify this tendency in early nineteenth-century
journalism. Temperance reformer Joseph Livesey (1794–1884) outlined
in his manifesto of 1838 the moral responsibilities of the press in a
country where factories and railways covered the land. Economic
growth, abundant employment and prosperity would, he emphasised,
not of themselves 'produce *happiness*, nor secure the tranquility (*sic*) or
safety of the state. Unless the people are morally improved, being now
brought into large masses, and possessing increased facilities for
mischief, the result, notwithstanding all other advantages, may, sooner
or later, be internal commotion, if not a national wreck . . . '.[9] Criticising
the 'fruitless agitation' of the Chartists, Livesey denied that the roots of
social unrest lay in poverty. Britain's difficulties lay instead in 'the want
of *mental culture* and *moral worth*' among her people,[10] and one of the
chief obstacles to social improvement was the poor quality of popular
journalism. Rather than dispensing sound advice and useful knowledge,
newspapers were each week displaying an unedifying combination of ire

---

[7] Christian Johnstone, 'Cheap Periodicals', *Tait's Edinburgh Magazine*, Sept. 1832, p.
722. On 15 June 1832, Warburton had argued in the Commons for a reduction in
newspaper taxation on the following grounds: 'Granting then that there are distributors of
poison, let us insure the cheap distribution of antidotes', National Political Union, *Taxes
on Knowledge*, p. 24.

[8] Charles Mackay, 'Periodical Literature of the North American Indians', *Bentley's
Quarterly Review*, June 1837, p. 534.

[9] *Livesey's Moral Reformer*, 6 Jan. 1838, no. 1. For the autobiography of Joseph
Livesey, see John Pearce, *The Life and Teachings of Joseph Livesey, Comprising His
Autobiography* (1885).

[10] *Livesey's Moral Reformer*, 10 Feb. 1838.

and mutual contempt for one another, the worst of the editorial quarrels being not between editors of opposing political positions, but among those who were competing for the attention of the same readership. While newspapers, being read by what he regarded to be 'a great proportion of the people', might not themselves be responsible for the 'spirit of rage' that was so prevalent in his society, their general conduct evidently was not calculated to reduce its virulence. 'Who does not think and feel', Livesey wondered, ' . . . in the current language of the paper which he is accustomed to read?'[11]

The correspondence between reading and the ways in which thoughts and feelings were internalised by the reader raised for Livesey two further problems for the social and moral order. The first involved the danger of being both psychologically *and* physically stimulated by reading while consuming alcohol. Drink and texts, he contended, served to intensify each other's intoxicating propensities. While drink reduced the reader's capacity for critical reflection, inflammatory writing legitimated the drinker's potentially violent and disorderly conduct. The second problem lay in the way in which readers elevated (the wrong) writers into popular heroes. Writers of strong, vivid newspaper prose were said at the time to be 'men of metal', whose 'mawling' and 'blacking' Livesey was appalled to discover were regarded as 'proof of superior talent.' Given his belief that newspapers exerted 'a large influence in forming the character of the people',[12] Livesey appears to be saying two quite distinct things here. In the first place, his words should be seen in their context, which was his attempt to launch a temperance penny paper, the *Moral Reformer*, in the early months of 1838. That is to say, the argument may be read as a sales pitch to persuade readers that his own product was qualitatively different from others available on the market. In that sense, he too was projecting himself as a 'man of metal' even to the extent of inserting his name into the first title of his publication, and thereafter reminding the world that it was his own individual spirit which moved through its pages. Because of, rather than despite, his protestations to the contrary, Livesey conformed to the most rudimentary of the individual-enhancing styles that surfaced in early Victorian journalism. At another level, however, his words can be read as reflections on the power of the newspapers press to change or confirm the beliefs of readers, and to legitimise certain forms of behaviour. Given what he described as the extensive circulations of newspapers in the late 1830s – the fourpenny duty on each copy had recently been reduced to one penny – Livesey had grasped the possibility that the cheap periodical

---

[11] Ibid., 3 Mar. 1838.
[12] Ibid.

press could also counter social practice, and contest the dominant assumptions about social conduct. For newspapers to become the agencies of 'progress', they required more than able editors and writers. Above all, they needed to be infused with the determination 'to *raise the moral tone* of the community'. To achieve this goal, newspaper journalism should be obliged to ensure the accuracy of its statements, and to reduce its political partisanship. '*Bad* party spirit', in the reporting of events, warped editorial judgement and suppressed truth. Political interest, accompanied by financial pressure, encouraged newspapers to follow rather than 'to correct, the taste of the public'. The losers in this market-place were newspaper readers who, Livesey implied, would 'prefer the simple truth without editorial colouring'.

> Were most papers *less political* they would at least be more *useful* to general readers. If the object of a paper be to give a true representation of passing events, and to afford a vehicle for useful information, I cannot see how this can be best accomplished by a continuous repetition of articles for or against this, or the other political party; or by giving so much importance to parliamentary and government affairs. Most of the daily papers are little more than the publications of the strivings of two political parties, and multitudes read the accounts with the same avidity as they would gaze at the contending horses galloping the course, while matters more immediately concerning their interests are passed over as unworthy of notice. In the provincial papers there is certainly a growing attention to the *internal* improvements of the country, though some of them are still absorbed in politics.[13]

This explicit call for a depoliticised press, and his hostility to the space allocated to crime reporting, challenged the news values of the time. While the superficialities of politics, as Livesy saw them, held the readers' gaze, they distracted attention from weightier matters that far more effectively governed the lives and affected the well-being of the people. But Livesey's critique of journalism was also a tribute to the newspaper as a powerfully transforming, as well as a confirming, medium of communication.

Livesey's belief in both the corrupting and redeeming qualities of popular journalism were shared by Charles Knight (1791–1873). Editor and proprietor from 1812 to 1822 of the *Windsor and Eton Express*, a newspaper founded with his father, Knight had recognised by 1819 that the popular press had been monopolised by 'anarchists' who had given that '*new power* in society . . . a direction'. That function, Knight had

---

[13] Ibid., July 1838, p. 156. The moral duties of journalists had been outlined five years earlier: 'the responsibility attaching to our profession is most important. We consider its duties as no light or perfunctory undertaking: we insist upon the necessity of performing them in an earnest, nay, religious, spirit of truthfulness', *Tait's* July 1833, p. 495.

concluded, should 'be taken out of their hands'.[14] To help effect that transformation, Knight in February 1820 launched *The Plain Englishman*, whose combative opening editorial condemned the Anglican Church through its 'supine' Society for the Diffusion of Christian Knowledge, for failing 'to meet the new wants created by the growing ability to read'. Knight, unafraid of the new reading public, set out aggressively to write about 'dangerous Science [and] more dangerous History'.[15] Eight years later Knight published *The British Almanac*, a two shillings and sixpence annual which had been 'purified' of the astrological predictions and other indecencies of the older Almanacs,[16] but his most important contribution to the journalism of moral reform began in 1832 with the publication of the *Penny Magazine*. Six years previously, in 1826, Lord Brougham and others has established the Society for the Diffusion of Useful Knowledge (SDUK) to extend knowledge to the new reading public by means of the distribution principally of cheap pamphlets and booklets. Proposals for a periodical, provisionally entitled *The Progress of the Press*, had been put to the society by David Booth in January 1829, but a solution to the problem of how to 'find a person who will undertake to produce the work without costing the Society a shilling'[17] eluded them until Knight, in the midst of the Reform Act crisis, undertook the venture. The *Penny Magazine*, which first appeared on Saturday 31 March 1832, and whose first task it was to undermine the unstamped 'contraband newspapers'[18] was not under the law of 1819 classified as a newspaper, and was thus not liable to tax. As advertised by its title, the *Penny Magazine* could thus compete with the unstamped weeklies at their own price level, and its circulation soon reached 200,000, three times that of the Society for the Diffusion of Christian Knowledge's *Saturday Magazine*, and more than ten times that of the *Poor Man's Guardian*.[19]

The moral strategy of the *Penny Magazine* was from the beginning clearly outlined in the weekly editorial column. Public demand had generated a huge variety of penny publications, 80 per cent of which had

---

[14] Charles Knight, *Passages of a Working Life During Half a Century, With a Prelude of Early Reminiscences* (1864, 1865; Dublin edn, 1971), vol. i, p. 235. For a fuller treatment of Knight's *Penny Magazine*, see Scott Bennett, 'Revolutions in Thought: Serial Publications and the Mass Market for Reading', in Joanne Shattock and Michael Wolff (eds), *The Victorian Periodical Press: Samplings and Soundings* (Leicester University Press/Toronto University Press, 1982), pp. 225–60.

[15] Knight, *Passages of a Working Life*, pp. 241–42.

[16] *The British Almanac*, 1828, p. 2.

[17] David Booth, SDUK MS 2628, Jan. 1829, University College London (UCL).

[18] Knight, *Passages of a Working Life*, vol. i, p. 192

[19] Robert Stewart, *Henry Brougham 1778–1868. His Public Career* (1985), pp. 183–94.

established regular sales. However, there was little evidence to suggest that public demand was strongest for the 'lowest class of writers', and thus the channel was open through which he and the SDUK might pour 'clear waters from the pure and healthy springs of knowledge' into the minds of a growing pool of readers.[20] Knight estimated that the potential for social transformation of such an intervention in the periodical market-place was immense, and reminded his readers that whereas Edmund Burke had speculated that some 80,000 people were regular readers in Britain during the 1790s, his own calculations suggested that the readership of the *Penny Magazine* alone at the end of 1832 approached a million.

Not surprisingly, the SDUK and its moral reform publications attracted criticism from a variety of sources. From one direction came the outraged voices of the radical press. William Cobbett, whose 'democratic journalism' had been a key target of Knight's campaign,[21] retaliated by charging the 'literary impostors' of the *Penny Magazine* with seeking to delude 'the working-people to be quiet, while they suck luxuries and riches out of the fruit of their toil'.[22] From another came the charge that the SDUK had unnecessarily and dangerously opened the sluice-gates of popular reading, and had, by means of the penny press inculcated 'profligate doctrines . . . amongst the manufacturing classes of the community, who have just enough of education to enable them to read the journals which contain the poison, but not enough to give them the power of reflection which might serve them as an antidote'.[23]

Mainstream newspaper jouralism too was disturbed by the apparent commercial successes of the *Penny Magazine*. An attack on the society in *The Times* in the summer of 1834 was welcomed by Knight as excellent publicity for his paper,[24] and was interpreted by him as evidence that 'the London newspaper autocracy' were terrified that they might shortly be obliged to compete against an SDUK sponsored daily newspaper.[25]

---

[20] *Penny Magazine*, 31 Mar. 1832. The *Penny Magazine* was intended to supplement, not to supersede, popular newspapers, and sought to make better use of the 'spare half an hour for the reading of a newspaper' by producing a weekly publication 'that may be taken up and laid down without requiring any considerable effort; and that may tend to fix the mind upon calmer, and, it may be, purer subjects of thought than the violence of party discussion, or the stimulating details of crime and suffering', *Penny Magazine* no. i, 31 Mar. 1832.

[21] Knight, *Passages of a Working Life*, vol. i, p. 185. Knight here describes Cobbett as 'half knave and half enthusiast', ibid., p. 186.

[22] William Cobbett, article written in Newcastle upon Tyne on 23 September 1832, *Rural Rides*, (Harmondsworth, 1967), p. 508.

[23] S. Carter Hall, 'The Penny Press', *New Monthly Magazine*, Feb. 1834, p. 178.

[24] Charles Knight to Henry Brougham, 16 Aug. 1834, Brougham MS 18, 19, UCL.

[25] Knight to Brougham, 21 Sept. 1834, Brougham MS 18, 19, UCL. For a satirical

That particular challenge to the national newspapers was never mounted. The SDUK was dissolved in 1846, mired in debts caused by massive overinvestment in the ambitious *Biographical Dictionary*. The directors of the society at their last meeting, however, attributed the discontinuation of the *Penny Magazine* in 1845 to a changed political and moral climate, one in which dissenters could attend the University of London, workers had access to Mechanics' Institutes, Roman Catholics were no longer excluded from public office, and slavery had been abolished throughout the dominions of the British Empire. The society's work was done, its greatest objects achieved. The *Penny Magazine* had undermined the appeal, and curtailed the circulations, of those many immoral cheap publications, and had introduced sound reading habits and socially useful knowledge 'into quarters where books had hardly penetrated'.[26] Charles Knight himself, however, was less confident about the morally uplifting consequences of his journalism. Writing in the last issue of the *Penny Magazine* in 1845, he confessed that the streams of moral pollution had not been dammed.

> There are manufactories in London whence hundreds of reams of vile paper and printing issue weekly; where large bodies of children are employed to arrange types at the wages of shirt makers, from copy furnished by the most ignorant at the wages of scavengers. . . . All the garbage that belongs to the history of crime and misery is raked together, to diffuse a moral miasma through the land, in the shape of the most vulgar and brutal fiction.[27]

The 'march of intellect' had not, as Brougham was to claim in a reflective speech on the achievements of the SDUK delivered in 1858, driven 'the vile publications absolutely out of existence', nor by that time had the taste for the 'excitement of horror' in stories of murder, seduction and romance been supplanted or even marginalised. But Brougham was speaking for a new consensus when he added that popular habits of reading had been transformed during the previous four decades. Writers such as Carlile and Paine, he speculated, no longer attracted the same proportion of readers as they once had, and the strongest demand lay instead for 'papers which combine harmless recreation with some

---

treatment of the SDUK see for example *The Penny Comic Magazine, of an Amorous, Clamorous . . . and Glorious Society for the Diffusion of Broad Grins*, 1832.

[26] SDUK, *Address of the Committee of the Society for the Diffusion of Useful Knowledge* (1846), p. 15.

[27] Quoted approvingly in Alexander Strahan, 'Our Very Cheap Literature', *Contemporary Review*, June 1870, p. 440. Strahan asked whether it was 'worth while to agitate for compulsory education, if, when people have learnt to read, they will content themselves with such poor innutritious stuff [as *The Sons of Britain or Boys of England*]?' Grudgingly replying to his own question in the affirmative, Strahan reiterated the SDUK argument that any text was legitimate 'if it furnishes a taste for reading', ibid., p. 458.

instruction'. Whether by way of 'narrative, of fiction, or of discussion' the press had become 'the vehicle of . . . sound doctrines', and the importance of newspapers in particular, by facilitating the legislative and policing procedures of civil society, had become incontestible.[28] What Brougham did not concede, however, was the argument put forward by a new generation of moral reformers in the 1860s that the society had committed a serious error in seeking to 'instruct the people without interesting them'.[29]

With the demise of the SDUK and the *Penny Magazine*, a revived Anglicanism intensified its own attacks on infidelity. Starting from the premise that while the readers' grasp of the written language in the mid-1840s might remain slender, with 'hard words . . . passed over, and punctuation and pronunciation . . . set at nought', working-class demand for newspapers and magazines continued to grow. Much of this journalism was undoubtedly the work of 'satan . . . corrupting and perverting' the urban poor, and the newly popular Sunday newspapers, regardless of their content, were charged with breaking the Sabbath by keeping 'many thousands of persons from the house of prayer'.[30] But having 'furnished the disease, by pouring forth its socialist and Chartist publications' the newspaper press was, in the minds of Livesey, Knight and others, 'ready to furnish the remedy'.[31] But whereas Livesey in 1838 has condemned as dangerously immoral the news values of the great majority of newspapers, but had offered few alternatives other than to reduce the coverage of politics and crime, neither of which were wholly plausible objectives even in the 1830s, the anonymous author of a pamphlet entitled *The Power of the Press*, published in 1847, proposed a more vigorous investment in the collection and dissemination of news as a means of protecting Christian civilisation, as embodied in the Anglican Church, against its many and active enemies. Advocating that the most talented ministers ought to 'devote themselves entirely to *teaching by the press*' as the only means whereby 'millions of minds' might be reached,[32] it was also argued that news-gathering should be

---

[28] Lord Brougham, 'Cheap Literature for the People', speech delivered at the annual conference of the National Association for the Promotion of Social Science (NAPSS), Liverpool, 12 Oct. 1858, pp. 9–14.

[29] Whately Cooke Taylor, 'Educational Results of Cheap Fiction', NAPSS, *Sessional Proceedings*, 1867–68 (1868), p. 50.

[30] Anon., *The Power of the Press* (1847), pp. 3, 5, 20–22.

[31] The editor of the *Monmouthshire Beacon* on the function of *The Journal of the Working Classes*, whose objectives were 'to instruct, to warn and to console and defend', in *The Journal of the Working Classes*, no. i, 1841 (pub. and edited by W.E. Painter, publisher also of *The Church of England Quarterly Review*).

[32] *The Power of the Press* (1847), p. 26.

pursued with greater care and sensitivity since most newspaper editors obtained their intelligence, particularly foreign correspondence, from 'polluted sources – from the Romanist, or Infidel journals of the continent'. Analyses and editorial opinions were thus founded on false or compromised information, and in order to ensure the purity of the editorial voice it was essential to control the sources and the channels through which news flowed into the newspaper office. Finally, the pamphlet acknowledged the greater power exerted by the daily newspaper. Whereas the weeklies were aimed at individuals, too busy and too poor to read more frequently than once a week, the daily newspapers were targeted at institutions and at 'those who *must* purchase it for the use of others' citing reading rooms and church congregations, and as such were both more influential and less price-sensitive than weekly newspapers.[33]

Gradually, during the 1830s and 1840s, the medium and its counter-insurgent possibilities were being explored and redefined. By the mid-1850s, when a sufficient consensus existed in government to deregulate a medium which by then was considered to be generally safe from seditious intent, fears of a resurgent urban radicalism focused far more on 'ill written detestable pamphlets' and the growing taste for reading works of fiction, than on dissident newspapers. A correspondent to the Manchester-based manuscript magazine *Odds and Ends* in 1855 remarked that, in contrast to the debilitating effects of speeches, pamphleteering and cheap fiction, newspapers in the city's reading rooms provided readers with 'all the news of the day, together with notices of all the discoveries and inventions which are continually being made and which have such an effect upon our social and moral wellbeing'.[34] Together with schools, libraries, mechanics' institutes, mutual improvement societies, savings banks and religious denominations, newspapers were now generally considered to be integral components of the strategy of social improvement.[35]

The historian Charles Macintosh concluded in 1859 that, within a comparatively recent period, an observable shift had occurred in the perceived social value of popular newspapers. Only 30 years previously, the large-scale dissemination of news had seriously been considered to be

---

[33] Ibid., pp. 36–41.

[34] Nelson Collier, 'The Evils toWhich Young Men in Large Towns Like Manchester Are Most Liable, and Their Remedies', prize essay, *Odds and Ends by A's and B's. A Manuscript Magazine*, vol. i, edited by G. Milner and J. Baker, St Paul's Mutual Improvement Society, Manchester, 1855, Manchester City Library, p. 43.

[35] Consider in this context the significance of such newspaper titles as *The Lever, or The Power of the Press*, first issued by William White, Hope Street, Shelton, North Staffordshire, on 25 Jan. 1851.

a cause of social disorder. Since then, that 'dogma' had decisively been overturned. Knowledge, instead, was commonly, if not universally, regarded as being conducive 'to the social and political welfare of the community at large'.[36] Whately Cooke Taylor, in a paper delivered to the National Association for the Promotion of Social Science in December 1867, attempted to account for that cultural shift by placing the recent development of the newspaper in the context of the growth of popular fiction. Warning that the social effects of cheap fiction were those about which he and his contemporaries knew least, he noted with alarm the very high levels of anxiety which the 'intoxicating' consequences of fiction had engendered during that year of parliamentary reform. The causes of such anxiety were, for Cooke Taylor, quite evident. Fiction was an 'unsubstantial and insidious' form of writing for which it was difficult if not impossible to lay down rules such as those that might restrict 'writers of facts'. In the absence of such disciplining structures, imaginative writing was effectively beyond social control, and enjoyed a liberty which might be abused with impunity. By the same token, the social influence of cheap fiction could not be measured simply by interrogating statistics of titles and circulation, nor could its contents be put to 'immediate tests such as could be applied to science, to art, to writings upon politics, economy, or morals'. He did, however, insist in the positivist manner that a combination of statistics and 'a true theory of the subject' would enable him to reach some important conclusions concerning the social uses of fiction. Acknowledging that some very positive educational benefits accrued from the reading of fiction – Cooke Taylor conceded that his own knowledge of history was derived almost entirely from that source – he argued that the only sound methodology for testing the adverse social consequences of cheap fiction was to consider its influence on the 'poorer portions' of society. In this way, numbers and theory were to be fruitfully combined to produce an analysis.

Cooke Taylor's statistics were drawn principally from a comparison between the range of periodical publications that contained fiction in the two years 1831 and 1860. In 1831 the annual aggregate circulation of the high-quality monthlies and quarterlies, including the *Edinburgh Review*, *Quarterly Review*, *Westminster Review*, *Blackwood's Edinburgh Magazine*, *Tait's* and *Fraser's*, amounted to a mere 125,000 copies. At the same time, cheap, unlicensed titles of a wholly 'treasonable, immoral, or irreligious cast' were rife. Sedition and indecency, moreover, 'was then considered the only literary nourishment

---

[36] Charles A. Macintosh, *Popular Outlines of the Press, Ancient and Modern* (1859), p. 221.

palatable to the humble, and a lower taste was supposed to be a necessary accompaniment of a lower class'. All attempts made to improve this literature was prevented by high newspaper taxes, and the taste for politics introduced in the turbulent years of 1830 to 1832 produced fresh demand for cheap newspapers which, in the period 1836 to 1855 flooded the market with 'stories of horror, mystery and crime', most notably in such Sunday newspapers as *Reynolds's Weekly Newspaper* and *Lloyd's Weekly Newspaper*. This lamentable state of affairs contrasted sharply with the considerably more promising condition of 'safe' popular fiction in 1860.

Table 5.1 Circulation of periodical publishers of fiction (in whole or in part) in 1860

Whately Cooke Taylor's categories	*Circulations per annum*
Monthly magazines devoted to fiction	2,200,000
Weekly journals, chief feature being fiction	700,000
Weekley penny romances	5,000
Immoral publications	52,500
Twopenny magazines (excluding religious, temperance and educational periodicals)	374,000
Total	3,341,500

Source: Whately Cooke Taylor, 'Educational Results of Cheap Fiction', National Association for the Promotion of Social Science, *Sessional Proceedings, 1867–68* (1868), p. 43.

By 1860, it was estimated that half of the two million copies of monthly magazines contained 'wholesome' fiction, whereas only 52,500 copies of 'immoral fiction' could be found, a figure that was further reduced to a barely significant 9,000 in the following year, when the paper duties were finally abolished. Furthermore, by 1864, only 5,000 copies of freethinking periodicals were circulating in the United Kingdom. Drawing on evidence obtained from the periodical retail trade by the author of a recently published text, *The Progress of the Working Classes from 1832 to 1867*, Cooke Taylor proposed a theory of progression in the reading habits of the poor and the young. Initially attracted to stories whose illustrated plates were daubed with yellow, red and blue ink, readers, he surmised, soon tired of such 'strong dishes' and searched for more wholesome fare. Furthermore, the worst, most vicious of the penny publications suffered from such low circulations that they were only barely profitable as marketable commodities. Thus, a statistical and historical survey led to the optimistic conclusion that fiction, far from corrupting readers, in fact served both to educate and, in a social and moral sense, to purify them. Even the person who occasionally read the worst of the cheap periodicals was 'on the high road to become a wiser and a happier man, and a better and a worthier citizen'.[37]

Not everyone was equally sanguine. The tramping printer Charles Manby Smith deplored the influence of the 'gallows press', whose coverage of executions reduced the majesty of the law to 'the punch-and-judy level', and which for the young was 'one of the most fruitful sources of demoralisation and crime'.[38] Concern for the moral condition of youth was a recurring feature of the debate on the influence of the press. In 1873, James Greenwood, who as a journalist was himself no stranger to sensational fictions, linked 'Penny Awful' publications to crime by citing the case of a schoolboy who had turned to theft in order to finance his addiction to *Tyburn Dick*.[39] Five years later, Mary Lewis found contemporary children's literature to be 'a reproach to the age of mental and moral culture' in which she lived,[40] and Thomas Wright's celebrated treatise on popular culture of 1881 was forthright in its denunciation of penny dreadfuls as a displacement activity for the young. It was not that reading cheap fiction necessarily criminalised or demoralised the reader (Wright sensibly remarked that 'boys who do *not* read dreadfuls sometimes rob tills'), rather it was that they 'usurped the place of the only reading by which . . . the foundations of a cultured taste could be laid'.[41] By the end of the 1880s, another despairing reviewer of popular fiction alleged that to allow sensational children's literature to proliferate and circulate unchecked as they had been hitherto would be 'deliberately [to] poison the springs of a nation's life'.[42] Thus, whatever the social scientists might argue, it was evident that concern about the influence of

---

[37] Whately Cooke Taylor, 'Educational Results of Cheap Fiction', NAPSS *Sessional Proceedings*, 1867–68 (1868), pp. 42–51. See also his earlier attack on the *Northern Star*, whose teachings he predicted would 'end in an entire breaking-up of the English system of social order'. The influence of O'Connor's paper, he warned, was 'very much underrated by the majority of people in the South', W. Cooke Taylor, *Notes of a Tour in the Manufacturing Districts of Lancashire in a Series of Letters to His Grace the Archbishop of Dublin* (1842), p. 41.

[38] Charles Manby Smith, *The Working Man's Way in the World*, (1967 edn), first published serially in *Tait's* Mar. 1851–May 1852, p. 269. See also review of the above in *Typographical Circular*, 1 July 1854, p. 27, and Simon Nowell-Smith, 'Charles Manby Smith: His Family & Friends, His Fantasies & Fabrications', *Journal of the Printing Historical Society*, no. 7, 1972, pp. 1–28.

[39] James Greenwood, 'Penny Awfuls', *St Paul's Magazine*, Feb. 1873, p. 165.

[40] Mary A. Lewis, 'Cheap literature for Village Children', *Macmillan's Magazine*, July 1878, p. 220.

[41] Thomas Wright, 'On a Possible Popular Culture', *Contemporary Review*, July 1881 pp. 25–44.

[42] Bennett George Johns, 'Literature of the Streets', *Edinburgh Review*, Jan. 1887, p. 61.

cheap fiction on the moral and social behaviour of its readers could not be alleviated merely by the manipulation of circulation statistics. The market for fiction needed to be changed and controlled as much in the 1880s as it had been in the 1820s, and, again, the development of the popular newspaper became the key to that process. News and fiction plausibly appealed to similar literary appetites and cultural sensibilities: both were melodramatic narratives of the unexpected, the one often being as vividly expressed and highly charged as the other. The distinction between the two, in the perceptions of some, lay in the greater capacity of news to extend social knowledge. Through the newspaper, a social understanding based on credible, if not always accurate, information about the world might be constructed which cemented rather than undermined social stability. A similar argument was proposed as a justification for the extension of popular education, but newspapers were perceived to have a very specific role to play in that more comprehensive strategy of socialisation. In the first instance, newspaper reading was itself a displacement activity, which at best drew readers entirely away from 'low' fiction. Alternatively, by printing serialised fiction and poetry alongside and amidst news reports, advertisements and editorial commentary within the format of the newspaper, readers were obliged to juxtapose and thus to distinguish not only between language registers, but also between epistemologically diverse kinds of text. But for this contextualising process to be effective, and for journalism to fulfil its role as a compensating and christianising influence on modern life, as the Revd Herford had counselled in his Manchester sermon in 1866, it was essential that readers should trust in the veracity of what they read. That trust, however, was predicated not so much on the honesty of individual reporters as on the perceived integrity and cultural status of the entire corpus of journalists. But if, in theory, the reporting of news was regarded as an effective counter to the morally debilitating effects of cheap fiction in the everyday diet of popular reading, the development of newspaper journalism during the second half of the nineteenth century was itself to generate new cultural anxieties.

Respectable practices

At a meeting of the Newspaper Press Benevolent Association, held at the Freemason's Tavern, London, on Saturday 13 July, 1839, Lord Brougham, Benjamin Disraeli, the Prince of Oudh and Lord Lyndhurst paid lavish tributes to those 'connected with the literary departments of the Newspaper Press of the United Kingdom'. Particular attention was drawn to 'the influence and good effects of the Newspaper Press' on the moral conduct of society, as demonstrated by the educational, civilising and calming effects of newspaper reading in the armed services. In the navy, newspapers maintained 'that good feeling between man and man so essential to comfort', and in the army they had been 'instrumental in taking the bayonet from the soldier when off duty'. While there was a discernible element of political ritual in these expressions of gratitude by politicians to an audience of appreciative newspapermen, they also conveyed a hint of menace and of implied criticism. Two of the speakers singled out the vexing matter of the respectability of the trade of journalism, and by so doing cast doubt upon it. Lord Lyndhurst began his oration with the usual hyperbole on the power of the press before inserting the following carefully phrased words of warning:

> There was no engine . . . that exerted a more powerful influence than the public press of this country. It directed, controlled, it governed public opinion of this vast empire. How important, then, was it to consider what it was, and the consequences to which it would lead! How important was it that the press of this country should be conducted and directed by persons of the highest character and of the greatest respectability! How important it was that its aid should be called for in defence of morality and of virtue! If it were a powerful engine for good, they must remember that it was also a powerful engine for mischief. Therefore it was, that they should do their utmost to enlist it in the cause of virtue and morality.[43]

Lyndhurst was followed to the podium by Brougham, who repeatedly emphasised for the benefit of the assembled journalists that 'the greatest service . . . which they could now render to the public [was] . . . raising by their means the respectability of the public press'.[44] But what did respectability mean in relation to journalism ? The truthful reporting of events was an important, though not the sole, consideration, as Lyndhurst's injunction that the press should also defend 'morality and virtue' clearly implied. Journalism could remain in harmony with the social institutions that ostensibly benefited from its services only in so far as it adequately represented their interests. The functionally useful role that newspapers were believed to have played in the armed services in the 1830s, for example, hardly applied in the midst of the Crimean War when critical front-line reporting in *The Times*, taken up and magnified

---

[43] *Report of the Second Anniversary Meeting of the Newspaper Press Benevolent Association, held at the Freemason's Tavern on Saturday, 13 July, 1839* (1839), pp. 5–7.

[44] *Report of the Second Anniversary Meeting of the Newspaper Press Benevolent Association*, p. 18. The Newspaper Society, representing newspaper proprietors, was established in 1836. For further details, see Edward W. Davies, *The Newspaper Society, 1836–1936: a Centenary Retrospect* (1936).

by other newspapers and magazines, had so infuriated army officers as to prompt Harriet Martineau to complain of their conduct which was 'so insulting about the press' which they 'hated . . . beyond all measure'.[45] Journalism impinged on the public consciousness in a number of ways, not least via the mythologies of the heroic journalist, whose exceptional risks in resisting repressive governments or in facing hostile action on the battlefield, from Cobbett to William Howard Russell, were transmitted vicariously to the reader. But changing public perceptions of journalism were also, in part, conditioned by the practices employed by journalists in the everyday gathering and presentation of news, and for much of the nineteenth century, these practices defined the level of 'respectability', as defined by Lords Lyndhurst and Brougham in 1839, which journalism was deemed to have achieved.

It was noted in 1841 that the three essential characteristics of a 'well-conducted Newspaper' were 'systematic order, terse condensation, and lucid arrangement'.[46] But, for much of the nineteenth century, formats of news presentation remained fluid, and the frontiers between them porous. In the early decade of that century, no clear distinction was made between news published in newspapers and in broadsides. In some cases, broadsides may be seen to have been directly linked to newspapers as extensions or addendas, written, issued and distributed by the same publishers. In the broadsides, news was expressed as entertainment, parody, self-reflection. Older and more popularly accessible than the newspaper, they were intended to be read aloud or sung in their entirety, linking, as Rohan McWilliam has perceptively observed, oral and literary culture in a way which rendered illiteracy no barrier to understanding or enjoyment of the text.[47] Newsmen's verses, for example, provide illuminating instances of a style of news presentation that mimicked the broadside tradition. Usually published annually, normally at Christmas, they were firmly locked into the production schedule of the associated newspaper, written by its editor or printer and hawked on the streets and in the taverns in much the same way as were copies of the newspaper itself. They drew on the events of the passing year, providing a synoptic, if idiosyncratic, and easily assimilable version of the immediate past, an end of year round up of news local, national and international, privileging

---

[45] Harriet Martineau to Frederick Knight Hunt, n.d. (F.K. Hunt died in Dec. 1855), HM488, Heslop Room, University of Birmingham Library.

[46] T.S. Houghton, *The Printers' Practical Every-Day-Book* (1841), p. 8.

[47] Rohan Allan McWilliam, 'The Tichborne Claimant and the People: Investigations Into Popular Culture 1867–1886', (unpub. PhD, Univ. of Sussex, 1990), pp. 254–85. For McWilliam, the broadside idiom engendered a 'culture of consolation', a moral language designed to provoke an emotional response, 'not a language of class and only dealt with economic issues very broadly'.

certain themes, usually political, and offering interpretations of their continuing significance. Thus the *Bristol Gazette* issued for Christmas 1819 the following lament recording the tragic events that had occurred earlier that year at St Peter's Field in Manchester.

> At *Manchester*, a sad affair
> Occurr'd within the passing year,
> The less that's said perhaps the better
> Your Newsman hates a galling fetter;
> New Laws are made, not very civil
> To Printer, Publisher or 'Devil'.
> And if again the People meet
> To hold their Confabs on the street,
> They mey depend, some of the Quorum
> Will recite their Orators before 'em,
> And if a Stranger chance to speak
> Like pig in gate he's sure to squeak . . .
> Adieu to *Cobbet* and *Gale Jones*,
> To *Thistlewood* and *Tom Paine's Bones*.[48]

The *Bristol Mirror Newsman's Address* for the same year offered a very different reading of the same events. Such pithy expositions sharpened the political differences between newspapers and the sentiments of their producers.

> Hey for the *Radicals* and *Doctor Slop*
> And *Hone* and *Carlile's* great Sedition Shop,
> Whence irreligion and her filthy crew
> Stalk'd, in broad day-light, all the nation through,
> Scat'ring their poison as they pass'd along,
> In picture, parody, in ode and song,
> Until th' Attorney-General's iron hand
> Cross'd their rebellious path, and bid them stand !
> Arrested Treason in her full career,
> And in her bosom plung'd Ithuriel's spear.
> Who but a Radical could ever guess,
> Pennies to get from persons *penniless*![49]

Newsmen's verses enable us to study the range of criteria employed to signify newsworthiness, and in December 1826, the *Bristol Mirror's* newsman referred to the value of 'the Printer's Art' as it 'dogs the heels of Time . . . Preserving, in a thousand different ways/The business, actions, follies, frolic, fun' and served up annually 'as a dish of doggerel rhyme' for one shilling per copy.[50] The practice of producing verses of

---

[48] Newsman's verses from the *Bristol Gazette*, 1812 to 1860, Bristol RO 11944 (3). For a typical example, see the illustrated *The Bristol Times and Felix Farley's Journal Newsman's Address for Christmas 1856*.

[49] *The Bristol Mirror Newsman's Address for 1819*, Bristol RO 11944 (3).

[50] Ibid.

this kind continued well into the Victorian period, and were not always comic. We find, for example, the *Bristol Mercury Newsman's Address* of Christmas 1839 sorrowfully regretting the actions of the 'Mistaken and misguided men [who] were led to die' in the Newport Rising of the previous month.[51] The efforts of newspaper writers to 'look back and versify the news'[52] in this way suffered along with other broadsides and ballads with the growth of popular newspapers, which ironically adopted some of their humorous and melodramatic styles.

Formulas for newsmen's verses were well established by the mid-1830s, as were other means of attracting the attention of the reading public, such as the prospectus and the opening address. Both signalled in a direct, if an all too predictable, way the intentions and self-perceptions of the printer or editor. For this reason, their blandishments need to be taken seriously as self-justificatory means of establishing an identity and a place in the market for the new or proposed periodical. Emphasis was almost always placed on the high moral tone and general utility of the paper, a preoccupation which had long infused the self-imagery of the press. When in October 1833 the Dissenting proprietors of a newspaper in Bradford were searching for a suitable editor, emphasis was placed on

> a man of high talent and information, of liberal reforming principles
> – neither a Tory nor a Radical who has . . . just views of religious
> freedom and the . . . alliance of church and state. A handsome salary
> will be given. A decidedly pious man would be preferred – a full
> recognition of all the great principles of our common Christianity is
> essential. Our object is usefulness – it is important that the press
> should be under such guidance, especially perhaps in such a district
> as ours, as will give so powerful an engine a beneficial influence.[53]

A similar piety was expressed in the opening addresses. The example of the *Daily News*, launched on 21 January 1846, if more restrained, is not untypical of its kind. It made clear that it sought 'to elevate the character of the Public Press in England', and to attain for it 'a much higher position' so that its conductors might be 'more respected as a class'.[54] Assuming that the press was in a dire condition, to be rescued by this new publication, it emphasised its respectability, its care for family values, and paid due homage to the intelligence of its target readers. Others dealt with the same appeal in a different way. The first issue of *Reynolds's Weekly Newspaper; a Journal of Democratic Progress and*

---

[51] Ibid.

[52] Ibid.

[53] Revd B. Godwin to Mr. Copley, n.d. Oct. 1833, West Yorkshire Archive Service, Bradford (WYAS), MS 9D77/5.

[54] This first issue includes the first instalment of 'Travelling Letters, Written on the Road' by Charles Dickens.

General Intelligence, of Sunday 5 May 1850, dispensed with an address, carrying instead a front page, signed article by the editor, G.W.M. Reynolds, on 'The Prospects of the Democratic Cause' which applauded the victory of the red republicans and socialists over the reactionaries in Paris, and extends the analysis to Spain, Portugal, Hungary, Austria, and the 17 continental countries that had risen in the revolutions of 1848. Revolution was once more on the agenda, and Reynolds urged the British workers to start 'agitating at *home*'.[55] This was as clear an indication of his intentions as a journalist as any. But early issues of *Reynolds's Weekly Newspaper* departed from the normally uplifting tone of its view of the journalist. In the fifth number, Reynolds, again in a signed article, castigated the glibness of the 'journalist who sells his talents to the cause of tyranny, coercion, and despotism!' In a withering assault on the repressive ideological and physical policing of the Chartist demonstration held on Kennington Common, London, in April 1848, Reynolds clearly identified the journalist as part of the problem.

> If the toiling serfs and proletarians assemble together, in the belief that they at least possess the privilege of meeting to proclaim their wrongs and petition for their rights, the newspaper-organs of the upper and middle classes raise the cry that 'society is in danger'; and in order to 'save society', the Duke of Wellington marshalls his troops to bayonet and cannonade the people. . . . Ah! how convenient a word is 'society' in the mouths of men who have monopolies to maintain and class-interests to defend![56]

However, leading articles of this kind, intended to continue to locate the editorial voice at the heart of the paper, and described by Fox Bourne in 1887 as 'the highest grade of newspaper work, short of editorship', were not always highly regarded by readers. When read at all, it was seldom 'for instruction as sermons in church are listened to', and the 'thundering' style of *The Times* and its imitators was reported to amuse and entertain, rather than overawe, its readers.[57]

The pursuit of the respectability claimed by journalists in their own presentation of news continued to challenge them for the remainder of the century, and it was to be dealt with in a variety of ways. One means was to combine the inherited narrative of press freedom with the distinct character of English newspapers. Contrary to the experience of other European states, where journalism was characterised as being at best opinionated and at worst shackled by government censorship, English

---

[55] It contained 3.5 cols of European news and only 0.5 cols of police news. The title was changed to *Reynolds's Weekly Newspaper* on 18 Aug. 1850.

[56] *Reynolds's Weekly Newspaper*, 2 June 1850, no. 5, front page signed editorial 'Society and Public Opinion'.

[57] H.R. Fox Bourne, *English Newspapers*, vol. ii, pp. 385–89.

journalism was described as being chiefly concerned with the anonymous reporting of news and the dissemination of 'intelligence'. *Punch*, in 1847, vividly perceived the difference:

> A French journalist has two great chances. He may either become a Prime Minister or an inmate of a Government prison. . . . An English journalist . . . has one great chance. He writes for a number of years; he influences public opinion; he exposes swindles; analyses the most plausible schemes; gives warning of a panic, or restores confidence when most needed; and his great chance is, if he has extraordinary talent, perseverance, and industry – to remain unknown.[58]

A decade later, Josiah J. Merriman, editor of the *Preston Guardian*, in a spirited lecture on 'The English Newspaper' delivered at the Young Men's Club in Preston in 1857, pointedly observed how 'the Continental newspaper [was] more like a political essay or pamphlet than a newspaper. . . . Even a murderer claims a very brief notice at the hands of a Continental editor . . . '.[59] Where Frank Harris in 1878 was to interpret this difference as one which distinguished the eloquence and high-mindedness of the continental press from the venality of its English equivalent,[60] Merriman measured the success of an English newspaper by its commercial viability, which itself was dependent on the newspaper's 'freedom from party ties'. Whereas *The Times* owed its success to its financial and thus its political independence, the Liberal *Daily News*, Merriman asserted, had been damaged commercially and politically by its 'presumed connection with certain leaders of the Manchester school, whose ideas are far from popular in society'.[61] Respectability, calculated here by success in the market-place, could thus be claimed by reference to England's particular legislative and social history, as related by the newspaper historians, which had produced a journalism that was perceived to be both distinctive and in certain respects superior to its conterparts elsewhere in Europe. For newspaper journalists, the historical peculiarities of the English press were themselves indicative of the intrinsic worth of their occupation.

But if there existed a degree of consensus regarding the distinguishing features of English and continental journalism, there was less agreement on the question of anonymity. Defended by some as 'the life and soul of journalism', anonymously published articles were held to remove authorial vanity from the newspaper and, in consequence, to enable

---

[58] *Punch*, vol. 13, 1847, p. 123.

[59] Josiah J. Merriman, 'The English Newspaper', *The Popular Lecturer*, vol. ii, n.s., 1857, p. 4.

[60] Laurel Brake, *Subjugated Knowledges. Journalism, Gender and Literature in the Nineteenth-Century* (1994), pp. 137–38.

[61] Merriman, 'English Newspaper', p. 4.

readers to judge those articles by their contents rather than their signatures.[62] Anonymity was also regarded as a device for imposing a necessary measure of control over the individual's egotistic 'rage for publicity, the universality of print'. 'Abrogate the anonymous, and introduce personality into the public life of journalism', *Blackwood's* fulminated in 1859, 'then the ballot may be called for to temper the excesses of the press. It would be the only refuge from the egotism, the intrusion, the violation of privacy which is the vice of confessed authorship in newspapers'.[63] This defensive response to the use of signature or byline arose out of the deep assumptions of a dominant tradition of journalism which, up until the 1860s, was essentially impersonal and pervaded by the collective presence of the editorial 'we'. Anonymity had provided that tradition with its code of honour. From the 1860s, however, public interest was aroused in journalism as an occupation, and in journalists as individuals, one consequence of which was that the collective authority of the newspaper title began to fragment. One 'old reporter' justified the publication of his revealing memoirs in 1862 on the grounds that '[m]ost people like to pry into the business of their neighbours – the curious public will possibly like to see just a corner of the curtain which shrouds the mysteries of the "fourth estate" lifted by a practical hand'.[64] Whether or not the reading public was as voyeuristic as W.H. Watts implied, newspaper readers increasingly demanded to see the names of correspondents appended to news items, especially in relation to reports of foreign events. The example provided by French journalism, where a byline was 'the passport to credibility', was almost certainly a major influence,[65] but equally significant was the impact on the English newspaper reading public of the war correspondents in the Crimea and the American Civil War.[66] The growth of West End clubs were also held responsible for the decline of anonymity. Through these clubs, journalists were socialised into polite society in such a way as to demystify their occupation, a process which arguably led to a diminution of their mystique and their

---

[62] Lord Broughton, speech notes, 1854, Brit. Mus. Add. MS 47230, ff. 43–46.

[63] 'Popular Literature – the Periodical Press', *Blackwood's*, Feb. 1859, pp. 188–89.

[64] W.H. Watts, *My Private Note-Book; or, Recollections of an Old Reporter* (1862), p. 2.

[65] Sir Hugh Gilzean-Reid and P.J. Macdonell, 'The Press', in John Samuelson (ed.), *The Civilisation of Our Day*, p. 281. Emile Zola, however, had defended the practice of anonymity in political articles, though not in literary ones, at the Annual Conference of the Institute of Journalism, 23 Sept. 1893, 'Anonymity in Journalism', *Sell's Dictionary of the World's Press* (1894), pp. 89–94.

[66] See Phillip Knightley, *The First Casualty: the War Correspondent as Hero, Propagandist, and Myth Maker From the Crimea to Vietnam* (1975), *passim*.

direct political power.[67] While the tension between the writer of 'polite letters' and the 'diurnal narrator of political events' may have continued into the second half of the century, partly as a result of such socialisation, newspaper journalists were no longer stigmatised to the extent that they previously had been as liars, spies and informers who, amidst 'contempt, and almost loathing', plied a 'dangerous trade'.[68] A limited overlap between the segments of the trade was thus both possible and remunerative. Anonymity, as Dr Laurel Brake has shown, served to protect the identities of a network of writers who contributed, often simultaneously, to monthly, weekly and daily periodicals, ensuring a degree of continuity of style and content between what were otherwise perceived to be distinct media forms.[69]

While signature and byline acquired greater prominence in late nineteenth-century periodicals, anonymity was not eradicated from the larger proportion of news or feature items in newspapers. Nor could it be given the increasing importance of news agencies and the armies of 'staff' and local reporters who supplied them with their articles. The 'middle ground' between anonymity and signed contributions[70] occupied by the newspapers was symptomatic of a greater fragmentation of the multiple forms of the periodical press, a process that was further intensified by attempts by newspaper journalists to define themselves as a separate profession. In the years following the Repeal of the Newspaper Stamp Act, it became increasingly evident that newspaper reporters comprised a recognisable occupational group, 'a class of themselves . . . a privileged order' about which, because they operated 'behind the scenes of society', relatively little was known. The increased deployment of the term 'reporter' from the 1850s denoted a clearly defined segment of the literary labour market, one which was exclusively employed in the domain of newspaper work. Concern continued to be expressed regarding the 'respectability', and in particular the sobriety, of this occupational group. In a lifestyle characterised by travel and opportunities to mix with very different social circles, the temptations offered by alcohol were strong and, as one temperance activist reported in 1874, 'in all the press there is no disturbing influence like the whisky in the brains of journalists'.[71] But reporters also possessed recognisable, if unusual, skills. For example, contemporaries were astonished by the detachment, 'the almost judicial coolness' with which 'the experienced

---

[67] George Augustus Sala, 'The Press: What I Have Known of It – 1840–1890', *Progress of British Newspapers in the Nineteenth Century, Illustrated* (1901), p. 203.

[68] Charles Isaac Elton, 'Early English Newspapers', *Cornhill Magazine*, July 1868.

[69] Brake, *Subjugated Knowledges*, p. 92.

[70] Ibid., p. 91.

[71] *Alliance News*, 15 Aug. 1874, p. 524.

reporter' was 'able to sit amidst the wreck of political elements or the crash of religious worlds'.[72] Reporters themselves, however, were rarely so stoical. The 'old reporter' W.H. Watts complained in 1862 that both the 'regular' and the 'dismounted', or freelance, reporters were poorly treated and remunerated, and that the very few prizes that the press offered to its members were not destined for the lowly news-gatherer.[73] For an insight into the subjectivities of news reporting we need to consider not the printed, sub-edited copy, nor the self-regulated and polished memoir, but the reporter's diary. Here immediate impressions, draft sentences and experimental phrases express the writer's irony and shifting moods from exhilaration to boredom. Few texts are so suggestive of the reporter's self-perception, cultural location and understanding of the priorities and definitions of the news story, yet few have been so neglected by historians. In the reporter's diary or notebook, the formality of the printed news report reveals its genesis. The Bristol reporter D.A. Darlington, for example, noted his visit in March 1878 to the Forester's Music Hall, Broadmead, 'a wretched place – where George Leybourne sings some comic songs of a very indifferent character and with no fun in them. In the middle of the performance two policemen came in and nobbled one individual'.[74] Later, in attendance at the 'uninteresting proceedings' of the 1878 session of the Trades Union Congress he was entertained by 'some lively squabbles', and wryly observed that 'there is no doubt that this is a rare opportunity for a holiday for those delegates who come from a distance'.[75] Influence over the public mind stemmed from such mundane, even banal, attitudes. But such work nevertheless gave reporters a privileged access to a wide range of information, and, given that in many instances the reporter's words were the only sources of news available to the reader, enabled their observations and reflections to modify and perhaps also to form opinion.

Particular readings of English history, an insistence upon the distinctiveness of English journalism, the partial decline of anonymity, the systemisation of the language of journalism and the emergence of a more clearly defined occupational identity for newspaper reporting within an increasingly industrialised literary labour market, each in conjunction with the other forged the process whereby journalism by the 1860s and 1870s had come to be regarded as a more respectable practice. In the course of the following two decades, that process was underscored   by   the   ritual   reiteration   of   the   mantra   of

---

[72] 'Reporting and Reporters', *Meliora*, vol. 12, no. 48, 1869, pp. 322–32.
[73] Watts, *My Private Note-Book*, p. 2.
[74] 'Diary of a Journalist', 27 Mar. 1878, Bristol RO 40301.
[75] Ibid., 10 Sept. 1878.

professionalisation. Defined as the possession of specialist knowledge and skills, professional status became not only the most highly valued and desperately sought after goal of late nineteenth-century journalists, but it was also regarded as the final step in the long process that would underpin the clearly separate identity of newspaper journalism within the nineteenth-century media world.

Already by 1882, Joseph Hatton could observe that the Potts of Dickens would be as difficult to find in the English provinces as the Shandon of Thackeray would be in London.

> As Bohemia has laid aside its long pipe and 'two of gin', its sawdust floors and pewter pots, so has journalistic London advanced from the tavern corner, the sponging-house, and the gutter, to take a foremost place in the best society of the time, combining with literary London to make an intellectual aristocracy that bids fair to hold, in general estimation, a standing equal to that of hereditary rank and fortune. Liberal Premiers and Liberal Cabinets are credited with showing a more genuine respect for journalism than their Conservative opponents, though both have long since ceased to keep the London editor where Lord Chesterfield detained Dr Johnson – a patient and despised waiter on greatness among the lackeys in the hall.[76]

James Greenwood in 1883 could without any sense of discomfort describe himself as a 'Barrister at Law, journalist, etc',[77] while in 1885 George Augustus Sala could with an equal lack of embarrassment be termed 'the Emperor of Journalism'.[78] Biographical profiles and portraits of the most eminent editors and journalists in London and the provinces, together with descriptions of the types of work conducted in the various departments of their newspapers, began to be published in such publications as *Sell's Dictionary of the World's Press*.[79] The creation by these means of a new élite of newspapermen was functionally important in the process of improving the public image and status of journalism, and it is evident that the success of the few was admired and emulated if not by the many then by a number of writers who turned in less elevated circles. John Burnley, editor of *Yorkshire Life*, recorded in revealing terms his own debt to Sala as a writer both of fiction and newspaper features:

> since I was quite a lad I have laughed with you, and rambled with you all over the world. In the <u>Welcome Guest</u> I followed the

---

[76] Joseph Hatton, *Journalistic London*, pp. 41–43.

[77] James Greenwood to G.A. Sala, 11 Apr. 1883, Sala Corr., Special Collections, Brotherton Library, University of Leeds (SC, Brotherton, Leeds).

[78] James Colbeck to G.A. Sala, 13 Aug. 1885, SC, Brotherton, Leeds.

[79] *Sell's Dictionary of the World's Press* (1889), *passim*.

adventures of 'the Slim gentleman, the stout gentleman, and the man with the Iron Chest', in the <u>Illustrated Times</u> I dipped with you into the 'Babbington peerage Romance' . . . since then your pen has become still more familiar to me, and even though you are content to dub yourself journalist instead of author I have been content to look up to you as my 'most approved good master'. In proof of my privilege I may mention that I have sketched myself into local popularity by <u>imitating</u> – I say the words boldly and unflinchingly – your lively essays on London Life in a series of papers I have written for the <u>Bradford Observer</u>.[80]

Notwithstanding the value of the direct emulation of what in the trade was considered to be best practice, the challenge posed by Brougham in 1839 could not be met merely by raising the standards of the few. A more concerted drive was necessary to ensure the elevation of the many.[81] The pursuit of professional status for the majority of journalists was furthered by the establishment of regional press clubs, such as the one established in Manchester in 1870,[82] and, from 1886, by the National Association (later Institute) of Journalists (IoJ). Under the guidance of its first President, Algernon Borthwick, with Lord Glenesk, President of the Newspaper Press Fund, and such early directors as Justin MacCarthy MP and John Thackray Bunce of Birmingham, the Institute drew up a 13-point programme. These included the devising of measures for testing the qualification of candidates for admission to professional membership of the Institute 'by examination in theory and in practice or by any other actual practical tests; the promotion of whatever may tend to to the elevation of the status and the improvement of the qualifications of all members of Journalistic profession'. The IoJ also undertook to keep a watchful eye on 'any legislation affecting the discharge by Journalists of their professional duties and endeavouring to obtain amendments of the law affecting Journalists, their duties or interests, and securing the advancement of Journalism in all its branches and obtaining for Journalists as such formal and definite professional standing'.[83] Technically, the ranking of journalism as a profession dates precisely from the granting of a Charter to the IoJ in 1889, although, as was noted shortly afterwards, while 'legally regarded as a profession in the same sense as Law and

---

[80] John Burnley to G.A. Sala, 17 June 1885, SC, Brotherton, Leeds.

[81] Ernest Phillips calculated that there were 8,000 newspaper reporters in the UK in 1895, Ernest Phillips, *How to Become a Journalist. A Practical Guide to Newspaper Work* (1895), p. 1.

[82] Manchester Press Club, *Fifty Years of Us: a Jubilee Retrospect of Men and Newspapers* (Manchester, 1922).

[83] Institute of Journalists, *The Grey Book*, 1898, pp. 8–9.

Medicine', it differed from both 'in being open to all comers'.[84]

The work of the IoJ was aided by the publication of its official organ, *The Journalist and Newspaper Proprietor*, which in addition to praising the achievements of journalists, also ruthlessly exposed their shortcomings. In 1891, for example, the paper devoted extensive coverage to the scandal of reporters obtaining gifts for services. Noting that the enjoyment by reporters of such privileges as free admission to concerts, dinners and similar events was standard, and quite legitimate, practice given the duties they were called upon to perform, the paper was more disturbed by the possibility that receiving Christmas gifts, admittedly more common in the larger towns than in rural areas, might involve the 'sacrifice of professional dignity'. It was reported that 'presents on an ample scale were . . . secured by hints from the reporter', and that, in country areas, 'pressmen were often the recipients of such private hospitality as must of necessity impel them to see the bright side of the things they were sent to observe'. Gifts of game, it was argued, 'were not . . . worth fighting against, provided that they were really spontaneous'. But in general the IoJ advised its members that

> the function of the journalist was a high one. They had no cheap welcome for the young man who took to reporting for the love of beer and skittles, thinking only of the freedom, the Bohemianism, the famous men and places he would see, the notorious women he might chance to meet, the free dinners and champagne. The days of this light-headed gentleman were past.[85]

At the same time, the IoJ was called upon to defend reporters against what were regarded to be unjustified assaults on their integrity. The trade union leader John Burns, during an excoriating attack on the conduct of the *Evening Citizen* in a speech in Glasgow, accused journalists of accepting bribes from the railway companies which had led them to give 'false accounts' of events during the recent railway strike. Insinuating that 'you cannot expect honour and truth to come out between sandwiches of Scotch £5 notes', Burns reached rhetorical climax by comparing the Scottish reporters (unfavourably) with prostitutes. At that point the reporters as a body rose from their seats and left the hall, 'jeered and hooted' by a hostile audience.[86] The IoJ was stung into retaliation, pointing out that Burns's public reputation had been made by the London press, reminding him that 'the representatives of which are

---

[84] Phillips, *How to Become a Journalist*, p. ix.

[85] Paper read by W.G.R. Stone, of Evesham, at the Birmingham and Midland Counties District meeting on 'Journalists and Their Privileges', *Journalist and Newspaper Proprietor*, 3 Jan. 1891, p. 6.

[86] *Journalist and Newspaper Proprietor*, 17 Jan. 1891, p. 15.

not likely to forget in a hurry that he compared their brethren in Glasgow and in other parts of Scotland to prostitutes'.[87] Outside London, too, reporters were aghast by the implications of Burns's Glasgow speech, and the Warrington sub-district of the IoJ resolved 'to refuse to report Mr John Burns in any shape or form until he has withdrawn his charges, which the Sub-district regards as affecting pressmen generally'. Burns's subsequent sympathetic comments on the long working hours of reporters were insufficient to satisfy the traduced journalists.[88]

But the principal function of a professional association was not solely to expose internal bad practices nor to defend the occupation from external assaults, but rather to establish an internal code of conduct which in the future would enable journalism entirely to avoid such conflicts. William Lehman Burdett-Coutts MP, in the immediate wake of the Burns affair, expressed the view that 'the power of journalism was, unquestionably, an enormous one, and he thought it was well that those who wielded it should, like other professions, adopt some system which would comprise a code of rules and establish a standard of conduct to be acted up to'.[89] Such self-criticism led to attempts by individual reporters to draw up their own rules of behaviour, such as those propounded by an anonymous correspondent with regard to 'Acts Discreditable to a Journalist'. These consisted of

> sending false news to the Press . . . the refusal of Editors or Proprietors to correct false statements, . . . the continuation by Proprietors, or their Managers, of advertisements, or parts of advertisements, after proof of their falsity has been given; . . . and allowing a newspaper to be made the vehicle of outrageous personal abuse, accompanied by statements distinctly libellous on the face of them.[90]

In conclusion it was added that 'if the Institute is to raise the *status* of journalism it cannot too soon begin to formulate inferentially a code of professional morality and etiquette'.[91] Anxieties that such informal

---

[87] Ibid., 7 Feb. 1891, p. 9.

[88] Ibid., 21 Feb. 1891, p. 5.

[89] Ibid., 21 Mar. 1891, p. 5. Formerly William Lehman Ashmead Bartlett, the Unionist MP for Westminster changed his name following his marriage to Angela Georgina Burdett-Coutts (1814–1906), daughter of Sir Francis Burdett. He was the brother of Sir Ellis Ashmead Bartlett, Conservative politician, chairman of the National Union of Conservative Associations and owner of the patriotic Conservative newspaper, *England*.

[90] Ibid., 4 Apr. 1891, p. 15. See also Arthur William à Beckett, *The à Becketts of 'Punch'. Memories of Father and Son* (1902), p. 293. Strong supporters of professionalisation and entrance examinations, the à Becketts proposed the creation of a distinct category of 'Pressman'.

[91] *Journalist and Newspaper Proprietor*, 4 Apr. 1891, p. 15.

guidelines were not being adhered to lingered throughout the 1890s, and reports of the 'squaring' of newspapers continued to appear with disturbing regularity in the *The Journalist and Newspaper Proprietor*. Many involved minor infringements, such as the court reporters of Nottingham who allegedly operated a system whereby they would charge each defendant one shilling for omitting to include potentially embarrassing reports of their cases in the local newspapers.[92] Yet for the IoJ such incidents were painful reminders that respectability acquired through professional status remained more an ambition than reality.

While the IoJ single-mindedly pursued its distant goal, the acquisition by newspaper editors and reporters of skills relevant to their work proceeded on a far broader front. Ever since Pitman's phonetic shorthand had been developed in 1840, journalists, as well as official reporters in government, the judiciary and other institution, had availed themselves of the opportunity provided by that new writing system to take verbatim reports of speeches and meetings. But in addition to providing its users with a transferable and highly employable skill, the ability to read and write shorthand also defined a user group with access to its own cultural productions. While journalists earned their living by writing, in the first instance, for an audience literate in English, they themselves could be instructed and entertained by a journalism to which few outside their occupational group could gain access. For the contents of the *Phonetic Penny Magazine* of 1847, the *Phonetic Friend; a Monthly Journal of Entertainment and Instruction* published between 1849 and 1850 and the *Phonetic Miscellany* of 1856 were written entirely in stenographic characters. Some 20 further phonographic journals were issued between 1852 and 1896, among them F. and M. Brettell's *Phonographic Sun*, printed in Rotherham in 1853, F. Pitman's *Phonographic Pulpit* which lasted from 1869 until 1876, and the *Journalist: a Monthly Phonographic Magazine for Journalists, Shorthand Writers, and Reporters*, which was in continuous publication from November 1879 to July 1881. One of the two longest surviving shorthand journals was Allen Reid's *Reporters' Magazine,* which first appeared in 1847. Retitled the *Phonographic Reporter* in 1849, it was edited by F. Nightingale from 1880 to 1883. The other, the *Illustrated Monthly Phonographic Meteor*, launched under the editorship of C.J. Payne in 1877, was taken over by J.H. Ford in 1882 and was continued as the *Illustrated Monthly Reporters' Journal* from 1887, the *Reporters'*

---

[92] *Journalist and Newspaper Proprietor*, 6 Nov. 1897, p. 359. According to a former vice-President of the IoJ, attempts to bribe reporters had by 1895 become 'very rare', but when they did occur, he recommended that they be met with 'an indignant refusal', Phillips, *How to Become a Journalist*, pp. 107–09.

Journal from 1892, and the *Reporters' Journal and Shorthand Magazine* from 1901. Phonographic shorthand was thus not only a useful tool of the reporter's trade, it was also a quasi-secret language which defined the journalists and others who had been initiated into its use as both a distinct interest group and a highly specialised segment of the periodical readership.

In addition to the shorthand magazines, journalists were targeted also as a growing section of the book market. Journalism handbooks and training manuals not only recruited new talent into the trade and improved the effectiveness of newspaper editors and reporters, but, like phonography, served also to assert the distinctiveness of their occupation. Although E.P. Davies had issued *The Reporter's Handbook* in 1884, J. Dawson's manual of 'practical journalism', published in the following year, claimed to be 'the first of the kind' (it had first appeared as a two part series in the *Bazaar*). Despite the 'taint of Bohemianism' that still attached itself to journalism, and which made it 'somewhat unpopular with parents and guardians', Dawson insisted that in newspaper work there were 'more rewards of moderate worth than [were] to be found in Law or in Medicine, or in the Church'. Moreover, it was made abundantly clear that journalism no longer relied on 'innate talent', and that it was a craft, like any other, whose skills could be learnt.[93] Many of the authors of these handbooks were themselves prominent journalists who worked for newspapers outside London. John Mackie, for example, of the Middlesbrough newspaper, the *North-Eastern Daily Gazette*, was an enthusiastic Fellow of the IoJ who, in addition to providing wholesome guidance to young reporters also deliberately sought to dispel the 'mystery' of journalism by revealing 'conditions of service and modes of operation in the various literary spheres or departments of newspaper enterprise', without abandoning the editor's 'right to secrecy' in the protection of sources.[94] Ernest Phillips, author of the highly successful manual, *How to Become a Journalist*, published in 1895, was also a provincial journalist, an assistant editor of the *Sheffield Daily Telegraph*, and a former vice-president of the IoJ. But while Phillips's book contained advice on paragraph writing, reporting inquests, courts of law, public meetings, sporting events and exhibitions, and included sections on district reporting, editorial work and opportunities for women, R.H. Dunbar in his preface remarked that the guidelines would only concern

---

[93] J. Dawson, *Practical Journalism, How to Enter Thereon and Succeed. A Manual for Beginners and Amateurs* (1885), pp. i, 1–3.
[94] John Beveridge Mackie, *Modern Journalism. A Handbook of Instruction and Counsel for the Young Journalist* (1894), pp. iv, 71.

journalism as practiced in the provinces. The truth is that there is little need of a manual for the London journalist. It is very rarely the case that beginners are admitted on the staffs of the London papers, which are manned by journalists who have, in the great majority of instances, obtained their knowledge and experience on the Provincial press.[95]

Even in this, 'the youngest and the freest of all the professions',[96] a rigid geographical hierarchy was already assumed to exist. The distance between London and the provinces, however, was measured as much in terms of style and conduct as in status. 'A Northerner', employed by an unnamed provincial daily in London, appealed in July 1891 for other provincial journalists to join him in 'putting down the Cockney clique' that comprised the 'bloated aristocrats of the profession'. Sickened by the 'Toryism of the London daily newspaper swell who has got a number of fat jobs in his hands', he objected to their evident scorn for 'enterprising evening papers that want news red-hot', and their attempts to compel newspapers to 'continue in the deep ruts of leisurely news gathering'. The bitterness of the tone may to some degree be explained by the contempt with which provincial reporters sensed they were being regarded by their London counterparts, especially in the Gallery of the House of Commons and in the law courts.[97] H.W. Strong, editor of the Birmingham *Daily Argus*, agreed that the Gallery 'was a terrible medley of provincial accents' but insisted that the 'all-round readiness and adaptability' of the provincial reporter distinguished him clearly from the over-specialised and thus more limited capabilities of 'the town-trained journalist'.[98]

The manuals were not only descriptive of the changing world of the press at a critical moment in its modern formation but, more significantly, they offered prescriptive definitions of journalism as it ought to be practised. Thus, in addition to revealing such tricks of the trade as taking notes in the dark, the manuals also counselled young reporters on their personal appearance and habits, and issued strong injunctions against the use of alcohol and other stimulants.[99] For Mackie,

---

[95] Phillips, *How to Become a Journalist*, p. iv. The book was first published in instalments in the *Reporter's Journal* (see above); for a review of this book, consult *Journalist and Newspaper Proprietor*, 7 Dec. 1895, p. 391.

[96] Phillips, *How to Become a Journalist*, p. ix.

[97] *Journalist and Newspaper Proprietor*, 4 July 1891, p. 11.

[98] Ibid., 18 Jan. 1896, p. 20. This impression was confirmed by W.W. Yates, of the *Dewsbury Reporter*, who praised the ability of the local reporter in the West Riding to 'turn his pencil to anything', ibid., 7 Dec. 1895, p. 387.

[99] Alfred Kingston, *Pitman's Popular Guide to Journalism. A Practical Handbook for All Engaged in or Seeking to Qualify for Professional Work on the Newspaper Press* (1898), pp. 103–05. For other manuals, see also A.A. Reade, *Literary Success: Guide to*

editors were the professors of the 'People's University', and the newspaper press as a whole carried enormous social and moral responsibilities. In a powerful concluding chapter on 'The Power of the Press and Its Mission', he explained that

> the profession is now engaged in a united effort to raise its status educationally as well as socially. But even already it can be truly said that the journalist is more than a recorder of daily events – more, too, than a critic of the affairs of social, public, and national life. He is a recognised public teacher and guide who moves along with the times . . . and who helps his fellow-men in all departments of mental study, literary and artistic, scientific and theological, while utilising all his knowledge and influence on behalf of morality and righteousness. . . . The men who exercise the higher functions of journalism not only directly instruct the public mind and purify the public conscience, but they directly and powerfully help, correct, and to no small extent control the most gifted intellects and the most dominant enthusiasms of the day.[100]

On a more immediately practical level, a third category of publication aimed at journalists in the last 20 years of the nineteenth century was the guide to the law of libel, which became an essential and career-saving text which all editors were nervously and all too frequently obliged to consult.[101] Sensing an important new market for legal texts, Joseph R. Fisher and J.A. Strahan broke new ground in 1891 with the publication of *The Law of the Press* which, for the first time, brought together in one volume legislation and legal precedent 'treated from the point of view of the Press as a great modern power and interest'.[102]

Journalism (1885); J. Pendleton, *Newspaper Reporting* (1890); W.T. Stead, *A Journalist on Journalism* (1894); H.G. Reid, *The Press* (1896); J.B. Lamb, *Practical Hints for Writing for the Press* (1897); Arnold Bennet, *Journalism for Women: a Practical Guide* (1898), written when he was editor of *Woman* magazine; Editor, *How to Write for the Press. A Practical Handbook* (1899).

[100] Mackie, *Modern Journalism*, pp. 125–27.

[101] Guides to the libel laws published during the last 20 years of the nineteenth century, and aimed primarily at journalists, included the following: G. Elliott, *Newspaper Libel and Registration Act, 1881* (1884); W. Blake-Odgers, 'The Law of Libel Amendment Act', *Sell's Dictionary* (1890), pp. 34–48; R.J. Kelly, *Law of Newspaper Libel* (1889); W.B. Odgers, *Law of Libel Amendment Act, 1888* (1890); G.W. Rusden, *Letter on the Law of Libel* (1890); F.T. Cooper, *Handbook of the Law of Defamation* (Edinburgh, 1894); W.B. Odgers, *A Digest of the Law of Libel and Slander* (1896); H. Fraser, *Principles and Practice of the Law of Libel and Slander* (1897); W.B. Odgers, *An Outline of the Law of Libel* (1897); T. Starkie, *The Law of Slander and Libel* (1897).

[102] *Journalist and Newspaper Proprietor*, 7 Feb. 1891, p. 11. University education would shortly become an important means of entry into London journalism. C.P. Scott was informed in 1908 that 'the supply of able journalists is steadily diminishing. Young men especially from Oxford and Cambridge are ceasing to come in. Even with the reduced number of organs there is a dearth of ability', W. Robertson Nicoll to C.P. Scott, 31 Mar. 1908, MS 128/22, C.P. Scott Coll., John Rylands University Library, Manchester.

The combination of specialised legal texts with shorthand magazines and a stream of training manuals, clustered around a new professional association, constructed for late nineteenth-century newspaper journalism a clear occupational identity. Defensive, and jealous of their newly won privileges, journalists in the 1890s reacted vigorously, for example, to the continuation of amateur reporting, a practice which had for so long been the essential core of so much Victorian journalism. Angered by earlier reports that Nonconformist ministers were being paid by the religious press to cover church events, a reporter for the *Western Independent*, sent to file a report on the Wesleyan Conference at Plymouth in July 1895, complained to the IoJ that 'the Press table [was] swarming with ministers, armed with all the paraphernalia of reporting, and as busy as you like in undermining the opportunities of the professional newspaper man'.[103] But the cost of assuming the status of 'the professional newspaper man' was high, as H.W. Massingham recorded in 1900. A friend had been appointed to work on a London daily, the zenith of a provincial reporter's career, but when Massingham began to read that newspaper in order to find traces of his friend's 'knowledge and intellect . . . [he] could not find any sign of him'. Gradually he came to realise that his friend had

> disappeared; that the machinery of the 'great daily' had swallowed him up like the reams of blank paper which its rotary machinery devours every night. Henceforth he would have to speak the average Fleet St language, think the average Fleet St thought, and find that his intellectual life had been completely mapped out for him'.[104]

It may be thought ironic that the decline of anonymity, and the reduction of individuality implied by Massingham and others at this time, were parallel developments. But where newspapers were concerned, they were mutually reinforcing processes in two quite distinct ways, both of which were consequences of the restructuring of the labour market that resulted from the growth of the corporate newspaper. First, whereas the status of the more distinguished journalist might be denoted by the bylined column, the reporter remained largely anonymous, subsumed into the paper's 'staff'. Secondly, by securing the power of the national over the provincial press, the power of Fleet Street was consolidated not only economically but as a state of mind.

But the expansion of the newspaper industry did more than to fragment what had long been a vaguely defined but clearly recognisable occupational group. It also altered the terms in which journalism was

---

[103] *Journalist and Newspaper Proprietor*, 3 Aug. 1895, p. 242; see also 'Ministers of the Gospel as "Blackleg" Journalists', ibid., 1 Feb. 1896, p. 37.

[104] H.W. Massingham, 'The Ethics of Editing', *National Review*, Apr. 1900, pp. 259–60.

judged. Looked at from the perspective of the 1840s or 1850s, it would appear that by the 1890s the organisational logic of capitalism's mode of production of newspapers had brought to the press a longed-for measure of respectability. And if that respectability were defined, by the practising journalist, as the effective policing of reporting standards by a professional consciousness and, by the observer and critic of journalism, as a condition which functionally reinforced rather than challenged dominant social formations, then respectability might be said to have been accomplished. But the size, shape and dynamics of the newspaper industry in the 1890s ensured that the criteria by which journalism was judged had also been transformed, and while the practices of journalism may have altered substantially since the days of newsmen's verses, unstamped journals and broadsides in the first half of the nineteenth century, social attitudes towards newspaper journalism at the end of century remained as deeply ambivalent as they had been in the 1830s and 1840s.

The New Journalism of the 1890s specifically raised a number of serious and divisive issues regarding the conduct of the press and the nature of its influence over English society. Characterised principally by the innovations of W.T. Stead as editor of the *Pall Mall Gazette*, as well as others such as Edmund Yates, T.P. O'Connor and Frederick Greenwood, the New Journalism introduced fresh formats, shorter news items with headlines and cross-heads and more 'human interest' stories, particularly by means of the interview. The economic, organisational and even technological foundations of the New Journalism had been laid in the 1850s and 1860s, and a number of its supposed innovations – especially its use of illustration, investigative reporting and the employment of news agencies – had been attempted by numerous publications during the previous half-century. The one true innovation of the Fleet Street press in the 1890s, however, was its prodigious scale and nationwide distribution.[105] Emerging so soon after the passing of the Third Reform Act in 1884, and the redistribution of parliamentary seats in the following year, the New Journalism acquired a political resonance which had been largely lacking in press discourse during the previous 50 years. On this occasion, however, the new moral panic was triggered by the possibility that a 'mass' press could shape a 'mass culture' that could now wield actual political power through the ballot box. The sense of triumph felt in the 1850s, when, despite some lingering reservations, it was thought that the beast of the 'immoral' press had been tamed by commercial news journalism, was transformed into a new anxiety. As

---

[105] Lucy Brown, 'The Growth of a National Press' in Laurel Brake, Aled Jones and Lionel Madden (eds), *Investigating Victorian Journalism* (1990), pp. 133–42.

early as 1891, *Sell's Dictionary* printed a critique of the new experiments in news gathering and presentation,[106] and in the following year the *Westminster Review* charged Stead and 'Steadism' with being a 'great danger' to British politics.[107] Fighting his own rearguard action, Ernest Phillips in 1895 denounced the new style for seeking 'simply to be smart' and for troubling 'little about truth and nothing at all about taste'.[108]

Truth and taste in newspaper journalism, however, were problematic commodities, both being complicated by changing perceptions of the appropriate functions of the press. Stead's purchase of a child prostitute in 1885 put each of these questions under the juridicial spotlight. But for the most part, criticism of the New Journalism turned not on its definitions of truth, nor on the ethics of exposure journalism, but on its language. Frank Taylor in 1898 complained of the 'eternal stream of inane gabble' that flowed daily from the national newspapers, and regretted that 'large masses of minds' were held in 'continued servitude . . . to phrases and catchwords'.[109] Such notions that the New Journalism was responsible for the vulgarisation of popular taste rested on two interconnected assumptions. One was that the dystopia envisaged by J.S. Mill on the eve of the Second Reform Act, where a democratic but philistine mass would dominate, intimidate and silence minorities, had finally come to pass. It was precisely at this point in the 1890s that Q.D. Leavis, writing in 1939, located the decisive shift in English literature away from the 'taste of polite writing' that had been engendered in English culture by such eighteenth-century periodicals as the *Tatler* and the *Spectator*. The responsibility for that transformation, she argued, lay with the newspapers, and those of Lord Northcliffe in particular, which had mobilised 'the people to outvote the minority, who had hitherto set the standard of taste without any serious challenge'.[110] Leavis's reading of the 1890s as a traumatic and decadent *fin de siècle*, and the definitions of literature and the concepts of social power that underpinned it, did not go unchallenged, but the fact that it remained in currency for so long reveals both the seductive nature of the cultural

---

[106] 'New Journalism – Where It Fails', *Sell's Dictionary* (1891), pp. 38–41.

[107] Cyril Aubrey Waters, 'Steadism in Politics – a Great Danger', *Westminster Review*, Jun. 1892, p. 619.

[108] Phillips, *How to Become a Journalist*, p. xix. The historiography of the 'new journalism' has expanded rapidly in recent years. J.H. Wiener (ed.), *Papers for the Millions: The New Journalism in Britain, 1850s to 1914* (New York, 1988), L. Brake, *Subjugated Knowledges*, and Judith R. Walkowitz, *City of Dreadful Delight. Narratives of Sexual Danger in Late-Victorian London* (1992) are particularly rewarding.

[109] Frank Taylor, *The Newspaper Press* (1898), pp. 25–26. See also H.D. Traill, 'Newspapers and English: a Dialogue', *Macmillan's Magazine*, Oct. 1884, p. 445.

[110] Q.D. Leavis, *Fiction and the Reading Public* (1939), pp. 122, 185.

critique which the 1890s had of itself, and of the pivotal significance that changes in newspaper journalism were considered to have had in effecting that cultural transformation. W.H. Mallock's *Memoirs of Life and Literature* (1920) may have contained one of the most memorable indictments of the political and cultural consequences of mass democracy, but his apologia for the much older Tory defence of social hierarchy as a bulwark against anarchy was shared also by writers as diverse as Henry James, George Gissing and John Ruskin, who echoed Mallock's concern that, by the end of the nineteenth century, the alienation of the working class actively threatened to undermine the social order and the values of liberal society.

A second motive for associating New Journalism with vulgarity stemmed from an Anglocentric contempt for 'Americanisation', and its implied erosion of the English newspaper tradition as the international paradigm.[111] New Journalism was, rightly in many respects, seen as an American import that had not only refashioned the English language but was appropriate only for a capitalist democracy. English reactions to it, both in the 1890s and subsequently, were to a substantial extent determined by the anxiety that the new press, with its new values, would act as a forcing-house for a structural transformation of English culture and society.

Its defenders, on the other hand, saw the New Journalism as a symptom rather than a cause of contemporary shifts in social structure. From a journalist's perspective, readers in the speeded-up world of the late nineteenth century no longer enjoyed either the opportunity nor the inclination of their predecessors to read lengthy articles and verbatim reports of speeches at leisure. As T.P. O'Connor memorably remarked in 1889, readers now lived 'in an age of hurry and of multitudinous newspapers'. Consequently, he advised journalists that '[t]o get your ideas through the hurried eyes into the whirling brains that are employed in the reading of a newspaper there must be no mistake about your meaning . . . you must strike the reader right between the eyes.'[112] W.E. Pine, of the Portsmouth *Evening News*, applauded O'Connor's counsel and urged newspaper editors to 'eschew long leaders in favour of crisp notes on current events' and to replace long reports of speeches with 'condensed descriptive accounts . . . illustrations . . . striking headlines, and a greater variety of home news'. The future, he added, belonged to the halfpenny evening newspaper.[113] Some readers agreed. A Miss March Phillipps, in an address on New Journalism delivered at the Pioneer Club

---

[111] Taylor, *The Newspaper Press*, pp. 21–26.

[112] T.P. O'Connor, 'The New Journalism', *New Review*, Oct. 1889, p. 434.

[113] *Journalist and Newspaper Proprietor*, 21 Mar. 1891, p. 6.

on 28 February, 1895, remarked that while she 'blamed the new journalism for pandering to some of the lowest and most vulgar desires of the public', she none the less regarded it as being 'considerably more readable than the old', and in the course of the ensuing discussion few in her audience displayed any enthusiasm for a 'journalism that dares to be dull'.[114] The English newspaper, which in the past had been 'edited in the interests of only a proportion of the community', William Morton Fullerton wrote in 1893, was responding positively to social change, and the new 'mass' readership no longer desired their newspaper to be 'conservative, conventional, respectable'.[115] Even criticism of the coverage of crime, which some thought excessive and might 'pander to the worst propensities . . . of the working classes',[116] had long since acquired a strong counter-argument based on the notion that it was better that 'evil things . . . should be known . . . [and] vice . . . set in its bare reality in the pillory of public exposure'.[117]

Two outstanding issues associated with the practice of journalism, however, continued to arouse public debate, although neither was specifically a response to the New Journalism. One was the question of the individual's right to privacy, the other involved the culture and morality of commercial advertising. The first struck at the heart not only of the reporter's remit in the pursuit of a story, but also at the dignity and privileges of the Victorian royal family. In the late 1840s, voices had been raised against the impertinence of inquisitive 'spy-journalists', hungry for 'court news', whose intrusions into the family life of the Queen had caused her some distress, and in 1848 *Punch* printed a satirical cartoon depicting a Paul Pry reporter-artist peeping through a key-hole at Balmoral.[118] But whereas the novelist William Makepeace Thackeray could later judge such coverage, in the light of contemporary reporting standards, to be neither 'vulgar nor impertinent', and to be a valuable means whereby 'loyal subjects' could 'rally in spirit' to the monarchy,[119] other critics of the 1880s were insistent that such examples of 'journalistic barbarism' dissolved the distinctions between the private

---

[114] Ibid., 16 Mar. 1891, p. 6.

[115] W.M. Fullerton, 'The Significance of the Newspaper in the United States', *New Review*, June 1893, p. 659.

[116] George R. Humphery, 'The Reading of the Working Classes', *Nineteenth Century*, Apr. 1893, p. 691.

[117] Revd Brook Herford, 'A Sermon on Newspapers', *Newspaper Press*, 1 Dec. 1866, p. 6. Delivered at Manchester, to the text of Paul's first epistle to Timothy, iv. 13: 'Give attendance to reading'.

[118] *Punch*, no. 376, Sept. 23, 1848.

[119] M.H. Spielmann, *The Hitherto Unidentified Contributions of W.M. Thackeray to 'Punch'* (1899), pp. 228–30.

and public spheres and undermined the ethics and institutions of society. The following extract from an American printer's journal was published without comment in the English periodical, *The Printer*, in May 1886. It was a prescient reminder of the moral dangers that might engulf the hard-won 'respectability' of English journalism.

> Time was when the hearth of home was hedged about with as much divinity as ever mythically surrounding a king. The fireside has no recognised barriers around it now. . . . Time was when marriage was not fulsomely paraded in type, even to the uttermost fraction of dress. We have sadly outlived such tenderness and respect. Time was when death was looked upon with awe and regarded as holy from outside inter-meddling, and curious and prying eyes were not turned upon tearful faces, sobbing breasts and broken hearts. We have unmercifully gotten beyond such reverence, and nothing is permitted to screen corpse and coffin.[120]

As a result of the audacity of news gatherers, who routinely offered bribes in exchange for stories, and for whom even the corpses of the dead were 'legitimate plunder', the private lives of all citizens were potentially vulnerable to unprecedented intrusions as if their homes had 'been turned into telephones' and connected to newspaper offices.

> One might as well live with open doors and windows, or have repeating speaking tubes leading from every room into the street that all who desired might listen . . . all the sanctities of life are ruthlessly violated by the 'satanic press', and for what? The only justification pleaded is enterprise; the gathering of news, the desire to place before the public everything of interest or importance.
>
> The theory is unsound; the premises false. . . . It is simply the abuse of a questionable custom. It is the overstraining of a self-made law that was monstrous in the conception, is infamous in its workings and deadly in its results. It is the 'put money in thy purse' doctrine without the slightest regard to the feelings or rights of others, to truth, manhood, honor or common decency. [121]

The financial imperative of the new transatlantic journalism, driven by competition between titles, was closely related also to the commercial ethos that sustained the newspaper industry. It was widely understood that for newspapers to succeed financially, it was more important for them to attract advertisers than readers.[122] It was also a view that was widely, though not always wisely, disputed. Charles Knight, in August

---

[120] 'Journalistic Barbarism', *Printer*, May 1886, p. 85. Reprinted from the *Inland Printer*, established in Chicago in Oct. 1883.

[121] Ibid., p. 85.

[122] 'Newspapers are in reality somewhat in a false position. They profess to sell news and give advertisements to boot. What they really do is to sell publicity for advertisements and to give news to boot', Thomas Gibson Bowles, *Fortnightly Review*, July 1884, p. 25.

1834, had proudly announced that 'no Advertisment whatever' would be inserted in his periodical, *The Printing Machine*,[123] while Joseph Livesey had denounced 'quack advertisements' as 'unfit for the public eye'.[124] William Owen, too, had opposed the principle of inserting advertisements into his weekly labour newspaper, the *Potteries Examiner*, in 1872, on the grounds that 'no trade union journal could command advertisements because they had to contend against that class who advertised in newspapers'.[125] In truth, however, Owen successfully attracted sufficient local advertisements to sustain an elaborate network of radical newspapers for the best part of a decade. Owen's compromise was one which all newspapers would have to make in order to survive in the market-place, particularly towards the end of the nineteenth century when other forms of income, such as high cover prices or party subsidies, were unreliable long-term options. Advertising, moreover, pioneered new ways of configuring the formats of newspapers. If, by the early 1880s, newspapers had become 'the general medium through which information is tendered and publicity attained',[126] Samuel Deacon's theory that

> the eye passes over long columns of type, but it is arrested at once by the dog's head of a dog-biscuit maker, the steel pen of a pen maker, or the illustrations of a fat child, which is placed as an attraction to the advertisement of some infants' food maker[127]

promised the delivery not only of consumers to producers, but also of votes to politicians. The implications of Macaulay's dictum that advertisements were the steam of trade, and newspapers the sinews of war, were not lost on either editors or the political image-makers who saw in advertising techniques methods of constructing new loyalties in an expanded and highly competitive electoral market. This, however, is a development to which we shall return in the next chapter. The cultural debate on advertising pivoted around the aesthetics, rather than the high political possibilities, of the dog's head and the fat child. Objections to the implicit tastelessness of advertisements, which in a related context had resulted in the banning of 'sky-signs' by the London County Council in 1893,[128] had predictably provoked the ire of the *Pall Mall Gazette*

---

[123] *Printing Machine*, 16 Aug. 1834, p. 286.

[124] *Moral Reformer*, July 1838, p. 156.

[125] *Potteries Examiner*, 15 June 1872.

[126] *Sell's Dictionary* (1883), p. 35. Henry Sell's *Philosophy of Advertising*, later incorporated into the *Dictionary*, was first issued separately in 1882.

[127] 'How to Advertise', Samuel Deacon, *Deacon's Newspaper Handbook and Advertiser's Guide* (1881), p. 19.

[128] Lady Mary Jeune, *New Review*, Nov. 1893, p. 477. See also Richardson Evans, 'The Age of Disfigurement', *National Review*, Oct. 1890, p. 182.

which thought the outcry 'against the "degradation" of art by the advertiser' to be absurd and motivated by 'a spirit of narrow exclusiveness'. 'The street hoarding', the paper argued, was 'the Poor Man's Picture Gallery' and the 'age of advertisement' was 'essentially democratic'.[129]

The issues of privacy and advertising exposed with exceptional clarity the line of fracture between the priorities of commercial and moral imperatives that had run continuously through the journalism of the nineteenth century, and which, more than any other, had defined the terms of the cultural debate about the conduct and influence of newspapers. That fracture, however, ran not between opposing groups of individuals but, as Masao Miyoshi has argued in relation to Victorian literature in general, within individuals who were divided against themselves.[130] While a correspondent to *The Printer* in 1885 might insist that the newspaper was a 'moral teacher', s/he reluctantly conceded that, 'in the modern newspaper management everything has to give way to L.s.d'.[131] And which, it was asked, was the more 'respectable' role: that of the investigator or the money-maker? The pages of the official organ of the IoJ remained open to those whose replies to that question were out of kilter with the times, as a report of A.E. Fletcher's lecture on 'the Influence of the Newspaper Press' of 1897 revealed:

> he would not accept the announcement that the object of newspapers was commercial. While it was the object of some, it was not true of all. . . . Mankind was ruled by social, moral and religious influences, and it was the function of the journalist to investigate those hidden forces, to record their most striking phenomena, and thus to help in the formation of a healthy public opinion.[132]

---

[129] *Pall Mall Gazette*, 6 Nov. 1889. Aubrey Beardsley agreed, 'Advertisement is an absolute necessity of modern life, and if it can be made beautiful as well as obvious, so much better for the makers of soap and the public who are likely to wash', A. Beardsley, *New Review*, July 1894, p. 55.

[130] Masao Miyoshi, *The Divided Self. A Perspective on The Literature of the Victorians* (1969), p. ix. Miyoshi proposes that between the 1830s and the 1890s, 'the investment of the Victorians in moral commitment was gradually withdrawn. The men of the nineties could see in High Victorian commitment little else than self-delusion and hypocrisy', ibid., p. xvii.

[131] *Printer*, Feb. 1885, p. 4.

[132] *Journalist and Newspaper Proprietor*, 6 Nov. 1897, p. 362. Consider also the views of Charles Grundy, a member of the St Paul's Literary and Educational Society in Manchester, who advised that newspapers should be read backwards to avoid 'bribery by advertisement'. The article defended the thesis that 'Editors of Newspapers wield an enormous power in influencing the people of the country, and so long as Commercial gain – which means a large circulation – is the one chief object of exploiting many of the newspapers to the sacrifice of the moral tone, so long will their influence be retrogressive', Charles A. Grundy, 'Modern Journalism', *Odds and Ends . . . a Manuscript Magazine*, vol. liv., 1908, p. 122.

What no critic of advertising could do, however, was demonstrate convincingly how journalists could undertake those investigative functions without the financial support that advertisers provided. But while some newspaper journalists and readers were demonstrably aware of the limitations and contingencies of the medium, the dynamic possibilities of commercial expansion proved to be a beguiling counter-narrative. The newspaper as symbol of capitalist modernity represented incremental progress and respectability at virtually every level of its operation. Even the noisy and much criticised hawking of newspapers on the streets had for some demonstrated the positive effects of the mass press on the urban poor, who, once dependent on poor relief, could now

> earn seven shillings in some four or five hours by the sale of papers. Boys of ten years old will earn ninepence in the morning early enough to permit them to go to school afterwards. The establishment of the penny papers has been of immense advantage to those wild, untutored, uncared-for children who are called the Arabs of the streets. They have now an occupation which suits their wandering habits and their love of independence. They are their own masters . . . [133]

Henry Mayhew, among others, admired the individualism and entrepreneurial ethos of the newspaper street-sellers who for him represented 'a vivid type of the commercial character of England'.[134] Much the same could have been said of the popular newspaper press as a whole in the second half of the nineteenth century.

---

[133] *Meliora*, vol. 5, no. 19, 1863.
[134] *Fleet Street Gazette*, 25 Apr. 1874, pp. 9–10.

CHAPTER SIX

The political debate

All's Whiggery now,
But we old men are massed against the world.

W.B. Yeats, 'The Seven Sages',
The Winding Stair and Other Poems (1933).

On the evening of 27 January 1837, Isaac Arrowsmith, radical printer,
erstwhile leader of the Worcester Political Union and founder of the
Worcester Typographical Society, issued a furious broadside to his
'Fellow-Citizens' denying that he had abandoned his 'Political Principles
for the sake of obtaining a situation on the *Worcestershire Guardian*'. He
confessed that he obtained better wages at his new post, and that he
contributed articles to the paper, but went on to insist that it had been
agreed at the time of his appointment that he would not be required to
share the Tory politics of the newspaper's editor and proprietors.[1] Isaac
Arrowsmith, publicly and in print, was here announcing his right to the
autonomy of his beliefs within the newspaper as workplace. In so doing,
he also acknowledged and articulated the intensely politicised nature of
newspaper work. Few artisan or professional occupations were so
openly demarcated by local or national political loyalties, and few were
so wedded to the notion of a collective political voice. By contesting that
homogeneity in the way that he did, with recourse to the broadside
rather than the newspaper, Arrowsmith was confirming the power of
that editorial voice. Yet, at the same time, he also drew attention to the
problematic nature of the idea of a political *newspaper* press. For the
political voices with which newspapers actually spoke to their readers
involved more than editorial posturing in leading articles. Complex
negotiations were necessary in the formation of the remainder of the
text, both editorial and advertising, and editors were themselves aware
of a gap that separated the proclaimed political position of a paper from
the material that was actually printed in its pages. Given that their
function was to select from 'a thousand topics which day by day present
themselves', editors could not 'dare look for a universal agreement
among their readers and their contributors in all that they touch upon or
put forward'.[2] Until effective sub-editing smoothed out the ideological

---

[1] Bristol RO, MS 40145/per/3g. Arrowsmith had joined the Political Union in 1830, and
the Worcester Typographical Society on 2 Sept. 1833.

[2] John Moore Capes, *The Rambler*, Jan. 1849, p. 329.

and grammatical irregularities in material submitted for publication by the contributors, the catholicity of the actual content of newspapers was often at odds with the notion of the unitary political voice. Editors remained hostages to their sources long after the days when the unrepentant radical Isaac Arrowsmith could insert his own articles in the conservative *Worcestershire Guardian*. The practice of split-printing with news agency stereotype, for example, effectively removed editorial control from an entire half of many mid-Victorian newspapers. In short, editorial political identity was complicated by the multiplicity of discourses embodied in the text of the newspaper.

With this complication in mind, it is worth investigating the changing ways in which contemporary journalists and readers understood the implications and effects of such designations as 'conservative', 'radical' or 'independent' when applied to nineteenth-century newspapers. There can be little doubt that the identity of the editor, where known, and his public visibility as a hustings speaker or pamphleteer, could powerfully reinforce the reader's response to a particular paper. The personalities of William Cobbett, Feargus O'Connor and Joseph Livesey, to name only three activist-editors, not only pervaded the editorial policies of their respective papers, but had rendered them well-known public figures outside their journalism. As we saw earlier, the choice of title, and of title-page iconography, were also intended to convey direct political messages. Such individual or symbolic expressions of identity were related to the readership in two distinct ways. In one respect, they were clearly intended to attract readers and to provide them with a brand identifier that would sustain their loyalty as regular readers. In much the same way, they acted as signposts for potential correspondents, advertisers and distributors. But in another sense they implied the editor's construction of the readership which, in turn, to some extent shaped the paper's mode of address in terms of format, selection of news and features and the style and functions of leading articles.[3] While the political identity of many newspapers sprang from the convictions of the individuals who had launched them, it was also evidently the case that editors calculated that a political 'badge of belonging' might retain for their titles both a readership and an advertising base. The practice of

---

[3] Pertinent reflections on the ways in which the efforts of newspaper editors were being diverted into 'an entirely new channel' by the need to ensure that opinion determined factual content may be found in Thomas Gibson Bowles, *Fortnightly Review*, July 1884. Bowles noted that 'Newspapers . . . are now less NEWSpapers than OPINION papers. The publisher has become lost in the advocate, and at this time a public journal is regarded less an instrument for providing general information for its readers than as an organ for promoting among them the special opinions of a Political Party, or a Social Class' ibid., p. 26.

providing subsidies and exclusive news stories to sympathetic newspapers, by both political parties and governments, offered another motive for editors and publishers, especially those close to the centre of power in London, to align themselves publicly or secretly with particular tendencies at certain times. Secret Service and Admiralty subventions were little more than bribes, but governing parties could also use official information as a currency, giving the lion's share of intelligence to supportive editors, while propitiating the less enthusiastic with the occasional scrap to encourage them to stay generally on-side.[4] Conversely, the possibility of exerting direct influence over political events and individuals was another attraction of partisanship. George Augustus Sala, looking back from the vantage point of 1900, described the 1820s and 1830s as a period when the metropolitan newspapers enjoyed more direct political power than at any subsequent period. By power, Sala meant 'the ableness to do a thing – by repeated onslaughts, by denunciations, and sometimes by unscrupulous misrepresentations and calumny', such as to turn one government out of office and usher in another. That power, however, had extended only over a tiny geographical area.

> St James's, Pall Mall, Whitehall and Palace Yard, Old and New, to the west, and Cornhill, Lombard Street and Threadneedle Street to the east. The Royal palaces, the Houses of Parliament, the Ministerial Bureaux, the Horse Guards, the Admiralty, the Clubs; the Royal Exchange, the Bank of England, the India House were the places – and nearly the only places – where the leading articles of *The Times*, the *Morning Herald*, the *Morning Post*, the *Standard* – then only an evening paper – the *Morning Chronicle*, the *St James's Chronicle*, the *Sun*, and the *True Sun*, were then read, rejoiced in, or dreaded by statesmen, placemen, Members of Parliament, bankers and merchants.[5]

Furthermore, unlike the mass-circulation dailies of 1900, 'the great London newspapers' of the early nineteenth century

> were written almost altogether for the governing classes – aristocratic, official, parliamentary, financial, and commercial – and were not read, to any very considerable extent, by the general public outside the charmed sphere of those governing classes. And the immediate and palpable sway exercised by these newspapers over the fortunes of politics was largely due to a strong belief among readers who were on the border-land between the governors and the governed, that the leading journals were to a great extent controlled

---

[4] See A. Aspinall, *Politics and the Press, c. 1780–1850* (1949), *passim*, for further details, including those on John Waters' *The Times*.

[5] George Augustus Sala, 'The Press: What I Have Known of It – 1840–1890', *Progress of British Newspapers in the Nineteenth Century, Illustrated* (1901), p. 202.

and contributed to by members of the governing classes themselves.[6]

For readers from that 'border-land', the consequences of such close ties between press and politics were only too evident. Most noticeably during periods of national emergency, it was government that set the news agendas and the editorial tone of the vast majority of metropolitan newspapers. Sala argued that during the Napoleonic Wars,

> the power of three-fourths, or, to speak more accurately, of eight tenths of the leading London papers was substantially the power of the Government itself. The wealthiest journals were to most intents and purposes the merest mouthpieces of the administration; and their permanent cue was to repeat, with scarcely any intermission, that the Continental Powers, so long as they were in alliance with Great Britain, should be largely and constantly subsidised; that paper money was infinitely preferable to a gold currency, that the National Debt and continuously increasing taxation were unmitigated blessings; that the Catholics ought not to be emancipated, nor the Pension List reduced, and that Napoleon Bonaparte was a murderer, a perjurer, a dastard, a robber and a villain. There was truly an opposition Press; but that it was practically powerless is shown to my mind, conclusively, by the fact that from the time of the rupture of the Peace of Amiens to the great surrender of the Duke of Wellington on the question of Catholic Emancipation, the programme laid down by the predominant party was rarely disturbed, and that it continued to receive the same vehement support from the Government Press.[7]

It must be remembered that, for Sala, this historical reading of party–press relations prior to 1815 was a device which effectively enabled him to distinguish between what he regarded as the corrupt and monopolistic past of his profession, and the open and diverse nature of its present condition. Much was to change in the intervening period. In the relatively tranquil political and economic climate of the late 1850s and the early 1860s, for example, newspapers came close to being regarded as alternatives to parliamentary politics. Public opinion, suggested one correspondent to the *Saturday Review* in 1861, was 'the growth of quiet times', during which newspapers represented far better than political parties the shifting, nuanced, subjective and inconsistent ways in which individuals made sense of the world.

> When the day of party warfare has almost died away, the reign of public opinion begins. The *Times* in the years of the reform agitation had not the power or the influence it possesses in these untroubled days. Men had their views and their theories chalked out before them, and would have thought it treason to unsay to-morrow what

---

[6] Ibid., p. 203.
[7] Ibid., p. 204.

was said to-day. But when the world is tranquil, there is less need of
politicians. It would be quite possible now-a-days for a journal to be
too political for its readers. Every man is his own politician; his
views are a matter not of scientific dispute, but of liberal instinct,
and he is prepared to swear allegiance to no master. What does it
matter if the *Times*, which is the organ of so many of us, contradicts
itself, and changes sides from day to day? Do not most people
contradict themselves? Is the opinion we form this morning on the
telegram which arrives from Paris so necessarily true or fixed that it
may not be shaken to-morrow? Men learn their intelligence from
hour to hour, and they must generalize upon it as it arrives. The
process of reflection and digestion goes on in public. The article
written upon the event that happened to-day represents the first
blush the matter wears to an ordinary mind. The article of to-
morrow represents what we thought on being taken by surprise to-
day, modified by the subsequent news that will arrive this
evening . . . what an Englishman wishes to get in his newspaper is a
common sense aspect of a question in which he is interested, put in
an agreeable and attractive form. He neither cares to know merely
what the Carlton thinks, nor what the Reform Club thinks, nor
what the Manchester school is thinking. He cares to know what he
and the people about him are thinking.[8]

Unfortunately for this view, the reporting of high politics increased as the
Second Reform Act and the 1868 general election approached. In part,
this was regarded as a means of adding lustre to a political system that
might otherwise appear dull. Sir James Fitzjames Stephen speculated in
1867 that the public greatly disliked the idea that the nation was being
'governed in a prosaic way', and that they preferred the more strikingly
dramatic rendition of political events in and out of Parliament that
appeared in the newspapers. This tendency had been satirically observed
a quarter of a century earlier, when a speech not delivered by Edmund
Burke, or anyone else, in the House Commons was reported fully and
sympathetically by a reporter who had not been present at the session:

But take, for instance, up the "daily" news–
How mind-subduing its magnetic arts! . . .
Here senators resort, well pleas'd to find
Their speeches modell'd better than they spoke,
And some reported which were never heard.[9]

According to this interpretation, far from being alternatives to politics,
newspapers served to privilege Parliament and to intensify public interest
in the affairs of State.[10]
Much of the debate regarding the political impact of the press was

---

[8] *Saturday Review*, 16 Feb. 1861.
[9] 'The Press, a Poem', *Compositor's Chronicle*, 1 Feb. 1841, p. 47.
[10] Sir James Fitzjames Stephen, 'Journalism', *Cornhill Magazine*, July 1869, p. 52.

focused on the major London newspapers. But the post-1855 expansion of the press saw a particularly sharp increase in the numbers of newspapers started outside London, in what were condescendingly known as 'the provinces'. Large numbers of these papers lent their support to the Liberal Party, with whom they forged the most important links during election campaigns. Up until the passing of the Corrupt Practices Act in 1883, newspapers could effectively be bought by candidates contesting elections, an arrangement which suited both the candidate, who was assured publicity, and the editor, who was able to clear any accumulated debts with the proceeds of the ensuing windfall. A structural connection between politics and the press thus effectively underpinned the doctrinal and personal loyalties of editors. It was, for a brief period, regarded as a winning combination. A correspondent to the *Fortnightly Review* in August 1880 explained the curious failure of the overwhelmingly pro-Tory metropolitan newspapers to rescue the Conservative Party from defeat in the general election of 1880 by indicating that 'the London press does not represent provincial opinion, which remained solidly Gladstonian'. The London press, having mistaken the mood of the country so discreditably, could as a result no longer be regarded as anything but 'a local authority as organs of public opinion'.[11]

After 1883, however, the Liberal hegemony of the provincial press began to be eroded. Not only did the Corrupt Practices Act, which imposed financial auditing on campaigning candidates and their agents, cause major difficulties for the funding arrangements of many newspapers, but the restructuring of political parties that followed in the train of parliamentary reform in 1884 also affected their political loyalties. One observer noted that many businessmen and holders of landed property in the county constituencies, the traditional advertisers and financial backers of local newspapers, had abandoned the Liberal Party for the Conservatives after 1884, and that as a result many of the older Liberal newspapers became noticeably 'less politically partisan, with less coverage of political questions'. Moreover, as 'a curious result of a wider franchise', when political questions were discussed in such papers 'the local application of arguments used' was regrettably ignored.[12] Instead, journalism was drawn increasingly into the vortex of what Frederick Greenwood termed the 'political machine' of Parliament and the parties, principally through the development of the Lobby.[13] In

---

[11] Wemyss Reid, 'Public Opinion', *Fortnightly Review*, Aug. 1880, p. 234.

[12] Henry C. Wilkins, 'Newspapers and Politics', *Journalist and Newspaper Proprietor*, 8 Jun. 1895, p. 190.

[13] Frederick Greenwood, 'The Press and Government', *Nineteenth Century*, July 1890, p. 109.

the 1890s, the divisive issue of Irish Home Rule further weakened the hold of Gladstonian Liberalism over the newspaper press. Few of the Liberal weeklies 'avowedly altered their political creed' overnight, but to one reader it was clear that a change had 'taken place in the tone of the leading articles of many journals. . . . The lessened intensity of advocacy of the party which supports the present [Liberal] Government has had its effect on Conservative papers, especially in the places where the Liberal journal is the best news-sheet, as it often is'.[14] The same writer, reflecting on the consequences of these changes, noted a paradoxical development. Whereas 'experienced newspaper managers' were placing a diminishing value on the support of political parties, the 'smaller politicians' were clamouring for ever greater political loyalty from journalists, demanding 'that their particular organ should be "more Liberal" or "more Conservative"'.[15] The tensions generated by this and other discrepancies between the expectations of journalists and those of politicians had, during the course of the nineteenth century, informed much of the debate on the impact of the press on the political order. Once more, however, those discrepancies were most readily explained by referring to the conflicting discourses of morality and the market, and the extent to which one or the other should dominate the assumptions that governed the conduct of newspapers.

Liberalism and the politics of the market-place

The relationship between morals and the market in journalism, before and after 1836, was mediated by the law. A correspondent to Joseph Livesey's magnificently titled unstamped journal, *The Moral Reformer, and Protestor Against the Vices, Abuses, and Corruptions of the Age*, questioned the right of an unstamped paper, which was by implication hostile to the law, to advocate morality, which was defined as 'loyalty, and submissive obedience to the higher powers'. In his reply, Livesey justified his actions by appealing to a higher 'moral law', while at the same time drawing his critic's attention to the fact that, in any case, the law he was breaking was 'a comparatively inoperative act of parliament'.[16] When that law was changed in 1836, reducing the stamp duty to one penny while increasing the penalties against its violation, conditions for the production of radical journals, especially those carrying news, worsened considerably. The experience of the *Bolton Free*

---

[14] *Journalist and Newspaper Proprietor*, 8 June 1895, p. 190.
[15] Ibid.
[16] *Moral Reformer*, 1 Jan. 1832, pp. 29–30.

Press was typical of many of the older unstamped papers that sought to re-establish themselves as legal newspapers in the changed environment of 1836 and 1837. Founded as an illegal penny newspaper in November 1835, the printer-manager of the *Bolton Free Press* received from local Radicals a £100 loan to keep afloat what was already regarded as 'an expiring political paper'. But even with this fairly substantial investment, and the appointment of a vigorous new editor who had agreed to work initially without salary, the *Free Press* failed to compete successfully against its more established local rival, the *Bolton Chronicle*, and after incurring debts that matched the amount of the loan, the paper was discontinued.[17] There was very little space in this more competitive market for a 'pauper press' to flourish, and those newspapers, such as the *Northern Star*, which were associated with the politics of radical reform, were founded as legal, stamped publications which had every intention of surviving the rigours of commercial competition.

The terminal decline of the unstamped after 1836, however, masked some important continuities in the culture of oppositional journalism. Principally, there remained the need to define the position of the paper in relation to what it opposed. This was achieved in a variety of ways. One was to associate the distribution network of a radical paper with the internal lines of communication of an organised popular movement. In this way, Chartist and Owenite periodicals were sold alongside radical pamphlets, books and portraits of radical leaders – 'the invariable ornaments of most working men's houses' – in such 'Chartist publications shops' as Bowker's on the Oldham Road in Manchester, the interior of which was vividly described by Edwin Waugh in a diary entry in July 1849.[18] Another method was to define the radicalism of the title by contrasting it to the conservatism of the established institutions, which included not only government and the Church, but also abstracted notions of 'the press'. The Christian fundamentalist flat-earthists of *Parallax*, for example, devoted their pages to attacking Newtonian physics and Darwinism, and pitted themselves against the 'anonymous hirelings of the public Press' who refused to discuss what they regarded to be the 'irrational theory . . . of a round and evolving world', adding darkly that 'when the whole Press of Great Britain conspires to avoid a particular subject there must be something mysterious and suspicious about it'.[19] An extreme case, perhaps, but one with whose sense of

---

[17] John Taylor, *Autobiography of a Lancashire Lawyer* (Bolton, 1883), p. 179.

[18] 'The Diary of Edwin Waugh', Mon. 16 July 1849, unpub. microfilm coll., Manchester City Library. For a stimulating analysis of this diary see Patrick Joyce, *Democratic Subjects. The Self and the Social in Nineteenth-Century England* (Cambridge, 1994), esp. pp. 23–82.

[19] *Parallax*, Mar. 1885, p. 13. This was a monthly journal edited by John Hampden and

alienation from the 'mainstream' many journalists and readers, who for whatever reason perceived themselves to be in opposition to the powers that be, had good reason to feel some sympathy.

Political reformers, trade unionists, religious dissenters had all needed to mark out in public and in print the moral ground on which they stood. The journalism of the temperance movement provides a useful illustration of this process. It began, first, by defining itself against the backcloth of a hostile 'public press', the tangible expression of 'the politics of drunkards'.[20] For temperance activists, the liberty of the press was imaginary, for in reality the press was 'not free . . . the tyrants custom, party, prejudice, and interest, give a tone to the sentiments of writers, and as effectually destroy its independence and usefulness, as the intervention of absolute power, or the most stringent acts of parliament'. Not only did newspapers profit from the investments made by publicans and beer shop-keepers through advertising, but 'the systems which support their trade, are upheld by editorial countenance'. Literally or metaphorically, too many newspaper articles were 'written under the influence of the wine bottle'.[21] Secondly, to construct a sober and effective counter-journalism of their own, activists established fresh stylistic guidelines. Temperance newspapers, Livesey advised in 1838, should be *well written*, in a plain, pithy, lively style' and the articles '*short* and *interesting*' and interspersed with woodcuts.[22] It was important also to publicise their intention to devote any profits that might be made form the sale of such attractive popular newspapers to the propagation of the cause. Temperance journalism, the public was informed, was decidedly not a vehicle for personal aggrandisement.[23] Thirdly, the temperance movement challenged the hostile majority of newspapers on their own ground. By corresponding with their editors, and circulating to them free copies of *The British Temperance Advocate and Journal*, it was hoped that temperance news and arguments might percolate through the columns of the 'mainstream' local and national press.[24] The lobbying of perceived opinion formers, principally

---

devoted to propagating the principles of Samuel Birley Rowbotham, founder of the Zetetic Society.

[20] *British Temperance Advocate and Journal*, 15 Mar. 1839.

[21] *Rechabite Magazine*, no. 24, n., Dec. 1844, p. 1.

[22] *Moral Reformer*, July 1838, p. 179. Livesey conceded that 'the expense of one of these cuts is considerable; but by getting one engraved, and then taking a number of *stereotype casts* from it, the expense would be divided so as to fall lightly upon each'. He estimated that woodcuts varied in price from £1 to £5, 'but divided should cost no more than 7s 6d each'.

[23] *British Temperance Advocate and Journal*, 15 Jan.1840.

[24] Ibid., 15 Aug. 1840.

clergymen, doctors, magistrates and 'all editors of newspapers', was a major function of *The British Temperance Advocate*, approximately half of whose 15,000 print-run in 1840 was distributed free to such individuals.[25]

Given that so much of the energy of the movement was being expended in the lobbying of newspaper editors, efforts were made to increase the general level of newspaper reading among its supporters. Members of reading clubs were encouraged to place orders for newspapers, and regularly to scan their contents. Rejecting as unwise the 'complaint of teetotallers about what was called the contempt of the newspapers', activists argued that 'while none could vindicate those papers who reviled abstinence principles, yet for the silence of others we had ourselves to blame'. It was suggested in 1844 that each temperance society should select a 'number of active individuals', each one of whom should recruit seven other sympathetic persons who would be willing to invest three farthings a week to buy a weekly newspaper to be read in their own homes. Should this be achieved, it was envisaged that 3,000 classes of eight readers, reading a total of 156,000 copies of weekly newspapers per year, would be in operation in every city the size of Glasgow.[26] But the fondest ambition of many activists was neither to lobby mainstream editors, nor encourage the reading of their newspapers, but to establish an independent temperance newspaper. As for so many other enterprises, the abolition of the Stamp Duty in 1855 enabled the *Alliance News* to do precisely that. Founded in 1854, and sanctioned to carry news the following year, the *Alliance* rapidly became known as 'the backbone of the entire organisation' and enjoyed a regular weekly circulation of between 14,000 and 15,000 by 1859.[27] In the opening address to its readers in July 1854, *The Alliance* insisted that it was 'no commercial speculation, and cannot possibly pay more than its bare expences (*sic*)', and reminded the world that the necessity for its existence sprang 'out of the exigiencies of an important but special movement – a movement which finds no adequate exposition and representative in the political and religious press of this country'.[28]

Nevertheless, once their own newspaper had been launched, there is little evidence to suggest that the earlier tactic of lobbying the 'mainstream' newspapers ceased. On the contrary, minutes of meetings of the Executive Council of the United Kingdom Alliance in the early

---

[25] Ibid., 15 Apr. 1840.

[26] *National Temperance Magazine*, vol. 1, 1844, pp. 436–37.

[27] Brian Harrison, *Drink and the Victorians. The Temperance Question in England 1815–1872* (1971), p. 236.

[28] *The Alliance. A Weekly Journal of Moral and Social Reform*, 8 July 1854, p. 1.

1870s reveal the extent to which their propaganda activities remained focused on the national dailies, either through persuasive pressure[29] or by buying space in their pages at commercial rates. Members of the Council were particularly anxious to ensure that 'the facts' of their campaign 'were duly reported in the London papers', especially in *The Times*, the *Daily Telegraph*, the *Daily News* and the *Morning Post*.[30] Other sources confirm the readiness of political activists simultaneously to criticise and utilise the commercial newspapers. The Chartist John Ripley, for example, had 'from early manhood, used newspapers freely to promulgate temperance doctrine, as well as his opinions on very many other subjects'. His signed and 'racy letters', on a wide range of topics, were almost invariably printed.[31] But in addition to Chartist and temperance activists, those engaged in social movements as diverse as the Anti-Corn Law League, the Liberation Society, the peace and anti-slavery movements, the campaign against the Contagious Diseases Acts, and the Suffrage and labour movements each targeted commercial newspapers as central planks of their agitational strategies. As Hugh Price Hughes, editor of the *Methodist Times*, confessed in a speech delivered at the Exeter Hall on the occasion of W.T. Stead's release from prison in 1885, newspaper journalism was a 'gigantic power'. Hughes recalled how, for 16 years, he and other opponents of child prostitution had 'fought against the conspiracy of silence, and they had made great progress, showing that even the Press was not omnipotent. At last one journal –

---

[29] Little work has been done to date on the ways in which popular organisations and pressure groups brought pressure to bear on the editors of commerical newspapers to alter their contents and editorial policies. One of the few items of evidence I could contribute to what would be a fascinating and suggestive study is a reference to a conversation that took place at a meeting of the Burnley Typographical Association on 8 Jan. 1884, where it was proposed that the local Trades Council should use its resources to 'check the sale' of the *Burnley Gazette* following its adoption of a strongly anti-trade union position during the 'crisis in the cotton trade', Minute book, Burnley Typographical Association, Lancashire RO, Preston, DDX 1380, acc 4642 box 2. The decision taken by neighbouring trade unionists to reject an application by newsagents to be represented on the Trades Council could only have weakened any future attempts to regulate the sale of hostile newspapers, Minute book, Nelson and District Trades Council, 17 Oct. 1893 and 19 Nov. 1893, Lancashire RO, Preston, DDX 1628, acc 5856.

[30] Minutes, Executive Council of the United Kingdom Alliance, 14 June, 1871. See also 25 Oct . 1871, when arrangements were made 'to occupy a page of the *Times* (inside) at a cost of £150 to £180 . . . ', and 15 May 1872; Institute of Alcohol Studies, Alliance House, 12 Caxton St, London.

[31] M.A. Paull Ripley (ed.), *Teetotaller and Traveller. The Life and Journeyings of the Late John Ripley* (1893), pp. 296–97. For the interconnections between temperance, politics and the local press in Lancashire see J.G. Shaw, *The Life of William Gregson. Temperance Advocate* (1891), pp. 243–50. Shaw himself, incidentally, was editor of the *Blackburn Times*.

the *Pall Mall Gazette* – spoke out. The situation was changed in a moment'. This moral victory had shown that 'the modern newspaper had to a great extent superseded both the pulpit and Parliament', and that if reformers were to have any influence on humankind, they 'must lay hold of that tremendous weapon'.[32] By reminding his audience that it had been Stead's commercial *Pall Mall Gazette*, rather than his own, specialist *Methodist Times,* that had transformed 'in a moment' public and political attitudes, Hughes was acknowledging the debt which he and other moral reformers had over the years owed to the 'mainstream' newspaper press. Declarations of hostility towards those newspapers, while no doubt sincerely felt, were also rhetorical devices which obscured a deeper relationship of dependence upon them.

However, not all explicitly reformist publications eschewed the commercial market and some, indeed, embraced it. The peculiar dynamism of mid-Victorian Liberal journalism has been the subject of an impressive body of historical studies in recent years, and it is not our intention here to replicate the wealth of evidence they have produced. Rather, a very brief survey will be offered of the ways in which the electoral utility of commercial newspapers were perceived by Liberal political activists, locally and nationally. John Bright was in no doubt of the importance of journalism for the politically aware and active person. Penning with a note of exasperation the following complaint from Newcastle upon Tyne to a Manchester colleague in August 1855, 'I have no newspaper this morning – so am in the dark as to the <u>latest</u> news', Bright confessed, however, that he read *The Times*, the 'Journal of the oligarchy', only with reluctance and bad humour.[33] The simultaneous need for news and sympathetic treatment from journalists led Bright and Richard Cobden, among a number of other Liberal politicians, to explore the feasibility of establishing their own newspapers as profit-making enterprises that would, none the less, be subject to their editorial control. In August 1855, for example, shortly after the abolition of the Stamp Duty, Joseph Sturge proposed that Cobden and Bright be loaned £2,000 to set up a penny daily newspaper, the principal object of which was 'to oppose the [Crimean] war and advocate the future nonintervention with foreign States and the settlement of international disputes by arbitration'. In all other respects, the proposed paper would represent Cobden's and Bright's political opinions 'as known by their votes and speeches in the House of Commons', and would be subject to their veto on the material which the paper could and could not carry.[34] It

---

[32] J. Gregory Mantle, *Hugh Price Hughes. A Strenuous Life* (1902), pp. 87–88.

[33] John Bright to George Wilson, 23 Aug. 1855, John Bright to George Wilson, 24 Aug. 1855, M20/23, George Wilson Papers, Manchester City Archives (Wilson MCA).

[34] Joseph Sturge to George Wilson, 22 Aug. 1855, M20/23, Wilson MCA.

was widely appreciated that such ventures involved grave financial risks, but the consequences for newspaper ownership and management of the passing into law in 1854 of a Limited Liability Act were closely examined, and the Act swiftly came to be regarded as a legal means whereby this kind of political control could be exerted on a relatively sound financial basis. The argument ran as follows: newspapers, being the representatives of defined bodies of opinion, relied heavily on the support of well-wishers who broadly shared the editorial world-view. Up until 1854, that moral support had been underwritten by the money invested in the venture by subscribers. Subscription, however, had not entailed a contractual relationship between the newspaper and its backers since the editor could not legally be obliged to be directly responsible to the subscribers. Those subscribers who thought their investments entitled them to make moral claims on a newspaper's management were 'frequently disappointed and discontented with the conduct of Journals originated by their aid'. Limited liability, however, permitted subscribers to become shareholders 'with clear control over the journal', without being responsible for more than the money each had invested.[35]

The capacity of the new market mechanisms to generate a politically more diverse newspaper press, subject to the availability of adequate financial resources, proved to be enormously attractive to members and sympathisers of the main political parties in and out of London. Of course, individual ownership was also in many respects politically determined. E.F. Collins, editor and sole proprietor of the *Hull Advertiser*, for example, felt 'morally bound never to part' with his paper unless he could be assured that it would 'continue to be the advocate of Liberal opinions'. Nothing could induce him 'to sell it to the Tories'.[36] But limited liability enabled far larger newspaper enterprises to be formed for primarily political reasons, with the prospect of transforming the political balance of the daily press. Even the *Daily News*, started in January 1846 by Charles Dickens, and known in the early 1850s as 'the

---

[35] Flyer for *The Sunday Paper*, 1 Oct. 1855, a 2d weekly 'to be conducted on principles of Popular Liberalism', M20/23, Wilson MCA.

[36] E.F. Collins to Joseph Sturge, 29 Sept. 1855, M20/23, Wilson MCA. A third option considered by some was co-operative ownership, where 'each new member on joining [the Co-operative Society] should agree to take a copy every week, which should be delivered to him with his weekly purchases', Landor Praed, 'Possibility of a Co-operative Newspaper', *The Social Economist. Industrial Partnership Record and Co-operative Review*, 1 Jan. 1869, a report of a paper delivered to the Newspaper Committee appointed at the Halifax conference, 1866 and 1867. For an earlier attempt to establish a co-operative newspaper, see proposals for the 'National Press', run on trade union rules, in *Typographical Gazette*, Sept. 1846, p. 83, also pp. 125, 155, 179, 238.

'Cobden Organ' due to its 'uniformly Liberal' politics and advocacy of free trade',[37] at one time considered the advantages of limited liability ownership. The editor, G.F. Smith, estimated that it was unlikely that demand for the high-priced London dailies would in future increase (the *Daily News*, having abandoned Charles Dilke's policy of reducing the price to $2^{1}/_{2}$d., sold for 5d. with the registration stamp, 'the ordinary price of the Daily London News Papers'), and that additional revenue could not realistically be expected from a higher circulation. Financial reorganisation and the creation of a limited liability company, he concluded, were the paper's only means of salvation.[38] Similar calls were made the following year, when Smith again proposed a 'largely diffuced [*sic*] Proprietary',[39] despite the fact that the paper was by this time comfortably in the black. The growth of cheaper newspapers, the hostility of *The Times* and an impending political crisis, however, rendered it desirable to gather 'in one nucleus enough mass of popular Liberal tendencies' to defeat the government. Only a popular Liberal newspaper, one that could challenge the dominance of *The Times*, could sustain such a political nucleus, and an enterprise of such scale and ambition, Smith argued, could only be undertaken by a 'larger Proprietary'.[40]

The formation of limited liability companies was clearly an attractive option for journalists and activists, particularly to those associated with the Liberal Party outside London where large numbers of new titles were launched by this means. The evidence suggests that local political leaders were able to exert a degree of editorial control over these publications, a facility which proved to be of particular advantage in the post-1867 electoral system. There were many uses to which newspapers could be put by politicians beyond the maintaining of a constituency-based publicity machine. The examples of two Liberal politicians, A.J. Mundella in Sheffield and Joseph Chamberlain in Birmingham, illustrate two facets of this utility. In Mundella's case, an extensive private correspondence with Robert Leader of the *Sheffield Independent* in the election year of 1868 reveal the hidden interconnections between press and politics in the construction of a politician's public image.[41] Stung, for

---

[37] Goldwin Smith to Harriet Martineau, n.d. 1856, MS HM836, Heslop Room, Birmingham University Library (Martineau BUL). In fact the *Daily News* at this time was anything but 'uniformly Liberal', having rejected the 'peace views of that party' and being 'an energetic opponent of their policy in that respect', ibid.

[38] G.F. Smith to Harriet Martineau, n.d. (?1857), HM822, Martineau BUL.

[39] Ibid., 19 June 1858, HM827, Martineau BUL.

[40] Ibid., 21 June 1858, HM828, Martineau BUL.

[41] A.J. Mundella to Robert Leader, 19 July 1868, 6P/58/1/8/i, Mudella–Leader Corr., 1868–1895, Anthony John Mundella Papers, Special Collections, Sheffield University

example, by the xenophobic allegations made against him by the Conservative supporters of Roebuck in the *Sheffield Telegraph*, Mundella vigorously urged Leader to use his paper to counter the cry of 'Mundella the Frenchman' that had been raised by his opponents. Retorting that he was 'just as much French or foreign as the Prince of Wales himself' Mundella explained to Leader that he had been born in the Midlands to an old Tamworth family, and his father, an Italian exile, had settled and been naturalised in Yorkshire.[42] The *Independent* complied, and Mundella later expressed his gratitude to the paper for having 'thrown the shield of Mars over' him during the election.[43] Mundella's sensitivity to press opinion, and his intimate alliance with a local newspaper, transformed his public image as well as popularised his Liberal politics. Many other political figures, most notably Gladstone himself, were to benefit from similar treatment at the hands of a politically imaginative newspaper press.[44]

The private correspondence, extending over 30 years, between Joseph Chamberlain and John Thackeray Bunce of the *Birmingham Daily Post* demonstrate a similar regard for the public construction of a political figure who in return fed the local press with stories and advice.[45] This was particularly significant for Chamberlain, who in 1885 faced the virulent personal assaults which, in the previous 20 years, had been reserved by the conservative press for John Bright and Gladstone.[46] But Chamberlain was also actively engaged in the construction of a network of sympathetic Liberal newspapers in the west Midlands. In February 1884, H.G. Reid of the *Midland Echo* wrote to assure Chamberlain that their joint endeavour to purchase the Wolverhampton *Evening Express*, the *Midland Counties Express* and the *Wolverhampton Chronicle* had been a success. These newspapers, Reid explained, enjoyed 'the most general and the largest circulation of any paper in Staffordshire – in constituencies returning 14 or 15 members to Parliament', and, equally importantly, that they were 'Conservative and valuable properties' which

---

Library (Mundella SUL). See also W.H.G. Armytage, *A.J. Mundella 1825–1897. The Liberal Background to the Labour Movement* (1951).

[42] Mundella to Leader, 8 Aug. 1868, 6P/58/1/14/i, Mundella SUL.

[43] Ibid., 5 Oct. 1868, 6P/58/1/37/ii, Mundella SUL.

[44] See for example Edward Russell to W.E. Gladstone, 10 Oct. 1878, Brit. Mus. Add. MS 44458 ff. 42, in which Russell described how he had countered in the *Liverpool Daily Post* criticisms of Gladstone made in the London newspapers.

[45] Chamberlain to Bunce Corr., 1870–99, JC 5/8/1–52, Joseph Chamberlain Coll., Heslop Room, University of Birmingham Library (Chamberlain BUL). See also in the same coll. his letters to W.T. Stead, from Apr. 1877, when Stead was still with the *Northern Echo* in Darlington, until they quarrelled in April 1891, by which time Stead had established himself at the *Pall Mall Gazette*.

[46] Henry Lucy (Sir), *The Diary of a Journalist* (1920), p. 1.

'would bring large political influence and a good revenue'. Reid triumphally concluded thus, 'Your bold conception of our enterprise and our interest in you and your work, prompts me to make this, the first, intimation of our conquest'.[47]

The experiences of pressure groups and aspiring Liberal politicians in their relations with the press indicated a shared and overwhelmingly optimistic faith in the capacity of newspapers to bring about change. At the core of that faith lay the belief that, particularly following the passage of legislation affecting newspaper taxation and company ownership between 1854 and 1861, the free market was the engine of diversity whose mechanisms might be used to challenge the dominance of the conservative London and county press. In the boroughs of Newcastle upon Tyne, Leeds, Manchester, Liverpool, Sheffield and Birmingham, new Liberal élites had emerged that sought to represent and reproduce themselves in part through networks of sympathetic newspapers. However, their attempts to harmonise the political possibilities of the medium with the imperatives of the market, though initially highly successful, were founded on an ultimately mistaken assumption that the politics of the market-place were essentially and necessarily those of the Liberal Party. The long and tortuous history of Conservative attitudes towards the newspaper press would eventually demonstrate how wrong that assumption had been.

The Conservative 'moral strategy'

As we saw in the previous chapter, the urgency with which the debate on the power of newspapers was conducted in nineteenth-century England reflected deep anxieties about their cultural impact and their effects on the moral order. Running counter to the historical teleologies and the trajectories of modernisation and improvement were some highly critical positions which regarded the popular press as a profoundly destabilising and dysfunctional element in a society whose composition was thought in any case to be changing too quickly and in unwelcome ways. Thus, in addition to the 'if we have it not we die' response of many Liberals, the newspaper was also denounced by others as 'a public curse – a monster embittering existence' that terrified and trampled on helpless individuals, and perverted their moral codes.[48] Described in 1785 by George Crabbe as a huddle of dissociated articles which, though amusing, brought 'irreparable injury . . . upon the characters of individuals', newspapers

---

[47] H.G. Reid to Joseph Chamberlain, 23 Feb. 1884, JC 6/4j/1, Chamberlain BUL.
[48] Lord Broughton, speech notes, 1854, Brit. Mus. Add. MS 47230, ff. 43–46.

were ruthlessly satirised for their capacity to expand their numbers, and attract and mislead their readers:

> Endless it were to sing the powers of all,
> Their names, their numbers; how they rise and fall;
> Like baneful herbs the gazer's eye they seize,
> Rush to the head, and poison where they please;
> Like idle flies, a busy, buzzing train,
> They drop their maggots in the weak man's brain . . . [49]

Fears that newspapers were destructive influences were given free rein during and immediately following the French Revolutionary crisis, when Lord Grenville, Edmund Burke and others charged newspapers with subverting the moral and social order in France, and for threatening to do the same in England. John Reeves was so dismayed by the 'circulation of Newspapers filled with *disloyalty and sedition*' in 1792 that he published a pamphlet urging 'all good Subjects, whether Masters or Private Families, or Keepers of Inns, Taverns, or Coffee-Houses, to discontinue and discourage the use and circulation of all such disloyal and seditious Newspapers'.[50] Similar concerns were expressed during the turbulent post-war years, when Tory MP Henry Banks complained in the Commons that the repressive and counter-insurgent Six Acts of December 1819, which introduced new duties on periodicals containing news, had not gone far enough in restraining the press, which he feared would remain 'a tremendous engine in the hands of mischievous men'.[51] These anxieties, by linking cheap, popular newspapers with social unrest, powerfully shaped aspects of Conservative thinking about communications well into the nineteenth century.

The model of journalism which had been so admired by John Wilson Croker (1780–1857) in 1829 had rested on the intimacy of relations between editors and government ministers. Cabinet members, by secretly advising editors on 'what to avoid, what to hint, what to deny, when to leave folks in their errors, and when to open the real views of the Government', effectively set the tone of a small but influential number of London newspapers.[52] Such examples of metropolitan

---

[49] George Crabbe, *The News-Paper: a Poem* (1785), p. 6.

[50] *Proceedings of the Association for Preserving Liberty and Property against Republicans and Levellers*, 12 Dec. 1792, Reeves MS 942.073 A.11, 1792–3, Manchester City Library.

[51] *Parliamentary Debates*, xxxv. 584 (24 Feb. 1817), quoted in Aspinall, *Politics and the Press*, p. 1.

[52] Louis J. Jennings (ed.), *The Croker Papers. The Correspondence and Diaries of the Rt. Hon. John Wilson Croker*, vol. 2 (1884), pp. 21–23. For Croker's involvement with the 'higher journalism', consult Joanne Shattock, *Politics and Reviewers: The Edinburgh and the Quarterly in the Early Victorian age* (Liecester, 1989), pp. 63–69.

exclusivity, however, were of little help to Tories outside the capital where the Tory press was gradually but noticeably being overtaken by newspapers associated with the opposition. In 1831, a correspondent to the Duke of Wellington was alarmed by expressions of 'unfeeling abuse of the peasantry' in a county conservative newspaper, and warned that 'if the Tory press is not conducted with more judgement, it will not be surprizing that all classes of the nation should gradually be deluded to array themselves on the side of their opponents'.[53] By 1834, the hostility of the Whig government obliged some Tories to rally to the defence of press freedom, acknowledging that 'the Conservatives are not now at least seeking to shackle the Press; they are not shewing any symptoms of fear or hatred of that magnificent engine'.[54] But the conversion to the rhetoric of the free press disguised deep uncertainties within Tory thinking, not only about the press, but more widely about the relationship between the party and the modernity that the press represented.

Among the first to address this issue was Sir Archibald Alison (1792–1839), the high-Tory Sheriff of Lanarkshire. In a measured and insightful article in *Blackwood's* in 1834, his exploration into the nature of press power raised some difficult questions for Conservatives. Starting from the premise that the press was intrinsically democratic, an assertion which he based on the 'immense' growth in the circulation of the leading liberal newspapers, he argued that the press was daily becoming more of a social problem. With 'strong and vivid pictures addressed to the passions and the imagination, incitements to sensual indulgence, and that fatal union of genius with voluptuousness which is the well known sign of a declining age',[55] cheaper, often unstamped newspapers were an inherently destabilising force. The question was what, if anything, could be done to arrest these unwelcome developments.

> These then are the grand characteristics of the press in these times. . . . Its democratic character shakes the foundations of government: its licentious tendency saps the bulwarks of morals; its ascendancy over property gives the victory over all the institutions of society. If we would combat its pernicious tendency, we must discover the means of resisting these methods of attack.[56]

In the new political age, in which news and opinion were commodities shaped by the tastes of what Alison characterised as a scarcely

---

[53] Mrs J. Westmorland to the Duke of Wellington, 28 Dec. 1831, quoted in Aspinall, *Politics and the Press*, p. 474.

[54] John Wilson, *Blackwood's*, Mar. 1834, p. 295.

[55] Sir Archibald Alison, 'The Influence of the Press', *Blackwood's*, Sept. 1834, p. 373.

[56] Ibid., p. 374.

governable multitude, property mattered less than numbers. With this in mind, Alison considered whether the failure of the propertied and educated élite to resist this movement was attributable to the nature of the newspaper itself, the 'peculiarity in the form in which knowledge is transmitted'. The fortunes of most newspapers, 'from which nine-tenths of mankind implicitly adopt their opinions', relied more on their circulations than on the intimacy of their relations with Ministers. Consequently, in their representation in the press, 'the superior number of the lower orders gives them a decided preponderance over all the better classes of society'. Despite an income of some £100,000 a year, a Conservative nobleman might subscribe to three or four daily newspapers, whereas ten Radicals, by pooling their resources and purchasing newspapers jointly, subscribed to as many newspapers as the aristocrat. Thus

> ten persons on the democratic side, whose united income is probably not £500 a year, neutralize one Conservative whose income is two hundred times as great as all theirs put together. . . . This gives a clear insight into the leading principle on this subject, which is that in influencing the daily press, the influence of wealth, talent or virtue, is almost nothing compared to that of numbers; and therefore it is, that so vast a preponderance of journals, in number at least, adopt the popular and licentious side. In every other department property can overbalance numbers. . . . The reason is, that no man can do more than read one, or at the most two, newspapers a day; and this can be done as well by a weaver or a coalheaver as a prince or a philosopher. This simple principle gives, and ever must give, an overwhelming superiority to numbers over property in determining the character of the public press.[57]

The structural nature of the problem, however, implied that a solution might be difficult to find. Was 'man inevitably expelled from Paradise by eating of the Tree of Knowledge' Alison wondered, or were there 'principles to be found in human nature' that were capable of being manipulated in order that the 'spread of the poison' might be prevented? Despite his conviction that 'the spread of democratic fervour and journal ascendancy [was] a stage in the progress of corruption' that followed the French Revolution, he discerned certain characteristics in the trade of journalism that augured well for the future. The first was that the inherently democratic impulses of journalists were based on a 'desire for gain' rather than revolutionary political convictions. Consequently, it was necessary to harness their essentially entrepreneurial instincts. Coercion, a measure 'fit only for a savage age', would inevitably fail. The only effective antidote lay in the expansion of

---

[57] Ibid., p. 375.

a cheap and popular Conservative newspaper press in all areas of the country.[58] For Alison this meant devising and implementing a 'moral strategy of the press', on the success of which rested 'the whole destinies of civilized society'.[59] This was a challenge to which other Conservatives were continually to respond throughout the remainder of the century.

Alison's theoretical dissertation of 1834 was followed in the same journal in the following year with a more concrete set of proposals. Despite the fact that newspapers had 'a perpetual tendency to be democratical', it was possible, slowly and with difficulty, to expel the venom from the body politic by adopting a three-point strategy. First, party leaders should define an essental ideological core by deducting 'Conservative principles from history and experience'. Secondly, the party faithful were to resist 'the revolutionary hydra in the periodical press' by keeping it under surveillance, 'exposing all its misrepresentations, and counteracting its infernal tendency in works read by millions'. Finally, the radicalism of the cheap weekly papers needed to be combated in the daily newspapers. Here Conservatives needed to discharge 'the necessary, and often painful duty of keeping the public mind right on passing occurrences; and deducing from the fleeting events of the moment those just and rational conclusions which are calculated to give them their due weight in the formation of public opinion'. The Herculean task that faced them of 'righting the national mind, after a progressive perversion of half a century' required 'all the genius, and energy, and perseverance, which the Conservative part of the nation' could produce.[60] By 1835, then, the Tory party had been furnished with both an analysis of newspaper influence and a means of changing the balance of forces back in their favour. For these lone voices, the idea that the party had a historic responsibility to convert voters to conservatism was not an alien notion.[61] With few exceptions, however, their advice fell on deaf ears. For a variety of reasons, that ranged from a reluctance to part with money to a deep disquiet about challenging the liberals on their own 'democratical' ground and the doubtful proposition that communication with an unenfranchised public was a political priority, the party leaders did not seriously take up Alison's call to modernise its means of public communication.

In the autumn of 1836, the year of the reduction of the Stamp Duty, the results of a survey of the post-Reform press revealed that Tory newspapers in Britain were outnumbered by those which expressed

---

[58] Ibid., p. 391.
[59] Ibid., p. 389.
[60] 'Conservative Associations', Blackwood's, July 1835, p. 5.
[61] Martin Pugh, The Tories and the People 1880–1935 (1985), p. 6.

support for liberalism by 184 to 202, and the evidence of Stamp Returns of the same year showed that although the Tory papers were reasonably secure in the counties, in the expanding urban and industrial areas the liberal press was growing ominously stronger.[62] Within five weeks of the reduction of the Stamp Duty, it was reported that there had been 'a very large extension of the power of the liberal press' and that the 'liberal journals have been increasing rapidly in circulation',[63] despite the grants reputedly awarded by the 'press fund' of the Carlton Club to Alaric Watts and others in the early 1830s to help revive the provincial Conservative newspapers.[64] The garrulousness of the newly confident anti-Tory journalists was also regarded with astonishment. Whig and Radical editors were in turn reviled by William Maginn as 'vermin', 'literary scavengers who took up the trade of assassin' and who displayed a 'filthy malignity' towards such great Tory writers as Wordsworth, Southey and Walter Scott, whose 'secret moving hand' behind a section of the Scottish press was subjected to particular criticism by the liberals.[65] Southey himself, referring to the need to defend the 'MORAL versus political economy', spoke of 'powerful counteracting forces at work . . . the destructive and conservative principles'.[66] But certain opportunities did present themselves in the later 1830s to carry out, albeit in part, Alison's moral strategy. Richard Carlile in 1837 noted 'a new feature in the state of things among the political parties', namely the regularity with which radical journals, endangered financially after 1836, were being bought by Tories. More surprisingly, in 'a plan to work those Radical papers more efficiently against the Whigs', their radical editors were being retained, among them Henry

---

[62] 'Public opinion as indicated by the newspaper press', *Tait's*, Oct. 1836, pp. 661–62. See also an index of Tory and liberal newspapers, listed respectively in blue and red ink, in Clarke and Lewis, *Advertisements Received for the London Gazette* (1836). Aspinall, *Politics and the Press* is an essential starting-point, but see also Jeremy Black, *The English Press in the Eighteenth Century* (1987) and William Speck, 'Politics and the Press', in Michael Harris and Alan Lee (eds), *The Press in English Society from the Seventeenth to Nineteenth Centuries* (1986), pp. 47–63. For a recent treatment of seventeenth-century Tory propaganda, see Philip Harth, *Pen for a Party: Dryden's Tory Propaganda in its Contexts* (Princeton, 1993).

[63] J.J. Darling, 'The Liberal Newspapers: Effects of the Reduction of Stamp Duty', *Tait's*, Nov. 1836, p. 692.

[64] Lucy Brown, *Victorian News and Newspapers* (Oxford, 1985), p. 65. For an account of the 'Charles Street Gang', the Carlton Club and the party's ambivalence towards the press, see Robert Stewart, *The Foundation of the Conservative Party 1830–1867* (1978), pp. 73–77.

[65] William Maginn, 'On the Profligacy of the London Periodical Press', *Blackwood's*, Aug.–Oct. 1824, pp. 180–81.

[66] David Eastwood, 'Robert Southey and the Intellectual Origins of Romantic Conservatism', *English Historical Review*, 104, Apr. 1989 pp. 322, 330 n. 3.

Hetherington and Bell. The *Guide* and the Newcastle *Northern Liberator* were, according to Carlile, also taken over by the Tories to serve the same end.[67]

The fate of the *Conservative Journal*, however, revealed the scepticism with which the party regarded a press that was too closely associated with it. Launched in 1839 to beard in its den the 'tiger' of the liberal press,[68] it was rancorously discontinued only four years later. The *Courier* newspaper fared scarcely better. Offered in 1840 to Francis Bonham, the Conservatives' chief election manager, as a 'party organ', the *Courier*'s publisher John Follett was in effect asking both for party assistance in circulating the paper and in defraying of publication expenses. Lord Redesdale, Tory chief whip in the Lords, and Sir Robert Peel were both dubious, and Peel, expressing his 'horror of money transactions with Newspaper proprietors' eventually terminated the negotiations. Despite Follett's willingness to compromise on the appointment of an editor, and his readiness to accept funds in the form of shares rather than a subsidy, which would have meant that 'the party would thus have control of the newspaper', the party leadership refused the approach on three grounds. First they argued that the party did not take kindly to appeals for money, secondly that it was not in the party interest to have a party organ for whose tone and language the leadership would constantly be held responsible, and finally that by privileging the *Courier* in this way, other Conservative-supporting newspapers might be alienated.[69] The following year, in 1841, the acting proprietor of the *Morning Post* proposed a less formal relationship with Peel's party. Seeking 'to serve the cause of the Conservative party' and to 'promote the efficiency of the Conservative press as a political engine', he urged Peel to consider 'the effect of journalism upon the Public mind' and to 'use it in addition to Parliamentary speaking for the purpose of guiding and informing the Public'.[70]

Despite such initiatives, some Conservatives believed that by the middle of the century the battle had been lost. Croker's was the most pronounced voice to articulate this despair, and to reflect on the

---

[67] Richard Carlile to Thomas Turton, 22 Nov. 1837, quoted in Theophila Carlile Campbell, *The Battle of the Press, as Told in the Story of the Life of Richard Carlile* (1899), p. 207.

[68] *Conservative Journal and Church of England Gazette*, 5 Jan. 1849.

[69] Robert Stewart, 'The Conservative Party and the *Courier* newspaper, 1840', *English Historical Review*, vol. xci, no. 359, Apr. 1976, pp. 346–50. According to G.R. Seale, Peel 'saw the press as a particularly remarkable triumph of capitalist enterprise', G.R. Seale, *Entrepreneurial Politics in Mid-Victorian Britain* (Oxford, 1993), p. 40.

[70] Eastland Mitchell (?) to Sir Robert Peel, 18 Aug. 1841, Brit. Mus. Add. MS 40486, f. 130.

implications for the party's relationship with the press. By 1854, he considered the House of Commons to be 'unmanageable', and the country 'ungovernable', and attributed this calamitous state of affairs to two overriding developments. First, the 1832 Reform Act had undermined the authority of monarchy and the 'deliberative functions of . . . government' by increasing the 'representative element'. The second cause of the weakness of government he attributed to 'the power of newspapers. This power', Croker argued

> was always great, but was in general so nearly self-balanced as not seriously to interrupt the functions of a government. Mechanical improvements, extension of education and of business, of literary taste and commercial intercourse, have developed the powers of the press to be an enormous influence – an influence the greater because it has become so subtle that we breathe it as we breathe the air, without being conscious of the minuter particles that enter into its composition.[71]

The combination of parliamentary reform and the growth of the press was, for Croker, an explosive admixture that struck at the heart of the traditional independence of the MP to such an extent that the Speaker, 'instead of demanding from the Sovereign freedom of speech, had much better ask it from the *Times*'. Worse still, reform and the press had

> erected into omnipotence what was formerly a valuable subordinate agent, now called public opinion: she was of old the queen of the world; she has now become its tyrant, and the newspapers her ministers; that is they assume that they represent public opinion, and of course the people, in a more direct and authoritative manner, than even the House of Commons.[72]

Croker's hyperbolic language no doubt crystallised the disappointment of a figure who by mid-century felt out of touch and ignored. Other Conservatives, however, were less despondent. Sir E. Bulwer Lytton, for example, had argued in the Commons debate on the abolition of the Stamp Duty in April 1855 that the Conservative press should take fuller advantage of the new technologies of newspaper production and distribution, and urged party members to start new papers that would advocate 'the robust and healthy principles of Conservatism [which] would have everything to gain by free discussion and the general diffusion of knowledge'.[73] Benjamin Disraeli had already been attempting to accomplish precisely that with the launching of the weekly Conservative

---

[71] J.W. Croker to Henry Brougham, 21 July 1854, *Croker Papers*, vol. 3 (1884), p. 338.
[72] Ibid., *Croker Papers*, p. 339.
[73] *The Press*, 28 Apr. 1855.

newspaper *The Press* on 7 May 1853. Disraeli himself wrote several leading articles, his last piece appearing in 1856, and Bulwer Lytton and George Smythe had also contributed articles. Disraeli discovered, however, that moral support was more forthcoming than revenue. In June 1854, he spent £1,500 to meet the paper's losses, a high price to pay to sustain a paper with a circulation of only 2,000. In 1858, back in office, Disraeli sold the paper, which survived for a further eight years. Musing ruefully on the experience of Disraeli's ownership of *The Press*, its editor Samuel Lucas reflected that 'journalists as a class are opposed to the Conservative party, and one element of their opposition is their common conviction that our Party is indisposed to treat them considerately'.[74]

The repeal of the Stamp Act in 1855 stimulated fresh thinking in Conservative, as in other, political circles. Tory journalist William Rathbone Greg in October 1855, in an attempt to seize the initiative from the liberals, presciently argued that the notion of a 'party' newspaper was outdated, and that the free market provided the surest basis for a thoroughly Conservative press. He began with an analysis of the social functions of the newspaper in modern society.

> Not only does it supply the nation with nearly all the information on public topics which it possesses, but it supplies it with its notions and opinions in addition. It furnishes not only the materials on which our conclusions must be founded: it furnishes the conclusions themselves, cut and dried – coined, stamped and polished . . . it *does all the thinking* of the nation; saves us the trouble of weighing and perpending, of comparing and deliberating; and presents us with ready-made opinions clearly and forcibly expressed.[75]

But while newspapers, by commodifying 'conclusions' as well as information, might prevent readers from thinking for themselves, they also provided a readily accessible means of expression to marginalised groups. The diversity of voices thus represented, in many respects uniquely, through journalism contributed to the richness and the stability of both popular and political culture.

> Journalism is needed as part and parcel of the *representation* of the country. . . . The holders of unusual opinions, or of moderate or philosophic doctrines, the votaries of 'comin' creeds, the members of minorities in a word, are unrepresented in Parliament. . . . We all feel that we could not do without the vent for expression which the Newspaper Press affords us. We should explode were it not for such an immediate and ample safety-valve.[76]

---

[74] Thom Braun, *Disraeli the Novelist* (1981), p. 126; Lee, *Origins*, pp. 147–48.

[75] William Rathbone Greg, 'The Newspaper Press', *Edinburgh Review*, Oct. 1855, p. 477.

[76] Ibid., p. 479.

Finally, Greg concluded that attempts to set up established party organs were based on a mistaken view of the way in which journalism operated. Party newspapers were invariably precarious, costly and condemned to low circulations precisely because journalism was 'not the instrument by which the various divisions of the ruling classes express themselves . . . [but] . . . the instrument by means of which the aggregate intelligence of the nation criticises and controls them all'.[77] For Greg, this inescapable truth had two consequences for Conservatism, in politics and in the press. The first was that political diversity in journalism was a 'natural' corollary of market forces, continued resistance to which was a damaging waste of political energy. The second was that the real danger lay in the monopoly power exercised by a liberal-oriented daily newspaper.

> Such a power then becomes something equally difficult of control and counteraction. A daily organ which has reached this paramount position, is read every morning by hundreds of thousands *who read nothing else*, who imbibe its doctrines, who accept its statements, and who repeat both to every one they meet, till the whole intellectual and moral atmosphere of the nation becomes insensibly coloured and imbued. It of itself forms, and is, the public opinion of the country.[78]

The attempt to reorient Conservative attitudes towards the newspaper press continued in *Blackwood's* in 1859, which welcomed the new age in which 'the universality of print, [and] the omnipotence of ink'[79] were acknowledged rather than resisted by the Conservatives. The popular press was a permanent, if uncomfortable, reality to which all Tories needed to adjust and to learn to use intelligently. If this were done, the 'deluge' of democracy could be survived.

> For good or bad, our future is in it . . . the rise of this great power in the State, the development of this strange form of public life, the exercise and the extension of this franchise, must be numbered among the our greatest political blessings. May it be so in the future! We, as Tories, can look forward to that future, if without exultation, yet also without fear. All the movements of the time tend towards democracy, it is true, and a free press is supposed to be the peculiar symbol and engine of the democrat; but when the dreaded deluge comes, perhaps it will be found to come with safeguards in the constitution of the English press, which no previous democracy has ever enjoyed.[80]

---

[77] Ibid., p. 487.

[78] Ibid., p. 492.

[79] 'Popular Literature–the Periodical Press', *Blackwood's*, Jan. 1859, p. 99.

[80] Ibid., p. 100. According to Lee, even Conservative journalists 'adhered to a basically

One of the more noticeable aspects of the shifting focus of the debate on journalism in the middle of the nineteenth century was a modification of the political language. In the 1850s, the vocabulary of 'sedition' and 'licentiousness', which had defined conservative attitudes towards the press during the previous half-century, was used with far less frequency. At worst, newspapers were regarded as a 'strange form of public life'. The softening of attitudes may be attributed to two underlying causes. The first implied that a rational, historical explanation for the imbalance between conservative and liberal journalism could allay the fears of the Right. It was noted in 1867 that the ascendancy which the Tories had enjoyed over the press between 1800 and 1830 had entered its long period of decline almost immediately after the Whigs had assumed power. In the opinion of the Revd George Robert Gleig, readers were attracted to the liberal press not by subversive intent, but, on the contrary, by the same instinctive loyalty to King and country that had led them previously to read the Tory papers. After 1830, the liberal newspapers had displayed their essential loyalty to the state by supporting the Crown's mainly liberal constitutional advisers. Their patronage had, in the course of 36 years, 'filled every permament place, from seats on the episcopal and judicial benches down to clerkships in the public offices'. Under such circumstances, 'the liberalisation of almost all the daily, weekly, monthly and quarterly literature of the country' had been unavoidable.[81] Gleig thus advised Conservatives not to rail against the people, whose liberalism was more a reflection of their loyalty to the Crown than a rejection of it. The proper duty of Conservatives was to adopt rather than reject the publicity methods of their opponents.

A second reason for the adoption of more tolerant attitudes towards the press followed the realisation that the expanding market for liberal newspapers after 1855 reflected a real constituency of support which Conservatives needed to address. This became even more imperative as the implications of the Conservatives' own efforts at parliamentary reform in 1867 dawned on the party, and in particular on the party's increasingly organised and vocal rank and file. Before 1867, the Conservatives had been relatively slow to grasp the importance of a cheap daily press, the first Conservative penny daily, the *Nottingham*

---

liberal ideology according to which the press was, as if by definition, an indispensable political weapon', although some Tories held that Conservatism was so deeply rooted that the party had no need of the press, Lee, *Origins*, p. 150.

[81] George Robert Gleig, 'The Government and the Press', *Blackwood's*, Dec. 1867, pp. 763–66.

Daily Guardian, being launched only in 1861. However, the pace of change quickened in the late 1860s, and although it slowed down again in the 1870s, accelerated once more in the 1880s to create the kind of dominance of ideology over press that was to be further consolidated in the twentieth century.[82] One of the key forums where this strategy was debated was the National Union of Conservative Associations (NUCA).[83] Founded in November 1867, it regarded its prime function as being to instruct 'the people as to the real meaning, intentions, and ideas, of Conservatives',[84] to defend the party against attack by the Radical press, and 'to increase and multiply the influence of the Conservative Press throughout the United Kingdom'.[85] One of its early leaders was J.E. Gorst, who was appointed the party's Principal Agent on losing his seat as MP for Cambridge City in 1868. A 'pushing, ambitious and prickly' 35-year-old, Gorst was alive to the problems of Conservatism among the urban working classes.[86] For him, as for other anti-Northcote 'Fourth Party' Conservative radicals, such as Randolph Churchill and Arthur Balfour, the National Union was a means of modernising the party, of recruiting middle- and working-class supporters alienated both by Gladstone and by the 'Old Identity', the landowning and aristocratic section of the Tory party.[87] If Tory democracy was to have any meaning, or any future, the National Union was the instrument with which it would be forged. Gorst, by this time also the part-time editor of the London *Standard*,[88] understood the practical utility of the newspaper press in this venture. In consequence, he and others in the National Union needed to acknowledge just how weak the Conservative press was in relation to its more aggressive and self-confident Liberal counterpart.

At the founding conference of the NUCA in 1867 an appeal was made

---

[82] Lee, *Origins*, p. 151.

[83] See, for example, Robert Blake, *The Conservative Party from Peel to Thatcher* (1985), p. 114.

[84] *Minutes and Reports of the Conservative Party Conferences, 1867–1946*, Archives of the British Conservative Party, Harvester Microfiche, (*Minutes*, ABCP), 1867, p. 72.

[85] *Minutes*, ABCP, 1867, p. 77.

[86] Gorst was a 'genuine believer in working-class Conservatism, which, not perhaps entirely correctly, he understood to be the essence of Disraeli's creed', Blake, *The Conservative Party*, p. 144, See also H.E. Gorst, *The Fourth Party* (1906).

[87] Blake, *The Conservative Party*, p. 147. See also J. Cornford, 'The Transformation of Conservatism in the Late 19th Century', *Victorian Studies*, September 1963. Gorst resigned as Agent in November 1884, and sat again as a Conservative MP from 1885 to 1906, a maverick excluded from office.

[88] In 1858 the *Standard* received a substantial loan from the Conservative Party in the form of a mortgage on premises and plant, the funds being put up by 'prominent figures in the party and organized by the party agent, Philip Rose', Brown, *Victorian News*, p. 63.

to all Conservatives to support what was claimed to be the only Conservative penny weekly newspaper in London, the *British Lion*. Started in June 1867 in response to Conservatives' deficiency 'in press representation among the masses', the *British Lion* was marketed as 'a popular Conservative working-men's newspaper'.[89] However, beyond aiding the circulation and voluntarily providing advertisements, it was agreed that no further action should be taken on the grounds that the party should not give priority to any individual title.[90] Professor Koss suggested that a reliance on such an obscure weekly was humiliating to the Conservatives present at the conference, but the debate as a whole also revealed an important distinction between the concerns of the rank and file with the threat posed by the radical weeklies, particularly *Reynolds's*, and those of the party leadership who were preoccupied with the rumours that circulated in high political circles in London.[91] However, even at this stage, it was misleading to suggest that the Conservative press was in a critically weak position. Mitchell's *Newspaper Press Directory* of 1866 reveals a number of weekly provincial newspapers advertised primarily as Conservative organs. The *Doncaster Chronicle*, for example, advocated 'the measures and principles of the Conservative party, of which it is the accredited organ in the district', whilst the *Liverpool Mail*, established 15 September 1836, was 'decidedly attached to the Church of England, in doctrine and discipline, [and] as an especial Tory and Conservative organ, it enjoys the patronage of that party to a considerable extent'.[92] The *Nottinghamshire Guardian*, established 1 May 1846, advocated 'a strong Conservative policy, and is attached to the principles of the Church of England',[93] and the penny *Blue Budget. A Weekly Conservative Newspaper* founded in December 1868, reported Conservative meetings, speeches, demonstrations, dinners and other activities across the UK, launching in particular an attack on Bradlaugh's 'atheism'.[94] The Anglican press also made its contribution to the cause of Conservatism, the *National Church,* for example, increased its circulation from under 4,000 to over 12,000 in the course of 1872, 'thus justifying the large and heavily subsidized print-runs of the earlier part

---

[89] *The British Lion*, 29 June 1867 (first issue).

[90] *Minutes*, ABCP, 1867, p. 88.

[91] Stephen F. Koss, *The Rise and Fall of the Political Press in Britain*, vol.1 (1981), p. 184.

[92] C. Mitchell, *Newspaper Press Directory*, 1866, p. 59.

[93] Ibid., p. 66.

[94] *Blue Budget*, 12 Dec. 1868. See also *The Conservative*, Oct. 1872, the first issue of which led with a definition of 'the Conservative creed'.

of that year'.[95] In 1870, Alexander Andrews noted that, despite the fact that 'the Conservative body for years persistently ignored the rising power of the Fourth Estate' it was probable that, in opposition, party leaders had 'at last discovered the full value of a cheap and popular Press'.[96] Their return to office in 1874 led to fewer new papers being started by Conservative enthusiasts, although the Conservative Newspaper Union continued to encourage and advise existing Conservative newspapers by producing for them a regular bulletin, the *Editor's Handysheet*.[97] According to Dr. A.J. Lee's calculation, only seven Conservative newspaper companies were founded in the decade beginning in 1870, whereas 19 were established in the course of the following decade.[98] At the constituency level, however, the discussion about the relationship between the newspaper press and the political fortunes of the Tory party continued unabated.

The search for the most efficient means of 'counteracting revolutionary opinions, and of inculcating an honest and manly political policy' remained a priority for Conservative workers on the ground.[99] Plans were laid by the Bradford Conservative Association in December 1870, for example, to establish a Conservative newspaper in the town, and agents were appointed in each ward in the borough to offer shares in the venture,[100] 3,718 of which had been applied for by the end of June of the following year.[101] A newspaper committee was then established to arrange premises, to appoint an editor and a manager and to set their salaries.[102] In December 1871, it was reported 'with satisfaction' that a Conservative newspaper had been launched,[103] and only two years later the *Bradford Chronicle*, a new morning newspaper, had joined the *Evening Mail* in the promulgation of 'the principles of the Association in the borough'.[104] Partly as a consequence of such local successes, calls for

---

[95] M.J.D. Roberts, 'Pressure Group Politics and the Church of England: the Church Defence Institution 1859–1896', *Journal of Ecclesiastical History*, vol. 35, no. 4, Oct. 1984, p. 571.

[96] *Newspapers Press*, 1 Feb. 1870.

[97] Koss, *The Rise and Fall*, vol. 1, p. 207. Such manuals may be compared to other kinds of primers, such as John Morley's *English Men of Letters*, which were 'works to empower a specific strategy for reading fiction, one formulated by a new class of professionals', John L. Kijinski, 'John Morley's "English Men of Letters" Series and the Politics of Reading', *Victorian Studies*, Winter, 1991, p. 205.

[98] Lee, *Origins*, p. 152.

[99] *Minutes*, ABCP, 1872, p. 7.

[100] Minute book, Bradford Conservative Association, West Yorkshire Archive Service, Bradford, (WYAS), 36D78/1, 12 Dec. 1870.

[101] Ibid., 26 June 1871.

[102] Ibid., 10 July 1871.

[103] Ibid., 18, Dec. 1871.

[104] Ibid., 14 Jan. 1873. The Bradford Conservative Association, founded in 1869,

a more efficient Conservative press were in 1874 again being heard from the floor of the annual conference of the Conservative Associations. The *Sun*, published 'under the auspices of some prominent members of the party in and out of Parliament, with the object of disseminating Conservative principles among the rural population', was commended to those present as a venture worthy of their support.[105] During the previous general election, the *Sun* had been enlarged and turned into a daily in order to keep the canvassers and candidates informed of the 'current points of controversy', and copies were sent to the offices of every local Conservative party engaged in a contested election, 'together with supplies of placards, posters, and pamphlets, treating on the political questions at issue'.[106] No doubt the party machine could swing impressively into action during elections, but Conservative activists were demanding something more consistent, an ideological offensive, a party and a press on a permanent war-footing. Signals from the party leadership, however, were not encouraging, and the party's treatment of the press was cavalier, to say the least, once the emergency of election times had passed. Even in 1874, the year of Disraeli's victory over Gladstone, E.A. Fitzroy, proprietor of the Conservative *John Bull*, complained that he was receiving few official advertisements, despite being on the government's list, and in the same year George Webster protested to Gorst about 'the gross neglect and positive ill-treatment of the Conservative press by the Conservative party'.[107] Despite these tensions, the Council of the National Union could assert in 1875 that it was keenly aware of the importance of developing the Conservative press as a 'means of influencing public opinion',[108] and later in the same conference, Wollaston F. Pym proposed a toast to 'The Press' in a brief speech in which he acknowledged 'the services rendered by the Press of

---

originated as the Church Defence Association in 1859. The Bradford Conservative Association was dissolved and reformed in Nov. 1880, 'so as to have the Borough thoroughly organised and the Conservative interest fully attended to', by being taken over by the Bradford and County Conservative Club. It was renamed the Bradford Conservative Registration Association in Aug. 1882. The *Bradford Chronicle and Mail* collapsed in 1883. Conservative Agent John Thompson backed a new Tory newspaper, the *Daily Argus*, in 1892. By 1895, the Tories were wealthier, better organised and possessed a better press than the Liberals who had hitherto dominated the politics of the town. David James, *Bradford. Town and City Histories* (Halifax, 1990), pp. 72–74. Other studies of Bradford Conservatism include D.G. Wright, 'Politics and Opinion in Nineteenth Century Bradford 1832–80', unpublished PhD, Leeds University, 1966, 2 vols, and W.D. Ross, 'Bradford Politics 1880–1906', unpublished PhD, Bradford University, 1977.

[105] Ibid., 1874, p. 4.
[106] Ibid., 1874, p. 5.
[107] Brown, *Victorian News*, p. 56; Koss, *The Rise and Fall*, vol. 1, p. 207.
[108] *Minutes*, ABCP, 1875, p. 8.

this country to the Conservative cause'.[109] The inconsistencies between conference rhetoric and practice can in part be explained by the uncertainties felt by the party at all levels with regard to the best way of propagating Conservative ideas among the voters in the country. In this respect the 1870s were years of experimentation. Sir James Fergusson had counselled the party to wait upon the consequences of the spread of education and the 'more accurate knowledge of public events among the people'.[110] But for the less patient activists, often in marginal constituencies, a more urgent policy was required.

The most effective form of communication between party and public was the subject of much debate during the 1870s and early 1880s. Despite Disraeli's injunction of 1878 that there 'ought to be no such name as working men's clubs',[111] the trend among Conservative activists in the 1870s was precisely towards intervening in local politics by means of such clubs. Intended to be more than sick or burial associations, these clubs were to be the hub of local political education and organisation. In Bolton, for example, the Conservative Club recruited young males 'as soon as they became of age to take an interest in political matters', and held regular social gatherings at which discussions on current affairs were encouraged.[112]

But positive as the influence of the club movement was undoubtedly believed to be, it was inadequate to confront the weight of the Liberal press, whose poison needed to be drawn by other means. One 'Working Man' remarked in 1879 that most working men read the newspapers, 'though perhaps not very regularly', and were incensed by their partisan content. 'I feel indignant, terribly indignant', he protested, 'that we working men should be insulted, *grossly insulted*, in this kind of manner. We are being treated as fools'.[113] More effective than clubs in meeting this

---

[109] Ibid., p. 48.

[110] Sir James Fergusson, *The Theory and Practice of Conservatism. An Address Delivered at Glasgow, 26 January 1877*, p. 16.

[111] Ibid., p. 24.

[112] Ibid., p. 24. Patrick Joyce notes how the Tories' 'great command of "geniality and bonhomie" struck a dominant chord in working-class life' in the north-west of England, where the integration of workers into Conservatism by way of the clubs brought political successes to the Conservative party from the 1860s, Patrick Joyce, *Work, Society and Politics. The Culture of the Factory in Late Victorian England* (1980), p. 286. Clubs were also the focus of political training and electioneering. At the 1880 conference, Earl Percy admired the 'arrangements of the Birmingham Radicals who had made a point for many years of training a number of men to election work, and of giving them experience by employing them in municipal contests', *Minutes*, ABCP, 1880, pp. 9, 10; Randolph Churchill shared the view that the National Union ought to be modelled on the Birmingham Caucus, R.E. Quinault, 'Lord Randolph Churchill and Tory Democracy 1880–1885', *Historical Journal*, vol. 22, no. 1, 1979, p. 160.

[113] A Working Man, *Who Are Insulting the Working Classes?*, National Union of Conservative Associations, 1879, p. 2.

challenge was the publication of pamphlets and leaflets, which figured increasingly prominently in the work of the National Union from 1867. Numbers of pamphlets and leaflets published reached their peaks in election years, but the secular trend was dramatically upwards, from 42,000 in 1872, to 387,000 a decade later, and leaping to 12 million in 1892.[114] The use of pamphlets, many distributed free by the National Union through the local associations (in 1873, 49,000 of a total of 86,500 publications were distributed *gratis* in this manner) was further encouraged by activists at the 1880 conference, many expressing the view that their availability to counter the propaganda of the better organised Liberal newspapers had proved decisive in a number of constituencies in the 1880 general election.[115] A third means of continuing the propaganda war was by means of lectures, which were, some believed, more valuable than newspaper articles 'as a means of imparting sound political information'.[116] The defeat of the Conservatives in Bristol was attributed to their failure to make sufficient use of the platform, and though there was general disagreement as to whether speakers should be national or local figures, in 1880 there was a degree of consensus that the public theatre of the political platform was still the most powerful form of electioneering. 'The power of the tongue', one conference representative argued, 'had completely eclipsed the power of the press within the last four or five years'.[117] However, while some continued to play down the 'utterances of a *high-toned Press*' in favour of the 'free exercise of the prerogative offered in the *Public Meeting*',[118] others took a more sophisticated view of the interrelationship between platform and press. Writing in the Conservative weekly, *England*, in November 1880, 'An Aggressive Conservative' was strongly in favour of 'good speeches', but insisted also that the press, 'especially the provincial Conservative Press' should both report these speeches widely and, more generally, 'aid the cause . . . by putting before Conservatives their proper course of action, as each fresh question presents itself, and by meeting the misrepresentations of the Radicals with denial, and their persistent misleading statements with concise and accurate facts'.[119] It was clear that, if the party was seriously

---

[114] *Minutes*, ABCP, 1872, 1882, 1892. The increase is substantial, though it should be placed in its proper perspective. Whereas grants amounting to £21 were awarded for the publication of pamphlets in 1879–80, conference and banquet expenses totalled £137.9s.0d, *Minutes*, ABCP, 1880, p. 6.

[115] Ibid., 1880, p. 10.

[116] Ibid., p. 22.

[117] Ibid., pp. 23–26.

[118] *England*, 6 Nov. 1880.

[119] Ibid., 13 Nov. 1880.

contemplating meeting 'the enemy with their own weapons',[120] then, whatever else might be done, the question of how best to reorganise the Conservative press could no longer be avoided.

If the objective of propaganda was to place arguments and knowledge in the hands of the voters newly enfranchised in 1867 and 1884–85, clubs, pamphlets and lectures by themselves were insufficient. Calls were again heard for the party to produce at least one national weekly paper as a means of counteracting the influence of such popular weekly newspapers as *Lloyd's* and *Reynolds's*. *England*, it was argued, had provided the model, in terms of format and content, but the party needed to be much more directly involved in the production of such newspapers.[121] One year later, the *People* was added to the Conservative list, introduced in order to challenge the Liberal monopoly of the popular Sunday press.[122] The party, however, remained evasive. Earl Percy ritually genuflected to the 'influence of the daily and weekly papers', and acknowledged that the Conservative papers were 'doing very good work', but as far as party support was concerned, he was confident that there was 'plenty of Conservative feeling in the country to support all these papers'.[123] Developments in the early 1880s, however, accelerated the pace of the discussion. Broadly, there were two contexts to this renewed activity by the party rank and file. The first, and the most important, was the extension of the franchise in 1884, and the second, closely related to it, was the reorganisation of the NUCA. As early as 1881 a delegate from Carlisle had warned the conference of the urgent need to prepare for the 'lowering of the Franchise'.[124] Three years later, the 1884 Reform Act created some 2.5 million new voters at a time of agricultural depression whilst the 'politics of deference' was further undermined by the consequences of the 1883 Illegal Practices Act and the redistribution of seats in 1885. The political complexion of the countryside, the traditional Conservative heartland, could no longer be taken for granted. Conservative governments were to offer a partial solution to this awkward problem by calling general elections at harvest times to discourage agricultural labourers from voting,[125] but it was

---

[120] *Minutes*, ABCP, 1880, p. 27.

[121] Ibid., pp. 20, 21. *England* was established in 1880 to counter the 'Raving of the Radical Press', adding that 'a study of the organs of the party in power is both amusing and instructive', *England*, 25 Sept. 1880. It was published by Ashmead Bartlett from Mar. 1881 to May 1898. On another front, the Patriotic Association was also at this time 'keeping public opinion informed and on the alert upon questions of foreign policy', *England*, 6 Nov. 1880.

[122] *Minutes*, ABCP, 1881, pp. 7–8.

[123] Ibid., p. 11.

[124] Ibid., p. 16.

[125] 'This strategy was employed at every general election from 1886 until 1906 when the

essential also not only to persuade the rural labourers, when they did cast their votes, to do so for Conservative candidates but, perhaps more importantly, to embrace Conservative values in general. But aside from the important question of the rural constituencies, the redistribution of seats in 1885 marked the beginning of the party's dominance over the boroughs, where half its parliamentary strength now lay, and provided the basis for its power as a governing party, with one brief Gladstonian interlude, for the next 20 years. The second context was the changing relationship between the NUCA and the central party machine. Randolph Churchill, as Chair of the NUCA in 1884, insisted, with Salisbury, that the National Union should act only as an advisory body to the party, and should remain the focus of local, not national, activity. Among its newly formulated six functions was 'the improvement and development of the local press', and emphatically did not include the conduct of elections, nor the selection of candidates. Propaganda in the constituencies thus became a key function of the NUCA.[126] Faced by these twin challenges, party activists began to demand a campaign of 'Political Evangelisation'.[127] The looming problem of the agricultural workers was evident as early as 1882, when attacks on Joseph Arch's National Agricultural Labourer's Union were intensified, and measures were taken to ensure that copies of sympathetic newspapers, including *England*, were distributed by local party activists to all public houses, reading rooms and coffee houses in such areas as south Warwickshire, where the union was strong.[128] At this moment of crisis for the Conservative rank and file, the question of the press as a means of propagating Conservative ideas and of affecting voting behaviour was once again raised, within and outside the NUCA.

The moving spirit behind the discussions of 1884 and 1885 was H. Byron Reed, the 'progressive' Unionist member for Bradford East, and a director of the Northern Counties Constitutional Newspaper Company, which published the Darlington newspapers, the *North Star* and the *Northern Standard*.[129] Fearing that the party would 'lag behind in the race', a resolution, moved in Reed's absence by T.S. Hudson of West Hartlepool, at the Sheffield conference of the National Union in July

---

Liberals called a January election', E.H.H. Green, 'Radical Conservatism: the Electoral Genesis of Tariff Reform', *Historical Journal*, vol. 28, no. 3, 1985, pp. 674–78.

[126] *Minutes*, ABCP, 1884, pp. 12, 13.

[127] Ibid., 1882, p. 16.

[128] Ibid., p. 19. The paper was also distributed further afield. In Oct, 1883 it was recorded that 'Mr Glossop read the report of the delegates to the Birmingham Conference and 150 copies of "England" were distributed among the delegates', Minute book, Bradford Conservative Association, 8 Oct. 1883, WYAS 36D78/2.

[129] Lee, *Origins*, p. 155.

1884, called for an internal committee of enquiry to be set up to investigate the condition of the Conservative newspapers in Britain. The frustrations of the local activists were forcefully brought into the open during the debate on the press in 1884. Angered by the contempt shown by the party leaders towards the issue, and infuriated by the success of the Liberal press, a speaker from Barrow-in-Furness told of the immense difficulties faced by Conservatives canvassing in a town which had four newspapers, every one of them of Radical persuasion.[130] Commenting sympathetically on Reed's resolution of 1884, Sir Algernon Borthwick, (Baron Glenesk, 1830–1908), proprietor of the Conservative *Morning Post*, argued in the pages of the *National Review* that the local newspaper was the most effective means of influencing the convictions of those working men who could not adequately be reached by pamphlets or public meetings. Even if working men did not at first read the leading articles, Borthwick surmised,

> if the paper in other respects satisfies their wants, they will do so in the end; and if the argument is plainly and clearly put, a great number of them will become convinced, not, perhaps, that the Conservative cause is the absolutely right one, but that much of what they have heard from their Radical friends and associates is untrue.[131]

The format of the explicitly partisan Conservative newspaper thus required some amendment. Specifically, less emphasis ought to be placed on Conservative meetings and speeches, and more stress laid on lively news stories that would give 'equal space to Gladstone and Northcote'. A readership could only be attracted if the press provided a good news service. Once that had been achieved, the influence of the paper in promoting Conservative views would 'follow in due time, as a matter of course'.[132] The one danger with this tactic was that the Conservative press would begin to resemble the host of neutral or independent newspapers whose value to the party was alleged to be minimal, to say the least.

---

[130] *Minutes*, ABCP, 1884, p. 118. The 1884 resolution read as follows: 'That the condition of the Constitutional newspaper press throughout England calls for the immediate and serious consideration of the Conservative Party; and this Conference directs the Council to appoint a Committee to obtain the necessary information to be laid before its recognised heads and officials, with a view to active steps being taken to remedy such evils and supply such deficiency as may be proved to exist', Sir Algernon Borthwick, 'The Conservative Provincial Press', *National Review*, July 1885, p. 634. Borthwick, Conservative MP for South Kensington from 1885, claimed that the idea of the Primrose League originated in his newspaper, see R. Lucas, *Lord Glenesk and the 'Morning Post'* (1910), *passim*.

[131] Borthwick, 'Conservative Provincial Press', p. 635.

[132] Ibid., p. 643.

Though Reed's resolution was unanimously carried in 1884, little if anything was done by the Council during the ensuing year. Opening the 1885 session, Lord Claude Hamilton MP nervously acknowledged from the chair that the condition of the Conservative press was the 'one great weakness in our organization',[133] but warned the conference of the danger of being overtly critical of the press in an election year and thereby running the risk of losing what newspaper support they did enjoy. Reed would have none if it. He bluntly reminded the conference of the extent of the political and cultural changes that had occurred in recent years, pointing out in particular the consequences of educational legislation which, he deduced, had 'largely added to the newspaper reading public'. This new reading public, he insisted, would not be attracted by the older literary forms, such as essays, reviews or pamphlets, but instead demanded news and newspapers. Again the argument was made that the existing Conservative press was too explicitly political to convince new voters of the validity of the Conservative message. A different strategy was once more demanded, an editorial policy led by news rather than heavy-handed political sermons. Reed's advice to give readers the news first, and political opinion later, was clearly meant as a criticism of existing efforts. In contrast, the Liberal newspapers were impregnating with radical ideas 'the rising generation of another decade who will be the thinkers, the voters of this country'.[134] The inferiority of the Conservative press, Reed inferred, was in the first place a consequence of ignorance of the true state of the political press, and he once more called for an internal commission of enquiry. Secondly, the party leadership underrated and 'despised' the very journalists on whom they depended to carry the party message to the constituencies. A cultural change was required at the highest levels of the party, and a new policy adopted which would encourage and nurture those writers in the popular newspapers who chose to support the Conservatives. Finally, since the two great press agencies were 'poisoned at their source by Radical hands',[135] the party ought, as a matter of urgency, to establish its own news agency. Reed, in effect was calling for a new and comprehensive press policy to be approved by the party and, more importantly, to be put into practice. Not for the first time, the attempt failed. Despite acknowledging 'the supreme importance of the press as a means of influencing public opinion',[136] other representatives were outraged by Reed's criticisms of

---

[133] *Minutes*, ABCP, 1885, p. 9.
[134] Ibid., p. 30.
[135] Ibid., p. 42.
[136] Ibid., p 43.

the existing Conservative newspapers and denied emphatically that they were 'in the slightest degree inferior to the press of any other party'.[137] Once again, it is likely that the issue was fudged. In any case, according to the extant documentation,[138] the committee of enquiry did not complete its report.

The debate on the press in 1884 and 1885, however, throws an intriguing light on both the organisation and the psychology of the party on the eve of the twin political crises of the Third Reform Bill and the Unionist schism within the Liberal Party. At one level, as Dr Lee points out, the debate may be interpreted as a rank-and-file revolt, a means of launching an attack on the style and the values of the Conservative leadership. At another level, the press as an issue provided a language and a mental framework within which party activists could express their satisfaction or, more usually, their dismay, in the aftermath of elections.[139] In 1889, the Liberal victory in November 1885 was blamed by the conference chairman on the party's failure adequately to 'confront a vast mass of uninformed voters and misguided opinion which had never been properly instructed in Conservative policy',[140] despite the publication of 12 million pamphlets and flysheets by the National Union in the course of the year. Sir Albert Rollit agreed that the defeat was the result of 'the inadequate expression of Conservative views through the Press', and cited as an example two seats that had been won for the party in 1886 'solely owing to the existence' of a Conservative newspaper established the previous year. 'You should all acknowledge the power of the Press' he proclaimed, and exhorted all Conservatives to support 'in every way possible' the owners and editors of sympathetic newspapers 'as a matter of party duty'.[141] For Sir Albert, such solicitude towards the press began at home, and at his suggestion reporters were allowed for the first time to attend all 'open' sessions of the conference.[142]

By 1887 it was becoming clear that the condition of the Conservative press was improving, though ironically this was not achieved as a result

---

[137] Ibid., p. 48.

[138] Minutes of the 1888 and 1889 sessions of the NUCA are unavailable, presumed destroyed.

[139] Lee, *Origins*, p. 156.

[140] *Minutes*, ABCP, 1886, p. 3.

[141] Ibid., pp. 12–13.

[142] Ibid., p.22. The admission of press reporters to the conference had been a matter of debate for some time. In 1882, a move to admit reporters failed to secure a seconder, ibid., 1882, p. 13. In 1885, the privacy of the conference was again deemed to be in the best interests of free discussion. Summaries of sessions were drafted by NUCA minute-takers, approved by the conference and delivered to the press 'as an official report for publication'. Lascelles Carr, editor of the Cardiff *Western Mail*, was given special dispensation to remain as he 'was not there as a representative of the press', ibid., 1885, p. 19.

of the efforts made by the Conservatives themselves. Indeed, the establishment of the Primrose League Printing and Publishing Company in 1887, and the publication of the *Primrose Gazette*, which benefited from a steady supply of news items from the party leadership, only intensified the competition among the Conservative papers.[143] The boost to the party's representation in the press came rather from the Unionist defectors from the Liberals,[144] and the fresh appeals that the Conservatives could now make to the patriotism of the Liberal working class. S.S. Phillips of Uxbridge, seconding Dixon Heartland's call to reinstate Byron Reed's Press Committee, however, warned the party that though the dailies were now predominantly Unionist, it was the weekly newspapers that would bring the richest rewards. The poor had neither the time to read nor the money to buy daily newspapers, but a weekly paper, he argued, would not only be read but kept, re-read and thought about for a whole week.[145] Heartland also made explicit the preferred nature of the relationship between party and press, in which the emphasis was placed not on ownership but on news management. While Conservatives should continue to advertise and buy shares in newspaper publishing companies, and otherwise help to increase their circulations, they should also, crucially, provide news stories and write letters and articles on a regular basis. Writing for the local press should no longer be regarded as a shameful activity shrouded by anonymity, but a public and political duty.[146]

By the early 1890s the Conservative party publicity machine was in markedly better shape. A National Conservative League, aimed at 'getting the working classes together' along the lines of the Friendly Societies had been established by 1890, along with such regional organisations as the British League in the North of England.[147] Local organisations of this kind were instrumental in ensuring that Conservative-supporting newspapers were being distributed in all areas. An activists' handbook of 1894 advised that should trustworthy local newspapers not be available in a constituency, London papers such as

---

[143] See Lee, *Origins*, p. 157; Koss, *The Rise and Fall*, vol. 1, p. 249.

[144] Koss, *The Rise and Fall*, vol. 1, p. 287.

[145] *Minutes*, ABCP, 1887, p. 178.

[146] The shift in attitudes itself raised the status of the press, and Conservatives were aware of the propensity of Liberal intellectuals to conduct arguments in the public domain through the 'lower journalism' of the weeklies and dailies. J.S. Mill, for example, published 430 pieces in newspapers, Stefan Collini, *Public Moralists. Political Thought and Intellectual Life in Britain 1850–1930* (Oxford, 1991), pp. 31, 228. For Mill's newspaper writings, see Anne P. and John M. Robson (eds), *John Stuart Mill, Newspaper Writings*, 4 vols (University of Toronto Press, 1986).

[147] *Minutes*, ABCP, 1890, p. 221.

England or the *People* should be introduced, and news clubs opened where a range of Conservative newspapers might be obtained.[148] A renewed emphasis was placed on newspapers as the most effective means of communicating Conservative values, and in 1891 James Rankin MP suggested that material previously circulated in leaflets and pamphlets should instead be carried by the local Conservative newspaper press, where it would reach a far wider readership.[149] Moreover, the need to 'compete week by week and month by month with the Radicals in the press'[150] had led by 1892 to 'political warfare' in which the 'nonsense' and 'cock-and-bull stories' of the Gladstonians were being far more systematically countered.[151]

The continuing vigour of the Liberal newspapers, and the aggressive response of certain Conservative activists and MPs, had, to some extent, overcome the inertia of the party leadership with regard to the formulation of an effective publicity strategy based on the cheap press. The 'moral strategy' of regaining the Conservative ascendancy in the press was, by the 1890s, approaching its completion. Liberal Unionist journalists had undoubtedly brought with them into the Conservative fold both the necessary experience and confidence to enable the party once more to take the initiative, but the arguments within the party over the years had also had their effect. Following in the footsteps of, among others, Alison in 1834, Gleig in 1867 and Reed in 1884–85, Henry Cust, who was both a Conservative politician and a newspaper editor, concluded in 1893 that subtlety was the key to successful political journalism. Persuasion was at its most effective when imperceptible, and the political demands of elections were minor compared with the proper purpose of the Tory press, the construction of a Conservative world-view, a Tory morality. The party press, he argued, 'must be Tory not alone by virtue of its polemics. It must be Tory because it teaches Toryism quietly, consistently, unobtrusively, by its method of presenting the reader with matter written to suit his powers and taste from the Tory point of view'. Above all, the political intent should be concealed, and

---

[148] Conservative Central Office, '*Hints for Conservative Workers (Boroughs)*', March 1894, pp. 1–2.

[149] *Minutes*, ABCP, 1891, p. 14.

[150] Ibid., 1890, p. 113.

[151] Ibid., 1892, p. 2. See for example, Conservative Central Office pamphlet, *The Government and 'The Times'*, Apr. 1889, ABCP Series 1, Pamphlets and Leaflets Part 1, 1868–1901, Harvester Microfiche, 1889/62 (henceforth ABCP Pamphlets); Conservative Publications Department, *A Radical Paper's Account of the Great Ulster Demonstration against Home Rule*, May 1892, ABCP Pamphlets, 1892/111; '*Ten Tongues' but One Tune. The Pall Mall Gazette on Mr Gladstone and the Newcastle Programme*, ABCP Pamphlets, 1892/92; *Another Cock and Bull Story. How Gladstonian Orators Try to Befool Their Audiences*, ABCP Pamphlets, 1892/82.

'the reader must never be allowed to get it into his head for a moment that a sort of apostle is preaching at him'.[152] For Cust, the lessons of the New Journalism were clear enough. Nevertheless, newspapers had for the whole of the nineteenth century presented the Conservatives with an awkward difficulty. Whilst the Marquess of Granby could confidently announce in 1895 that 'nowadays the Electorate can only to a very large extent be educated by means of the Press',[153] it was far from clear, even at this late stage, whether others in his party agreed that this was an appropriate way for Conservatives to conduct themselves politically. Residual sympathy remained for the view expressed by W.B. Yeats that the 'love of print and paper' was perverse and exaggerated, at odds with a more organic and communal society, and representative of a culture of modernity which he and they rejected.[154]

---

[152] H. Cust, 'Tory Press and Tory Party', *National Review*, May 1893, p. 367. Eighty-five years later, Stuart Holland agreed that 'the dominance of a particular ideology does not have to be explicit', Stuart Holland, 'Countervailing Press Power', in James Curran (ed.), *The British Press: a Manifesto* (1978), p. 95.

[153] *Minutes*, ABCP, 1895, p. 23.

[154] Linda Dowling, *Language and Decadence in the Victorian Fin de Siècle* (Princeton, 1989), p. 277. The 'commodification dilemma' identified by Searle distressed both Conservatives and Liberals, for whom the production of news and opinion as commodities clashed with their intention to provide 'honest', propagandist journalism of enduring political and social value, G.R. Searle, *Entrepreneurial Politics in Mid-Victorian Britain* (Oxford, 1993), pp. 300–01.

CHAPTER SEVEN

Journalism and public discussion

The newspaper is the only efficient means of diffucing [*sic*] political information. The regularity of its publication allows it to handle every topic of present importance, the various nature of its contents adopts it to all readers, and the style and brevity of its disquisitions will often command the attention of those who have not leisure for the continuous reading of a regular treatise. . . . To furnish from time to time materials which shall aid all inquiring persons in the formation of their opinions or important political questions, is one of the most useful services that the editor of a newspaper can render.

Quoted from the *Sheffield Times* in *The Typographical Gazette*, 1 May 1846, p. 29.

The present glory, – the present social, moral, political and educational superiority of England in the great family of nations, is, in a vast measure, owing to her free, untrammelled, outspoken, and patriotic newspaper press.

W.S. Robinson, 'The Press: Its Achievements and Influence', Address to the Liverpool Chatham Society, 23 Dec. 1858, Liverpool RO 374 Cha/8/2.

The belief in the power of newspapers to influence society was taken to be axiomatic among nineteenth-century journalists, authors, printers, and other stakeholders in the newspaper business. Whether journalism corrupted or empowered readers, politically and morally, rather depended upon circumstances, but virtually all those who were engaged in the writing, production and distribution of newspapers colluded in shoring up the view that their commodity was in one way or another a socially powerful agency. That these assumptions were shared by advertisers increasingly became an essential precondition for the survival and growth of the industry, and were, as has been shown, both implied in the content and style of the newspaper, and reflected upon more explicitly by journalists and others in a wide variety of other formats. The object of this influence, as expressed in these reflections on the power of newspapers, was the reader. This reader, however, was not a socially situated human being. He, and less frequently she, was an idea implanted in the writer's mind and implied by the text's mode of address. Journalists who targeted short, accessible articles at those 'who have not leisure for the continuous reading of a regular treatise' were in actuality targeting an imagined type of a working or lower-middle class reader-in-a-hurry. Some even explicitly addressed the illiterate consumer, presumably in the expectation that the text would be read out to them. Joseph Livesey, for example, opened an article aimed at 'females employed in factories' by confessing that he realised that hardly any of them could read. Linking illiteracy with uncivil tongues, he then went on to rebuke factory women for being 'addicted to *swearing, damning,* and indulging in *obscene* expressions'.[1] Those men and women who actually read newspapers, or listened to newspapers being read to them, in their homes, or in public houses, reading rooms or train carriages, were rarely if ever consulted. Market research by means of interviews and questionnaires are a more recent feature of commodity marketing, and the dearth of documented evidence relating to the responses of readers as consumers to the newspapers which they read renders historical enquiry in this area at best partial and at worst purely speculative. With these limitations of the evidence very firmly in mind, this final chapter considers the changing patterns of newspaper reading in nineteenth-century England, and the shifting attitudes of readers to the contents and general functions of the newspaper press. It argues that, in addition to the 'formal' discourses of the law, journals, memoirs and so forth, which were drawn upon in the preceding chapters, there existed a lively 'informal' and largely oral tradition of criticism of newspaper journalism and of reflection on its role in a changing society.

Newspaper reading

'The right use of time', Thomas Cooper dourly advised young working-class men in 1855, 'is to get knowledge'.[2] But knowledge, as we have seen, was not an unproblematic category. It had been observed in 1822 that a more widespread public taste for reading had been accompanied by 'a growing disrelish, if not antipathy, for metaphysical analysis and elaborate disquisition'. In their place, the public demanded biography and narrative, inferior types of text which created 'a superficial standard of self-improvement, equally unfavourable to erudition, originality, and a sound judgement'.[3] In the same year, another critic was forced to accept

---

[1] *Moral Reformer*, 1 Feb. 1832, pp. 42–43.

[2] Thomas Cooper, 'Letters to the Young Men of the Working Classes', *Northern Tribune*, 3 Mar. 1855, p. 55. For accounts of literacy in nineteenth-century England, see David Vincent, *Literacy and Popular Culture. England 1750–1914* (Cambridge, 1989), R.D. Altick, *The English Common Reader* (Chicago, 1957), and A. Ellegard, *The Readership of the Periodical Press in Mid-Victorian England* (Goteborg, 1957).

[3] Thomas Finch, *Elements of Self-Improvement, Composing a Familiar View of the*

not only that a public taste for reading had been formed, but that the process was an irreversible one. The only thing that could be done to combat the social consequences of popular reading was to 'employ caution in providing, as far as is within the power of individual exertions, that mischief should not arise to principle from the gratification thus allowed to imagination'.[4] But the control of what some exasperated contemporaries described as a '*mass* of printed matter', much of which was feared to be 'false, trifling or absurd, so much that is not worth telling at all . . . or wearisome or disgusting by the method and style in which it is treated', was to be complicated by the increasingly 'mass' character of the readership itself.[5] In the last decade of the nineteenth century, when both printed matter and its readership vastly had been expanded, Sir Walter Besant identified the demands of the 'the great bulk and mass of the nation' as being, in order of priority, politics, local news and fiction.[6] Newspapers, which he described as the private libraries of the poor, supplied all three regularly, cheaply and in copious quantities. This is not to say that newspaper editors targeted their imagined readers in a socially undifferentiated way. On the contrary, as newspaper advertisements and opening addresses reveal, editors defined their consumers in class, and sometimes even in narrowly occupational, terms.[7] By the end of the century, however, 'narrowcasting', or niche marketing, were increasingly regarded as means of identifying specialist spaces left uncovered by the otherwise totalising presence of the New Journalism dailies, rather than as moral correctives to the insidiously 'mass' forms of print. The nature of the relationship between the extension of public knowledge, 'mass' newspaper reading and social harmony (or disharmony) thus rested as much on the response of the reader as on the content of the newspapers themselves. If the excesses of the latter could be constrained only within the parameters set by the libel laws and the structure of the market, then it followed that inappropriate

---

Intellectual Powers and Moral Characteristics of Human Nature: Principally Adopted for Young Persons Entering into Active Life', (1822), p. 3.

[4] A review of *Influence: a Moral Tale, for Young People* by 'A Lady', (2 vols, 1822) in *The Monthly Censor or, General Review of Domestic and Foreign Literature*, June–Nov. 1822, vol. i, pp. 462–63.

[5] Eliza R. Walker, 'County Reading Societies', *New Monthly Magazine*, Mar. 1828, p. 216.

[6] *Journalist and Newspaper Proprietor*, 14 Sept. 1895, p. 299.

[7] This was particularly true of craft newspapers. *The Industrial Partnerships' Record*, *Specimen Number* of Apr. 1867 explained that 'Between the *Record* and [the much older] *Co-operator* there is no rivalry – no antagonism – no relations but the most friendly. Each has its distinct and independent sphere specially defined. The *Co-operator* appeals more particularly to the intelligent working classes; – we appeal to the middle and upper, and commercial classes generally'.

'readings' of their content might be averted if influence could be brought to bear on the intellectual context and the physical environment in which the act of newspaper reading occurred.

One means of helping readers understand what they read, and of guiding their attention to those titles and sections of titles that were deemed to be of greatest utility to them, were the newspaper companions. Charles Knight of the SDUK was among the first to issue such guides to newspaper reading with his *Companion to the Newspaper, and Journal of Facts in Politics, Statistics, and Public Economy*, published monthly from 1833 to 1836.[8] Others followed, including Francis Lathom's *Read and Reflect. The Newspaper and General Reader's Pocket Companion* of 1855, which coincided with an increase in such self-improving literature as *Live and Learn: a Guide for All Who Wish to Speak and Write Correctly*, which went through 11 editions between 1855 and 1868. Some 20 years later, Henry Axon, proprietor of the *Bolton Express* issued *The Newspaper Readers' Index of Reference* which enabled readers to assemble their own catalogue of useful articles in daily and weekly newspapers, and thus to think of the 'better' newspapers as permanent and valued records rather than as throwaway ephemera. But the influence of such external material on popular newspaper reading habits were doomed to be at best marginal. Reading rooms were of far greater significance, at least until the habit of individual newspaper purchase for private reading became virtually universal with the coming of the morning and evening halfpenny papers in the 1890s. Many reading rooms had their origins in local discussion societies, whose objectives, such as those of the Literary and Philosophical Society of Preston, founded in 1811, were 'to acquire a knowledge of the properties of matter, and the mechanisms of mind, of the constitution of civil society, and the scheme of moral obligation'. Making knowledge of this nature 'useful to every description of men'[9] was also the stated aim of many newspaper editors, and it is hardly surprising to find that such societies began to adopt the practice of reading and discussing newspapers as a key aspect of their activity. But the consequence of including such naturally disputatious organs as newspapers into club life were not always harmonious, and conflicts over the appropriateness or otherwise of purchasing individual titles often broke out among the members. The Bristol Institution for the Advancement of Science and the Arts, which had argued rancorously

---

[8] Initially a segment of Knight's *Printing Machine*, it was conducted separately by the SDUK from Aug. 1834.

[9] 'President's Opening Address', *Transactions of the Literary and Philosophical Society of Preston*, 13 May 1811, pp. 51–52, Dr Shepherd Coll., Harris Library, Preston.

over the respective merits of the two major Paris Liberal journals, the *Journal des Debats* and the *Constitutionnel*, from 1829 until 1840, were equally sensitive to the contents of the English newspapers. Confessing to a sense of 'delicacy' in admitting *John Bull* after having formerly rejected the paper, the committee was in October 1831 of the opinion that its 'altered character' fully justified its acceptance by the institution. But a political balance among the newspapers admitted to the reading room still needed to be maintained, and as a consequence of the adoption of the *Liverpool Standard* in May 1837 it was resolved that 'a paper supporting another political party' be ordered, 'with the view of preventing unpleasant feelings being mixed up with the proposed alteration'. Distribution agencies were aware of the political senstitivities of their clients, and in order to facilitate a politically balanced selection, Clarke and Lewis, of Threadneedle Street, London, one of the principal suppliers of newspapers to reading rooms such as the one run by the Bristol institute, helpfully printed in their catalogues the titles of Conservative newspapers in blue ink and Liberal papers in red.

Table 7.1 Number of newspapers, with their political and regional distribution, available to reading rooms via the Clarke and Lewis agency, 1837

Politics	England	Ireland	Scotland	Wales	Islands	London
Lib.	121	36	29	5	11	26
Con.	85	34	21	3	6	18

Source: Bristol Institution for the Advancement of Science and the Arts. Proceedings of the Sub-committee for the Legislation of the Reading Rooms, 3 May 1837, Bristol Record Office, 32079/14.

If the reading rooms provided for their members by the comparatively wealthy social élites of Bristol stood at one end of the spectrum, less ambitious local initiatives such as that undertaken by Thomas Grundy in Redvales, Bury, stood at the other. Grundy, in the midst of the Reform crisis of 1832, had simply rented a small room, fitted only with table, stove and gas lighting, and had appealed to those who were 'wishful to learn what [was] passing in the political world, to become members'. He had soon attracted a hundred subscribers, whose donations of three-half-pence weekly enabled them collectively to buy three daily and eight weekly newspapers, including *Cobbett's Register*.[10] But the great majority of reading rooms fell into an intermediate category, many of them being administered by Mechanics' Institutes under substantial

---

[10] *Moral Reformer*, 1 Mar. 1832, p. 99.

middle-class or professional supervision. The Bradford Mechanics' Institute, for example, also established in 1832, numbered five church ministers among its 19-strong management committee, and E.C. Lister MP among its seven patrons.[11] Membership subscriptions were more than twice those of Grundy's informal arrangement in Bury, except for apprentices and youths under eighteen who were allowed to become associate members for six shillings a year. Despite the Bradford Institute's emphasis on the importance of reading, described by the Revd J. Ackworth on the occasion of laying the foundation stone of the Mechanic's Hall in Bradford in April 1839 as 'one of the most extraordinary phenomena of our age, abounding as it does in what is strange and surprising',[12] it is perhaps astonishing to learn that both fiction and newspapers were banned from the reading room until 1853,[13] a period of liberalisation which also for the first time saw the admission of women into the institute.[14]

Other Mechanics' Institutes were less reticent about the value of newspapers. The Institution established at the Black Bull Inn in Haslingden, Lancashire, in February 1846, almost immediately opened a news room which took three daily, one twice-weekly and six weekly newspapers. By April 1855 the number of titles available in the reading room had risen to 20.[15] In 1854, a boys' reading room was also opened in an effort to encourage the practice of regular newspaper and periodical reading among the under-16s.[16] Stocked with such worthy improving literature as *Cassel's Illustrated Family Paper*, the *Working Man's Friend*, the *Sunday at Home*, the *Leisure Hour*, the temperance *Alliance*, the *Band of Hope Review* and the *Commonwealth*, the venture was abandoned in May of the following year 'in consequence of the rude behaviour of the Boys'.[17] Undeterred, the Institution's president, Dr

---

[11] *Rules of the Bradford Mechanics' Institute; or, Society for the Acquisition of Useful Knowledge, Established 1832* (Bradford, 1832), WYAS Bradford 70D87/1, p. 2. See also Minute Book, Bradford Mechanics' Intitute, 10 Feb. 1832, WYAS Bradford DB 39 case 10 no.1

[12] *Laying the Foundation Stone of the Mechanics' Hall*, Bradford, 1 Apr. 1839, WYAS DB 39, case 10, no. 2.

[13] *Twenty-Third Annual Report*, Bradford Mechanics' Institute. A Newspaper Room was opened in 1854, separating newspapers and periodicals due to lack of space, WYAS DB 39, case 10, no. 3.

[14] Women numbered 43 of a total membership of 1,249 in Mar. 1854, and 64 of 1,507 in Mar. 1855, Minute book, Bradford Mechanics' Institute, WYAS DB 39, case 10, no. 3.

[15] Minute book, Haslingden Mechanics' Institution, 1 Jan. 1847 and 13 Apr. 1855, Lancashire RO, Preston, MBH/5/5.

[16] Minute book, Haslingden Young Men's Institute, 10 May 1854, Lancs. R.O., Preston, MBH/5/5.

[17] Ibid., 2 Mar. 1855 and 7 May 1855.

Binns, expressed at its New Year tea-party on 2 January 1856 his continuing faith that 'the growing literature of the times' would exert a positive, even revolutionary influence 'amongst the masses', while another speaker at the same event inferred that while by individual exertion humanity might improve 'like a snail creeping', co-operative educational and political endeavour enabled individuals to progress with 'Railway speed'.[18]

High-speed, steam-driven progress, however, required its own abundant source of power, namely knowledge in the form of news. Gathered and packaged by journalists, who potentially brought the world – locally, nationally and internationally – to the attention of each individual, news was regarded as the essential fuel which allowed the wheels of political, social and moral improvement to turn. But newspapers were not the sole conveyors of news, especially for organisations which could afford the higher costs of more immediate forms of transmission such as the telegraph. The Bristol Institution for the Advancement of Science, Literature and the Arts, established in 1824, after much discussion reluctantly decided in July 1855, on purely financial grounds, not to install an electric telegraph machine in their library.[19] This aborted attempt to circumvent newspapers by acquiring news directly from the telegraphic agencies was pursued more successfully elsewhere. In Bradford in May 1854, the management of the Mechanics' Institute resolved to invest heavily in the new technology and opened negotiations with the Electric Telegraph Company to supply 'London News' by telegraph directly to their reading room.[20] The value of the expensive telegraph machine was called into question three years later, however, when it was discovered that the editor of the *Bradford Advertiser* was secretly but routinely appropriating, without payment or acknowledgement, intelligence supplied by telegraph to the Mechanics' Institute for the exclusive use of his own newspaper.[21] The coming of cheaper newspapers following the abolition of the Stamp Duty in 1855 no doubt contributed to the greater economy of newspaper-buying as against on-line telegraphic provision, but cheaper and more abundantly available newspapers may also have played their part in the gradual decline of some reading rooms. The Bristol Institution, for example, noted with alarm in January 1859 that whereas the population of Bristol had doubled during the previous 50 years, membership of the society

---

[18] Minute book, Haslingden Mechanics' Institution, 2 Jan. 1856.

[19] Minute book, Bristol Institution for the Advancement of Science, Literature and the Arts, 6 May 1847, 10 July 1855, 6 Jan 1859, Bristol RO, 32079/14.

[20] Minute book, Bradford Mechanics' Institute. 4 May 1854.

[21] Ibid., 2 Apr. 1857.

had halved to less than 170 members.[22] New patterns of newspaper reading, where individuals increasingly bought and read their own copies of newspapers, rendered even the worthiest attempts to shape the reading habits of the public difficult if not redundant.

Reader-critics

The privatising of reading, however, did not dull the critical reflexes of readers. On the contrary, criticism of newspapers continued to sustain a lively sub-culture of letter writing, manuscript journalism, lecturing and public-house debating throughout the century. But like Yeats, who could hear the 'great song' of the nineteenth century only as the 'rattle of pebbles on the shore',[23] these less formal traces of the nineteenth-century 'long argument' about where in the culture newspapers ought to be situated are at best obscure and indistinct. The most evident source of reader response to the form and content of journalism may be found in readers' letters printed in newspapers. 'Writing to the paper' was a veritable cottage industry in nineteenth-century England, motivated in part at least by the readers' ambition to see their words and names appear in print, and correspondence columns occupied substantial proportions of newspaper space, particularly in the local press. Cheap for the editor and diverting for other readers, letters were, in the view of John Mackie, among the most socially useful sections of the newspaper, being a more accurate indication of what occupied the minds, or the passions, of different sections of the community than 'the platform speech or the public demonstration'.[24] Gilzean-Reid and Macdonell agreed, seeing in letter columns a means of publicising 'needs and grievances' that otherwise would not get a public airing, and thus expressing 'in some measure the feelings and desires of the average man'. Readers' letters were the 'very health element in the English newspaper', an essential means of 'feeling the national pulse'. The governments of those nations such as Germany, whose newspapers did not routinely carry unsolicited readers' correspondence, were deemed to suffer the longer-term consequences of disregarding the shifts in public opinion that were capable of being expressed in this way. Readers' correspondence was thus regarded not simply as an inexpensive space-

---

[22] Minute book, Bristol Institution for the Advancement of Science, Literature and the Arts, 6 Jan. 1859, Bristol RO, 32079/14.

[23] W.B. Yeats, 'The Nineteenth Century and After', *The Winding Stair and Other Poems* (1933).

[24] John B. Mackie, *Modern Journalism. A Handbook of Instruction and Counsel for the Young Journalist* (1894), p. 74.

filler conveniently provided by the passionate or the vain but, more importantly, as a form of political representation which, if not so decisive as the casting of a vote, was more sensitive and complex.[25] Political activists were well aware of the lobbying power of the carefully planted letter, and the facility with which the form could be used to fly political kites and to canvass support for candidates in elections. The following extract from a letter printed in the Wallingford weekly, the *Berks and Oxon Advertiser* of 23 August 1878, however, illustrates the difficulties involved in interpreting the intended meaning of an unsolicited 'letter to the Editor'. Note in particular the inconsistencies of spelling, and the writer's repeated apologies for his 'bad writing'.

> It is a long time ago that I have attempted to write a letter, and I am a very poor hand at it, not having any schooling, having had to go to work as soon as ever I could earn three-pence a day . . . how ham I to live and pay my way, and pay into a club to support me if I should be ill?. . . . Therefore brothers let us vote freely, fearlessly and conseanasly. . . . Please sir excuse by bad writing and spelling for since I have found out that we laborers was sold last time I do most sencerely hope and pray God that we shall do write this time, and give all our votes to Mr Walter Wren the Liberal candidate is the sincer disre of your humble sirvent AN AGRICULTURAL LABOURER.[26]

In the autumn of 1878, this letter was selected for special treatment by being extracted from the newspaper, reprinted separately, solipsisms included, and distributed as a broadside. Whether or not it had been the original intention of the author to make an explicitly propandist intervention in the lead up to an election campaign, that is precisely how this letter was used. There are other oddities present in the text. While substantial numbers of agricultural labourers in the English Midlands were members of trade unions in the mid-1870s, only 1,226 of the adult inhabitants of Wallingford were enfranchised prior to the Reform Act of 1884. Gladstone, for one, was suspicious of the letter's provenance, and expressed doubts regarding its authenticity. In comments written on the margin of the printed broadside, he pointed out the inconsistencies of the spelling and inferred that the Liberal Party was being made to appear, no doubt by its political enemies, as the party of the volatile and barely-literate poor.[27] Forgeries, precursors of the 'Zinoviev letter' of 1924, may

---

[25] Sir Hugh Gilzean-Reid and P.J. Macdonell, 'The Press', in John Samuelson (ed.), *The Civilisation of our Day. A Series of Original Essays on Some of Its More Important Phases at the Close of the Nineteenth Century, by Expert Writers* (1896), p. 285.

[26] *Berks and Oxon Advertiser*, 23 Aug. 1878. Wren narrowly won the 1880 election with 582 votes against the 541 cast for the Conservative candidate, E. Wells. The election was declared void on petition, F.W.S. Craig, *British Parliamentary Election Results, 1832–1885* (1977), p. 316.

[27] Printed letter, Gladstone Coll., Brit. Mus. Add. MS 44458 ff 128.

thus not have been uncommon features of the correspondence pages of nineteenth-century newspapers, and it is evident that readers' letters were read by contemporaries with scepticism and suspicion as well as pleasure.

However, at a time when the press was itself the subject of political debate, readers' criticism was also aimed at the content and conduct of newspapers. James Cowen, for example, urged all political reformers in 1857 to 'write . . . to your Press not to sell itself to every bidder that commands a so-called position in society'.[28] But criticism of editorial policy could take a number of forms, some of them dramatically symbolic. In February 1859 James Eadie, a representative of the Northern Reform Union in Newcastle upon Tyne, wrote privately to W.C. Marshall, proprietor of the *Northern Daily Express*, in terms not 'altogether in accordance with the etiquette of newspaper correspondence', to explain why copies of his paper had been publicly burned on the platform of a Reform meeting. Members of the Reform Union, he explained, had been offended by the 'unfairness' and generally unbecoming political conduct of Marshall's 'servant, the Editor', who had consistently refused to insert letters by local Liberals in the correspondence pages of the newspaper. 'Refused access to your columns to defend ourselves', Eadie explained by way of justification, 'we burnt your journal to mark our contempt of its one sided advocacy'.[29] Louis Blanc, the French Liberal journalist then based in London, suggested in 1867 a less violent form of redress by proposing a legal 'Right of Reply' to attacks made by newspapers on individuals.[30] He found few supporters in an industry preoccupied with its own rights freely to publish both news and comment. Deprived of the automatic right to space in the organ which had initially caused offence, some dissatisfied readers devoted entire pamphlets, published at their own expense, to the shortcomings of those titles. In 1872, for example, Francis Neale issued a 16-page attack on the *British Workman* in a pamphlet appropriately entitled *Pious Puerility*, in which a torrent of abuse portrayed the paper as

> one of those 'goody goody' publications which issue from Paternoster Row, and owes much of its circulation to pious spinsters, who divide their time and attention between pet poodles and the Lamb of God . . . Sunday school teachers . . . fanatic

---

[28] *British Slaves' Journal*, 29 Feb. 1857, p. 5.

[29] James Eadie to W.C. Marshall, 15 Feb. 1859, TWAS MF818/C515. See also the response of the Preston Trades Council to the 'villification' (sic) of the labour movement in the *Preston Herald*, minute book, Amalgamated Trades Council, 27 Jan. 1869, Lancashire RO, Preston, DDP acc 6318, pp. 4–5.

[30] *Newspaper Press*, 2 Sept. 1867, p. 188.

followers of Fiddler Joss, Methodist tub thumpers, Scripture readers, and converted blacklegs.[31]

Critical comment on the condition of journalism was also made in a variety of other contexts, including private diaries, where Edwin Waugh praised the 'excellent extracts in the <u>Examiner</u> [on] the unnatural condition of human development in our day',[32] in trade union meetings, where, in contrast, in March 1892 the Nelson and District Trades Council condemned 'emphatically . . . the stale news that appears in the "Cotton Factory Times" weekly from Briersfield',[33] and in manuscript magazines. The latter deserve far greater historical scrutiny, being local, small-scale vehicles for stimulating 'the free discussion of all questions' unhindered by the technology, or the costs, of print. Commonly associated with local improvement societies, such examples as *Once a Month. A Manuscript Magazine*, first issued by the Rusholme Road Young Men's club *circa* 1860, attempted to construct for necessarily small groups a controllable media environment, one in which the subscribers were both readers and writers.[34]

'Everybody is reading', *Blackwood's* noted in 1859, 'every class is writing. . . . An immense number of people, with little practice and no skill, are trying to compose, are ambitious to appear in print. . . . The people, in fact, are writing for themselves'.[35] But it is evident that 'the people' were, in addition to writing, also talking, listening and arguing among themselves about the contents and purposes of newspaper journalism. Sources for such public discussions are, naturally, scarce, and the breakfast-table controversies alluded to by Lord Broughton in his speech on newspapers of 1854 remain largely unrecorded.[36] But records do exist of discussions held in more organised settings, including, for example, meetings of the Royal Agricultural Society, at whose banquet in 1871 Dr Evory Kennedy JP argued that the Society 'was quite within its province to occupy itself in considering in a broad and philosophic spirit what the Press really is, and the mutual relations which should exist between it and the public'.[37] Similar discussions were held in a

---

[31] Francis Neale, *Pious Puerility* (1872); see also the rejoinder in the *British Workman*, 1 Dec. 1872

[32] Drawing on his reading of letters by 'Eclectic' in the *Examiner*, Waugh mused on how 'foolishly fashionable it is to think it impossible to be robust and hardy in body . . . and beastly in mind at the same time!', Diary of Edwin Waugh, Saturday, 19 Aug. 1848, Manchester City Library, MF 802.

[33] Minute book, Nelson and District Trades Council, 15 Mar. 1892, Lancashire RO, Preston, DDX 1628, acc 5856.

[34] *Once a Month. A Manuscript Magazine*, no. 11, Jan. 1861, p. 342, Misc 746, Manchester City Library.

[35] 'Popular Literature–the Periodical Press', *Blackwood's*, Feb. 1859, p. 188.

[36] MS of speech by Lord Broughton, 1854, Brit. Mus. Add. MS 47230, ff. 43–46.

[37] *Newspaper Press*, 1 May 1871, p. 105.

variety of forums, the most accessible to historians being literary and philosophical societies and local debating clubs. Membership of many such mutual improvement societies were deliberately kept low. Rowland Hill, originator of the postage stamp, had as a young man in Birmingham in 1816 established a Literary and Scientific Society which not once exceeded a membership of five.[38] The Leeds Conversation Club, founded in July 1849 by Edward Baines Jr and a group of his friends, also confined the membership to 12 men, who met regularly to discuss their week's reading over dinner.[39] Despite the small numbers involved, however, the minuted discussions of such groups do provide some minimal indication of trends in nineteenth-century public opinion on a wide variety of subjects. And, in any case, there prevailed among social reformers an ambition to extend such voluntary societies 'far beyond the lowest verge of the trading class into the higher divisions of the working class'.[40] By the mid-1860s, there appeared to be some evidence to suggest that this was occurring. In an intelligent evangelical study of religious scepticism in working-class culture, which involved a survey of debating societies, public discussion groups and cheap literature, James Dawson concluded that

> in many large towns mechanics and others of the working classes have of late evinced marked partialities for the profound subtleties of such writers as Paley or Butler. Among others is manifested a taste for poetry, description, narrative and argument. These are familiarizing themselves with the exhibition, the clothing, and the working out of thought, after the manner of educated minds.[41]

Until Christian preachers recognised and attuned themselves to the realities of such social trends, Dawson argued, they would fail to make any impression on their audiences, who 'in harmony with the spirit of the advancing intelligence of the times . . . [expected] to be made to think'.[42] Thus, while the numbers of individuals involved in structured and minuted discussions may have been small and self-selected, they may none the less signal significant shifts in popular mood.

Products of the eighteenth-century Enlightenment, literary and philosophical societies had been established in one form or another in

---

[38] The Society met each Sunday morning in the summer house in Hill's father's garden, and brought a quarto edition of Johnson's *Dictionary* and a subscription to the *Edinburgh Review*; George Birkbeck Hill, *The Life of Sir Rowland Hill and the History of Penny Postage* (1880), p. 68.

[39] Edwin Kitson Clark, *Conversation Club [Memoirs]* (Leeds, 1939), p. 4.

[40] Sir E. Bulwer-Lytton to Sir Edward Baines, 6 Oct. 1882, Edward F. Baines Coll., Leeds Archive Service MS 17.

[41] James Dawson, *Pulpit Power* (1865), p. 139.

[42] Ibid., p. 143.

all the major centres of population in England by the early nineteenth century. In Sheffield, the Literary and Philosophical Society hosted at least eight lectures a year, some delivered by members, others by 'eminent professors' from elsewhere. For one guinea a year, men (women were admitted as full members only in December 1868) were invited to enjoy lectures on subjects drawn 'from any branch of literature and science, excluding all discussions on politics or religion', the first, delivered to an audience of 400 on 21 February 1823, being a lecture on the history of literature.[43] Others included a lecture on the influence of fiction (6 April 1832), and papers on 'the Mind and the Senses, and their liability to Deception' (21 February 1834),[44] daguerrotype photography, with a demostration of the apparatus (4 August 1843) and early Sheffield newspapers 'with specimens exhibited' (1 June 1855).[45] Membership of these societies fluctuated widely: that of the Leeds Philosophical and Literary Society grew most rapidly in the period 1860–64, when membership increased from 260 to 650, peaked in 1875–76 with 730 members, and began to decline from the mid-1880s.[46] The Bradford Literary Club, established in February 1876 at the height of the enthusiasm in nearby Leeds for such activities, enshrined the objective of the club in its founding constitution, namely to secure 'the free interchange of ideas, chiefly on literary and philosophical topics; it being understood that every member is prepared to listen to the most outspoken expression of opinion on every subject', among which 'expressions of opinion', in October 1877, featured a defence of anonymous journalism by the proprietor of the *Bradford Observer*, William Byles.[47] The condition of journalism was also a popular subject among lecturers in a number of other local mutual improvement societies, examples of which may be found throughout the nineteenth century. In Liverpool, lectures were delivered 'on the conduct and abilities of newspapers' in 1819 and on the American press in 1822, through to discussions on 'the Fourth Estate' in 1896 and 'English Essays and Journalism' in 1902 (which complained of the 'dullness and

---

43 Minute book, General Meetings of the Sheffield Literary and Philosophical Society, Sheffield City Library 192, pp. 10–22

44 Ibid., pp. 98–111.

45 Ibid., pp. 203 and 342.

46 Edwin Kitson Clark, *History of 100 Years of Life of the Leeds Philosophical and Literary Society* (Leeds, 1924), p. 235.

47 Minute book, Bradford Literary Club, WYAS Bradford, 33D77. For William Byles, see David James, 'William Byles and the *Bradford Observer*', in D.G. Wright and J.A. Howitt, *Victorian Bradford. Essays in Honour of Jack Reynolds* (Bradford, 1982), pp. 115–36; Henry Nathaniel Byles, *William Byles: by His Youngest Son* (Weymouth, 1932); Donald M. Jones, 'The Liberal Press and the Rise of Labour: A Study With Particular Reference to Leeds and Bradford: 1850–1895', PhD, University of Leeds 1973, *passim*.

Table 7.2 Sample of motions debated at the Great George Street
Literary and Debating Society, Liverpool, 1872–79

Date	Motion	Yes	No
11.3.72	Ought Home Rule to be granted to Ireland?	4	11
25.3.72	Has the present Government [Gladstone] maintained the confidence reposed in it at the election of 1868?	11	4
18.11.72	Is Phrenology True?	5	11
10.3.73	Ought women to have equal electoral rights to men?	9	8
10.11.73	Are Trade Unions for the benefit of the community?	6	10
9.2.74	Ought a national System of Education to be Secular or Religious?	Sec. 11	Relig. 8
23.3.74	Ought Governments to purchase and work the Railways?	7	9
8.11.75	Ought capital punishment to be abolished?	15	18
6.12.75	Has novel reading an injurious tendency?	8	7
21.2.76	Is woman mentally inferior to man?	13	14
20.3.76	Ought the House of Lords to be abolished?	27	25
9.11.79	Ought the Country to support the Present Government [Disraeli]?	6	11

Source: Minutes, Great George Street Literary and Debating Society, Liverpool,
Lancashire Record Office, Preston, CULi.

want of enterprise [of] Provincial Journalism').[48] In the Colne Literary
and Scientific Society, founded in 1899, the first paper delivered was an
impassioned defence of the value of daily newspapers, which, citing as
proof the *Manchester Guardian* of that day which contained articles on
Dante and the Egyptian *Book of the Dead*, were said to contain the
finest examples of current literature.[49]

The records of debating clubs reveal, in addition to the subjects of

---

48 Index of lectures, Liverpool Literary and Philosophical Society, Liverpool RO 060
Lit/8/1, and Minute book, Liverpool Literary and Philosophical Society, 1812–23,
Liverpool RO 060 Lit/1/2 and 060 Lit/1/11.

49 Minute book, Colne Literary and Scientific Society, 16 Feb. 1899, Colne Library,
Colne, Lancashire. See also lantern lectures by C. Coates, Liverpool, on 'The Production
of a Newpspaer', with commentary on the 'revolution in type-setting since 1890' and 'the
wonderful linotype machine and the system of stereotyping', 28 Jan. 1910; and James M.
Smeeth, Manchester, on 'The Story of Printing' from the Bible to the modern newspaper,
28 Mar. 1911.

Table 7.3 Debates held on issues relating to journalism at the
Manchester Literary Society, 1829–73

Date	Motion	Yes	No
13.10.29	Is the influence of Newspapers and Reviews upon Public Opinion warranted by their merit?	1	4
13.12.36	The Newspaper Press – Will the recent reduction of Stamp Duty raise its characer?	9	2
16.1.38	Does Oratory exert a more powerful influence over Society than General Literature?	Gen.Lit. 5	Oratory 4
22.10.44	Would the immediate formation of the railways now in projection, be beneficial to the Country?	5	7
7.11.48	Is the tendency of the literature of the present day in England to elevate and enlarge the public mind?	16	2
17.3.63	Is not our Newspaper Press as at present existing more mischievous than beneficial?	5	10
29.3.63	Has Novel-writing as an Art and as an Educational influence progressed in this Country?	7	5
7.1.73	Can we affirm a principle of Mental Progression in Historic Man?	5	9

Source: Minutes, Manchester Literary Society, Manchester City Library, MS f
062 M3.

discussion, the climate of opinion among those present who voted at
the conclusion of the debate. Occasionally, the main points raised by
the proposers and opponents of motions were minuted, as were some
of the contributions made from the floor, but in general only the title
and the voting record were logged. The sample of debates (shown in
Table 7.2) held at the Great George Street Literary and Debating
Society, Liverpool, in the 1870s (it was established in 1869) provides
an impression of the range of issues which were deemed to be
sufficiently interesting and important to discuss formally.

Among the diversity of matters discussed in such debating clubs was
the power and significance of the newspaper press, usually measured
against other institutions and practices. One was the jury system, the
motion 'would the abolition of the Trial by Jury or the Liberty of the
Press be the most injurious to this Country?' being the problem discussed
by the Preston Debating Society on 22 December 1817, the members of
which sensibly resolved that, of the two, trial by jury was the most

'invaluable Priviledge' (*sic*).[50] Another relatively common device was to pit the press against the pulpit, as was done at the Great George Street debating society on 14 February 1870. Following a discussion on whether 'the Pulpit or the Press [had] done most to secure the Progress of Society', eight voted for the pulpit and ten for the newspaper press. When exactly the same debate was held nine years later, on 24 February 1879, six voted for the pulpit, and only one for the press.[51] Evidence provided by the Manchester Literary Society, however, suggests a different trajectory. Established in 1826, this was essentially a radical institution. Chaired in 1837 by Richard Cobden, the Manchester Literary Society debated and found in favour of democratic government (31 October 1837), the abolition of the death penalty (*nem con* on 11 November 1845), and the desirability of 'political action on the part of the Masses' (28 January 1868).[52] The results of its inquiries into the effects of the press on social behaviour, however, were far from clear, although a more charitable view of the standards achieved by newspapers was taken from the late 1840s.

Another debating club with radical associations, which met each Sunday evening from 1854 to 1886 at Robert Edmonds' Hope and Anchor Inn, Navigation Street, Birmingham, devoted much of its energies to reading and reflecting on the contents of newspapers.[53] At the time of its closure in January 1886, three of its most prominent members, Allan Dalzell, Mr Sketchley and Mr Lampard were happy to be described variously as Chartists and 'wild socialists' who opposed the Liberal 'dogma of Free Trade in favour of fair trade'. Political reforms, Dalzell insisted 'must be of a sweeping character and not a miserable tinkering to suit the middle class only'. The club honoured a proud history of political activism, and one of the earliest debates, held during the Crimean War, had led to a petition

---

[50] Minutes, Preston Debating Society, 22 Dec. 1817, Manchester City Library MS 374.24P1.

[51] Minutes, Great George St Literary and Debating Society, Liverpool, 14 Feb. 1870 and 24 Feb. 1879, Lancashire RO, Preston, CULi.

[52] Minutes, Manchester Literary Society, Proposed Questions vol. 7, Manchester City Library MS f 062 M3. It was also decided *inter alia* that 'the characteristics of Races' were eradicable (30 Mar. 1847), and that 'the Phenomena attributed to "Spiritualism" [were] worthy of serious investigation' (23 Dec. 1873).

[53] Separate debates were held each Sunday evening (unless adjourned) until the Franco-Prussian War of 1870–71, after which debates were extended over lengthier periods, were more directly concerned with 'events of the week', with fewer votes being taken, Minute book, the Sunday Evening Debating Society, Hope and Anchor Inn, Navigation Street, Birmingham, Archives Dept., Birmingham Library Service, MS 103138 (two vols) 3 January 1858 to 24 January 1886. (Minutes, Hope and Anchor Debating Society.) No records were located of proceedings between 1854 and 1858. See also Brian Harrison, 'Pubs', in H.J. Dyos and Michael Wolff, *The Victorian City: Images and Realities*, vol. 1, pp. 179–80.

being sent 'from the members of the Society to the Govt. that was [in] great measure the cause of the relief of our soldiers and sailors who were then suffering from the incompetence of our Generals'. Suspicious of its activities, the Birmingham police had sent spies to the meetings, and on the basis of their reports successfully prosecuted one of its speakers, George Hunter Mantle, who in consequence suffered two years of imprisonment 'for his advocacy of the people's rights'. Other visiting labour leaders had included George Odger, George Howell, and Harold Cremer. Above all, the members valued the opportunity the society had given them 'to educate each other', and one long-term member described it fondly in 1886 as 'the best Sunday School for politics that had ever been established in our town'.[54] Against this political background, the public-house debaters of the Hope and Anchor addressed a vast range of urgent contemporary issues (see Appendix). When it was proposed that 'Winter or no winter – which is the best' should be the subject of a future debate, the suggestion was brusquely dismissed for being 'a waste of time to discuss [such] a question'.[55] Debates which directly involved the scrutiny of the press included those in Table 7.4, which demonstrate a clear commitment to the view that the expansion of the press was a socially liberating process.

Table 7.4 Debates relating to journalism conducted by the Sunday Evening Debating Society, Hope and Anchor Inn, Navigation Street, Birmingham, 1859–69

Date	Motion	Yes	No
17/04/59	Has cheap Literature added to the spread of Civilization and Morality?	20	3
29/04/60	The Immorality of the Age – Would it be better kept in checque (*sic*) by Parliamentary Enactments – or by Moral suasion Example and Education?	Enact. 6	Moral 25
5/08/60	Is a Knowledge (through the association and observance of every walk in life) necessary for the development of social morality?	10	4
12/09/69	Would the establishment of a working man's newspaper in the midland counties be beneficial, and was the proposed plan to start, 'the Radical' commercially sound?	'almost unanimously' in favour	

Source: Archives Department, Birmingham Library Service, MS 103138.

---

[54] Ibid., 5 Oct. 1879, 17 Jan. 1886, 24 Jan. 1886.
[55] Ibid., 23 Sept. 1860.

Discussion of journalism by the Hope and Anchor debaters, however, was not confined to those debates most directly concerned with the newspaper press. We find, for example, criticisms of the local press for refusing to print letters sent to their editors by 'the labour party' in a debate on the condition of the Birmingham Liberal Association in January 1876.[56] But most significantly, newspapers provided the necessary information which enabled the debaters to extend the range of their subject-matter beyond the local. 'Political events of the week' was a common subject for discussion from the later 1860s, and it is evident that much of the material discussed was drawn from local and national newspapers and journals, in particular the *Birmingham Daily Post*, *The Times*, the *Spectator* and the *Daily Telegraph*. The latter was especially valuable, and controversial, in debates on foreign affairs, especially those regarding events in the Balkans in the period 1875–78. Strenuous efforts were made to discredit the 'exaggerated accounts' of the war that were printed in the *Telegraph* – 'who could believe that paper?', one speaker ruefully asked in 1877 – yet it was reluctantly acknowledged that 'the Rowdy Paper' accurately reflected 'popular feeling', in contrast to the growing unpopularity and dimunition of circulation suffered by the anti-war *Daily News*.[57] Newspapers such as these fuelled an astonishing range of debates on foreign events.

Note in Figure 7.1 how few local matters were discussed in the period 1858–62, in contrast to the time expended on international politics and domestic social policy issues. There can be little doubt that both the programme and the contents of debates in clubs such as the one that met in the upstairs room of the Hope and Anchor Inn in Birmingham were determined to a significant extent by the regular reading of the newly affordable and more news oriented journalism of the post-Stamp Act period. At the same time, the participants recognised that whatever truth there might be in the news was mediated by the politics and the personalities of journalism, and while debate informed by news journalism was a way of exploring different truths about the world, reasoned argument was also a means of talking *about* journalism, and thus of contesting in some measure the power of the press.

Evidence supplied by two other Birmingham debating societies reveal the extent to which attitudes towards the question of press power differed. The Birmingham and Edgbaston Debating Society, established in 1846, and with which the young Joseph Chamberlain was for a time associated, hosted a number of debates specifically on the influence of newspapers. The majority, as shown in Table 7.5, took a benign view of

---

[56] Ibid., 23 Jan. 1876.
[57] Ibid., 26 Sept. 1875 and 29 July 1877.

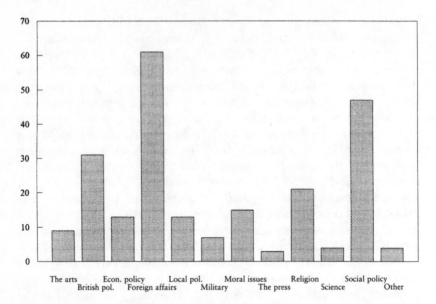

7.1 Numbers and categories of subjects debated at the Hope and Anchor Inn, Birmingham, January 1858 to December 1862.

Source: Abstracted from Minute book, the Sunday Evening Debating Society, Hope and Anchor Inn, Navigation Street, Birmingham, Archives Department, Birmingham Library Service, MS 103138.

their social role.[58]

In contrast, the Birmingham Ladies Debating Society, established by Mrs Alfred Osler in October 1881, while being of the view that socialism was 'the true remedy for existing evils', carried motions to the effect that 'the liberty of the press should be curtailed', and that 'the modern development of the English Press is undesirable'.[59] These divergent approaches raise the possibility that social attitudes towards journalism in the nineteenth century may in some respects have been gendered, and that women may have taken a more sceptical view than men of the much vaunted 'liberties' of the press. But, however tantalising, the evidence is currently too insubstantial to enable us to do more than speculate on the broader ramifications of these snapshots of opinion.

---

[58] Minute book, Birmingham and Edgbaston Debating Society, Birmingham Library Service, Local Studies and History L50.7. Records for 1859 may be found in the Joseph Chamberlain papers, Heslop Room, University of Birmingham Library. Membership in 1894 stood at 274, although attendances at debates averaged around 36, ranging from *c*.18 to *c*.50 per week.

[59] Minute book, Birmingham Ladies Debating Society, 19 Apr. 1890, Birmingham Library Service, Local Studies and History L50.7.

Table 7.5 Debates on journalism held by the Birmingham and
Edgbaston Debating Society, 1886–1903.

Date	Motion	(C)arried or (L)ost
1886	That the Liberty of the Press in England has of late been shamefully abused, and should be restricted by law	L
1889	That newspapers are a curse	L
1890	That the modern intellectual taste is degraded by the increase of ephemeral literature	C
1894	That the increase in the circulation of the modern newspapers is detrimental to literature	C
1899	That the influence of the Press at times of national crises has a tendency to evil rather than good	L
1903	That in politics, cartoons have more effect than leading articles	L

Source: Birmingham Library Service, Local Studies and History, L50.7.

Members of debating societies may also have participated in what
Edward Said has termed 'guerilla interference' in the media. Beyond
reading and talking about the press, some debaters actively sought to
manipulate the news agendas of local newspapers. In Sheffield, a socialist
secret society known as the March, formed in 1881, had by 1890 taken
over the Forum debating club by throwing 'chunks of Henry George and
H.M. Hyndman about until the old gang were quite knocked out'. At the
same time, the 40 or so members of the March, mainly teachers, bank
and office clerks and engravers, wrote copiously but in an organised way
to local editors, criticising, 'scaring' and proposing alternatives to the
ways in which news stories were covered. Tragically, their minute book
was burnt at their final meeting *circa* 1891, when, fuelled by paranoia,
they feared imminent arrest.[60] But debating clubs were also subject to
manipulation by journalists themselves, who could also be organised to

---

[60] William Armitage, 'Sheffield Secret Society', Sheffield Newspaper Cuttings, vol. 9, pp.
328–29, item dated 15 Jan. 1921, Sheffield City Library Local Studies and Archives Division.
The account, by an erstwhile member of 'The March', is confused. Armitage attributes the
abrupt termination of the society in *c*.1891 to 'Fenianism . . . the Clerkenwell explosion and
the fatal affray in connection with the prison van in the streets of Manchester', events which
had occurred in 1867. 'The police in all the big towns were put on the *qui vive*. We had done
nothing that we need be ashamed of – but we felt that being known in our minute book only
as numbers we might be compromised if our meetings became known, and the book
discovered. So we decided to retain our sanity, and at our last meeting we popped the minute-
book into the stove and stood around until it was reduced to ashes.'

participate in defence of their occupation. A motion debated at an East Grinstead club in 1895 proposed that newspapers were not 'conducive to the Elevation of Public Morals' on the grounds that crime reports, and space devoted to sensational trials, racing and betting took precedence over 'news of a moral and religious nature'. Commercial newspapers, the proposer argued, 'played down to its advertising clients instead of adopting a tone in advance of the current standard of morality.' The ensuing debate, however, went almost entirely against the opening speaker thanks largely to the presence of 'several local journalists . . . who championed their own cause'.[61]

Amateur parliaments provided another forum where the content of newspapers could both be used as the basis for discussion, and, in turn, evaluated and criticised. These voluntary societies replicated the form of the House of Commons, often in highly elaborate detail. The Newton Heath Parliamentary Debating Society in Lanchasire, for example, established in November 1881, comprised 72 Liberal, 31 Conservative and 10 Independent MPs, and elected its own Speaker and Whips.[62] Amateur parliaments, moreover, by issuing Bills and holding public debates, often overlapped with 'real' politics, locally and nationally, thereby enabling individuals, some of whom were not enfranchised prior to 1884, to engage in a parallel politics which shadowed but was at the same time autonomous of Parliament. This engagement with actual parliamentary politics brought amateur parliamentarians into contact with the press in a particularly direct way. Not only were their own activities extensively covered by local newspapers, but the treatment of party politics, and of party leaders, was a matter of immediate concern. During a debate on the ways in which W.E. Gladstone had been represented in the local press, held during the 1881–82 session of the Sheffield Amateur Parliament, it was noted that

> the Tory Journals (notably the <u>Sheffield Telegraph</u>) have spared no effort to perform the odious task of depreciating the greatest statesman of his age. It is to be said in their favour that they are at all events obeying their true instincts. Mr Gladstone is representative of all that they hate most. . . . To the Tory Journals . . . the world exists for the good of a privileged few, and all the arrangements of political and social life must be adapted to their convenience.[63]

---

[61] *Journalist and Newspaper Proprietor*, 9 Nov. 1895, p. 363.

[62] Minute book, Newton Heath Parliamentary Debating Society, Lancashire RO, Preston, DDX 1014/10.

[63] Minute book, Sheffield Amateur Parliament, 1881–82 session, Sheffield City Library Local Studies and Archives, MS 808.5S. Amateur parliaments also issued their own periodicals, for example *The Bradford Debater. The Weekly Organ of the Bradford Parliamentary Debating Society*, est. 8 Oct. 1881, WYAS Bradford, 81D77/1.

Amateur parliaments formed part of that undergrowth of thought and activity which enriched the largely municipal political culture of Victorian England, and comprised, along with letter writers and participants in reading and debating clubs, 'the new tribes' which *Tait's* had witnessed as early as 1822 'invading and conquering the regions of mental culture' and forming the 'origins of literary democracy' as a direct consequence of 'the uprising of this FOURTH ESTATE'.[64] Their readiness to contest readings of the news, and to question the form adopted by the newspaper as a medium of communication, qualifies to some extent the notion that the late nineteenth-century newspaper readership was, as Frederick Greenwood implied, 'easily impressed and quite uncritical'.[65] They also infer that the emergence of a mass commercial press did not necessarily restrict or close the more open, spontaneous and democratic forms of communication associated with pre-literate, oral popular culture. In certain respects, and the historical record provides access only to very small, if active, minorities, the growth of the newspaper generated rather than silenced oral communication by stimulating creative thought and by introducing new subject-matter for political argument, casual conversation and humour. While newspapers and other popular forms of print had undermined the autonomy of the oral tradition within popular culture, they did not automatically shut down autonomous forms of thinking and behaving. By engaging critically with the medium, nineteenth-century newspaper readers effected a shift in the uses of orality as well as of literacy, and thereby engendered, to borrow Habermas's term, a structural transformation in the public sphere.

The documented responses of the readership, however, constituted but one dimension of the 'great song' of criticism that greeted the coming of the mass newspaper in nineteenth-century England. That 'long argument' effectively redefined the newspaper, which, in the course of the nineteenth century, found for itself a place not only in the market but also in the culture. By the turn of the twentieth century, the daily newspaper stood in a commercially dominant position in relation to other forms of print, such as the journal, the pamphlet or even the book, and the authority exerted over the world media by Fleet Street, its symbolic representation, was unquestioned. The transitory, evasive life of the newspaper as a fugitive literature within English print culture was over. Brash and energetic, the highly profitable and ubiquitous dailies of

---

[64] *Tait's*, July 1833, pp. 491–95.

[65] Frederick Greenwood, 'The Newspaper Press', *Nineteenth Century*, May 1890, p. 840. See also the observations of W.T. Fullerton, 'the newspaper in England is becoming representative of a larger constituency, and it is becoming more democratic and more of a NEWSpaper', *National Review*, June 1893, p. 659.

the early 1900s were integral, though often awkward and controversial, components of daily life, as necessary to the enjoyment of popular leisure as they were to the conduct of high politics. The newspaper's monopoly over the dissemination of news, however, was short-lived, and would soon be challenged by the first of many new, non-print based forms of communication. These new media forms would themselves also be the subjects of moral anxieties and of lengthy processes of cultural negotiation. The 'long argument' about newspapers in the nineteenth century was doomed to be reiterated, often in tediously repetitive form, in our own century with the coming of cinema, radio, television, video, interactive computer software and the Internet. What this study has suggested is that the agenda for addressing the social influences of these media forms in the twentieth century was set in the nineteenth. The lineage that connects William Cobbett and Feargus O'Connor to Frederick Greenwood and W.T. Stead, and hence from Lords Northcliffe and Beaverbrook to Rupert Murdoch and Ted Turner, is a lineage that also connects the threads of a social argument that defined the media's problematic place in our society. The fundamental questions about the modern media were initially asked about newspapers. They were the first forms of 'mass' communication to be subjected to a sustained public investigation into their uses, their reliability, their funding, their legal rights and obligations, the interests they served and the means by which they could be made accountable and to whom. One suspects that this argument was at times not so much a 'great song' as a great song and dance, a means of talking of other things, from the failures of political leaders to the causes of a perceived decline in moral standards. But it could also be argued that not only did this argument take place in public, but that it also helped to shape a public. The many levels at which the argument was conducted, from the parliamentary speeches of the political élite to the contentions of bar-room debaters, from weighty journal articles to angry letters sent off in haste to editors, and from novels to satirical prints, indicate a considerable degree of social participation.

Through the newspaper, readers as well as writers found new ways to communicate. In consequence, it was possible for them to imagine a public, a constituency beyond the individual, the family or the locality, an integrated social whole whose cohesion was underpinned *inter alia* by its access to a common stock of regularly revised knowledge about the world. The newspaper's ability to provide what George Steiner termed the 'alphabet of culture', the shared stories and cultural references which enable social life to occur, made the nineteenth-century concept of the public possible. But by reflecting upon and criticising this process, individual users of newspapers were themselves acting as a public in the interests of a perceived public good. A socially constructed category, the public began to acquire an identity and a penchant for self-reflection in large part through the uses it made of newspapers. No doubt this dual process of situating the newspaper within the culture and, simultaneously, of constructing a public of reader-critics was undertaken in a variety of ways at around the same time in other countries, and comparative studies of the diverging trajectories taken by the 'long argument' in other national newspaper markets would reveal much about the evolution of different cultural and political traditions in Europe and beyond. In England, however, the critical response to the growth of newspapers fed into a discourse of power and social order which, in relation to more recent technologies, continues to influence the terms in which the news media, indeed all media, are regarded.

The transformation of the popular newspaper from a fugitive literature which prowled the margins of social consciousness, to a professional and pervasive form of communication which, in terms of its political acceptability, commercial success and cultural value, was considered to have acquired mainstream status, was substantially effected during the period between the 1820s and the turn of the twentieth century. But if the newspaper by that time was no longer a fugitive, neither was it any longer regarded as a form of literature. Unlike the literary and political journal, the newspaper's industrial mode of production, its socially undifferentiated market and its ephemerality excluded it from the narrowing definition of what constituted English literature. Journalism, understood increasingly as news journalism, acquired its distinctive place in the lexicon precisely in order to make room in the language for a construction which would shortly be broadened to include other products of 'mass communications'. The origins of the distinction between literature and popular culture in the twentieth century may be traced in part to the separation of literature and journalism within late Victorian English literary discourse, a process which was itself a response to the material growth of the cheap newspaper press during the previous half-century. By situating the nineteenth-century newspaper in its own historical and theoretical contexts, it becomes necessary to rethink those later categories and by, so doing, to open up fresh possibilities for the cultural politics of our own time.

Appendix

The Sunday Evening Debating Society, held at the Hope and Anchor Inn, Navigation Street, Birmingham: debates conducted during its first year, 3 January to 26 December 1858

Date	Motion	Yes	No
03/01/58	What should be the future Government of India, a representative principal (*sic*)?	24	7
09/01/58	Are Theatrical and Operatic Performances conducive to the Morals of the People?	Aff. *nem con*	
10/01/58	Will the interest of Great Britain be injured by the marriage of the Princess Royal with the Prince Frederick William of Prussia?	11	11
17/01/58	Are the Americans justified in going to war with the Mormons?	14	6
24/01/58	Should Government Education be given apart from religious teaching?	26	8
31/01/58	Is the Emperor Napolian (*sic*) justified in demanding the expulsion of Political Refugees from this Country?	12	15
07/02/58	Does a knowledge of the inductive sciences conduce to the happiness and welfare of Man? (Supplementary: 'If so – in what ratio should they be taught – and should the State provide the means through the government schools – or should they depend upon individual or co-operative means for support?' Result not recorded)	32	6
07/02/58	Which is the greatest incentive to action Hope or Fear?		
	Hope	9	
	Fear	1	
14/02/58	The Attack upon Mr Leach near Bristol		

in the previous week was a conspiracy
on the part of the Revd Mr Smith and
his Wife to rob and murder the said Mr
Leach. (Education debate adjourned.
Mr Leach was a member of the society)   22   1

07/03/58   What amount of Reform may we
reasonable (*sic*) expect from the
Ministry now in power. The measure
of reform to be expected from Lord
Derby are of that indefinate (*sic*),
treacherous and subtle character to
this nation which does not warrant
the change of the Administration from
Lord Palmerston to the existing one?   11   10

(Won on the chair's casting vote against the view that Derby would
'reform . . . the Indian Government', and at home 'extend the Franchise'
and 'alter the mode of voting')

14/03/58   Which has the greatest power of
elevating the human mind to its
appreciation of a supreme power,
Principles taught by the works of
nature, or by Ideas taught and
framed by religious dogmas?
Nature   21
Religion   4

21/03/58   Which is the greatest precursor of
Civilization the Press or Platform?
Platform   16
Press   14

28/03/58   Is the presence of the Bishops in the
House of Lords conducive to the
interests of the Country and should they
cease to sit there?   12   29*

*(they should not cease to sit there)

04/04/58   Is the ballot desirable under present
circumstances?   21   10

11/04/58   Has the Government of Napoleon
been beneficial to the   7   13
Interests of Europe?

18/04/58   What should the Alies (*sic*) do with
Canton?
Retain as a colony   2
Return it to China to increase trade   15

25/04/58	Government sponsored free emigration being the best means of throwing off the pressure under which the skilled labour of this country is now placed	9	1
02/05/58	Which would be the most Beneficial to this Country, Septenial (*sic*) or Trianial (*sic*) Parliaments?		
	Septenial (*sic*)	7	
	Trienial (*sic*)	15	
09/05/58	Will the result of the Trial of Dr Bernard add to the character of England for its independants (*sic*) or will it lower her in the Opinions of Surrounding nations?		
	Adds to the character	28	
	Lowers the character	1	
16/05/58	Is the present Law of Property Qualification right or wrong?		
	Right	18	
	Wrong	7	
23/05/58	Is Lord Ellenboro (*sic*) justified in the Position he has taken with regard to Lord Cannings Proclamation?	18	12
30/05/58	Which would be the best method of defending the shores of England in case there should be an Invasion?		
	A large standing army	4	
	Arming the people of the south coast	1	
	Increase the size of the navy	10	
06/06/58	How can we enhance the reception of her Majesty on her visit to the Borough of Birmingham so as to give general Satisfaction?		
	Alderman to appear in robes	Carried *nem con*	
	40,000 children on a platform	Carried *nem con*	
	Dinner for 2,000 unemployed, 'the recipients to bring their own knife fork and cup'	14	2
	'Two fine bullocks' bought by the Commitee and labelled 'meat for the poor'	1	14

	Procession of the unemployed led by a band	1	15
13/06/58	What course of Policy should the British Government pursue in the present American Despute (*sic*) as regard the Right of Search? That the Government should maintain the same vigorous and firm Policy that has been adopted since the Year 1836	Carried *nem con*	
20/06/58	Has the action of the present Government been worthy of the appreciation of the people?	5	6
27/06/58	Which would be the best Method of supporting the Established Church?		
	Reduce incomes of Bishops	11	
	Disestablishment	7	
04/07/58	Would a Repeal of the Paper Duty be politic and more advantageous to the promotion of education?	17	1
11/07/58	Has England received any substantial Benefit from the result of the Paris Conference?	14	7
18/07/58	That the present condition or state of British rule in India is more precarious than before the outbreak in Oude, and that the tardy manner in which the present Government are legislating to meet the difficulty adds doubt as to the ultimate success of the measure devised for suppressing the mutiny and giving a speedy restoration of the mercantile interests of the two countries?	17	12
25/07/58	Debate adjourned		
31/07/58	Is it judicious for her majesty to go to Cherbourg on the present occasion?	20	4
05/08/58	Are the teachings and practices of the High Church party in this country in accordance with the doctrines of the New Testament and the Book of Common Prayer or conducive to the Interests of the Established Church?	2	22
15/08/58	Does the Mind of Man eminate (*sic*)		

	from the Brain or from a higher Source?		
	Higher source	26	
	Brain	10	
29/08/58	Has the employment of a British Squadron on the coast of Africa for suppressing the slave trade attended with such beneficial results as would justify the Government sanctioning further operations?	22	2
19/09/58	Was Cromwell a Patriot and did the Removal of Charles the 1st conduce to the spread of civil and Religious Liberty?	35	3
26/09/58	Does the present state of Society indicate that Education and Morals have kept pace with each other?	26	8
03/10/58	Is Capital Punishment necessary?	17	16
10/10/58	Which of the two Sciences Astrology or Astronomy has the greatest influence on the minds of the People of Great Britain?		
	Astronomy	27	
	Astrology	5	
17/10/58	What kind of Reform Bill will be most suitable to introduce in the next Session of Parliament ? That a Reform will be satisfactory to the nation that provides for the distribution of the Electoral (*sic*) franchise and an appointment of Representation according to the population of the Boroughs and Counties ?	18	2
24/10/58	Have the British colonies been worth the acquisition of them and has their relationship to the Parent country been beneficial alike to both ?	27	3
31/10/58	That it is the opinion of this meeting that means should be provided for the Elementary and Industrial Education of the People. But that compulsory Education would be arbitary, unconstitutional and unEnglish and		

	would interfere with liberty of the subject and as such cannot be supported	28	17
07/11/58	Is centralization compatible with the forms and principals (*sic*) of popular and liberal Government?	8	16
14/11/58	The State Church of England at the present time is incompatible with the religious and moral wants and requirements of the age ?	23	3
21/11/58	Which of the three conditions Rich Poor or Middle conduce most to the Virtue and well being of Society?		
	Rich	0	
	Poor	18	
	Middle	8	
28/11/58	What is Political Economy?		
	Study of production, distribution and consumption	17	
	Full remuneration to labour and capital	14	
	Reduction of National Debt	2	
05/12/58	Which of the two, the Laity or the Clergy have contributed most to the Literature and Science of this Country?		
	The Laity	Carried *nem con*	
12/12/58	That the present mode of Education of the Female portion of the Children in Government and other schools is not conducive to their further welfare and well being in Society?	Carried *nem con*	
19/12/58	Is the present Policy of the French Government in enforcing the laying up of a three months supply of wheat calculated to meet the requirements of the People or add to the Mercantile Stability of the Empire ?	No *nem con*	
26/12/58	Affirm that the discontinuance of Transportation of convicts to the British colonies is Politic and		

that the Penitentiary
system at home has proved of
advantage to the reform of the
criminal and to the security and
well being of the country?   Carried *nem con*

Source: Archives Department, Birmingham Library Service, MS 103138
(2 vols) 3 January 1858 to 24 January 1886.

Selected Bibliography

Archival sources
(With abbreviations used in the footnotes)

Archives of the British Conservative Party (ABCP), Harvester Microfilm

Birmingham Library Service, Local Studies and History Dept.
Birmingham and Edgbaston Debating Society
Birmingham Ladies Debating Society
Sunday Evening Debating Society, Hope and Anchor Inn

Birmingham University Library (BUL)
Harriet Martineau Papers, Heslop Room
Joseph Chamberlain Papers, Heslop Room

Bristol Record Office
Bristol Philosophical Society
Bristol Typographical Society
Bristol Institution for the Advancement of Science, Literature
   and the Arts
'Diary of a journalist'
Newsmen's Verses

British Museum Add. MSS
Gladstone Coll.
MS 40486 f. 130   MS 44458 ff. 128
MS 44574 f. 107   MS 47230 ff. 43–46
MS 44458 ff.42

Brotherton Library, University of Leeds
Sala Coll., Special Collections

Church of England Record Centre, London
Church Defence Institution

Colne Library, Colne, Lancashire
Colne Literary and Scientific Society

Harris Library, Preston
Literary and Philosophic Society of Preston, Dr Shepherd Coll.

Institute of Alcohol Studies, London
Executive Council of the United Kingdom Alliance

John Rylands University Library, Manchester
C.P. Scott Coll.

Lancashire Record Office, Preston
Amalgamated Trades Council
Burnley Typographical Association
Great George St Literary and Debating Society, Liverpool
Haslingden Mechanics' Institution
Nelson and District Trades Council
Newton Heath Parliamentary Debating Society

Leeds Archive Service
Baines Coll.

Liverpool Record Office, Liverpool City Libraries
Liverpool Chatham Society
Liverpool Literary and Philosophical Society

Manchester City Archives, Manchester City Library (MCA)
Diary of Edwin Waugh
George Wilson Papers
Manchester Literary Society
Odds and Ends ... a Manuscript Magazine
Preston Debating Society
Reeves Papers
St Paul's Mutual Improvement Society

Sheffield Archives, Sheffield Libraries and Information Services
Leader Papers

Sheffield City Library, Local Studies and Archives
General Meetings of the Sheffield Literary and Philosophical Society
Sheffield Amateur Parliament

Sheffield University Library
A.J. Mundella Papers, Special Collections

Tyne and Wear Archive Service, Newcastle upon Tyne (TWAS)
Joseph Cowen Papers
Literary and Philosophical Society, Newcastle upon Tyne

University College, London (UCL)
Society for the Diffusion of Useful Knowledge Coll.

West Yorkshire Archive Service, Bradford (WYAS)
Bradford Conservative Association
Bradford Literary Club
Bradford Mechanics' Institute

Newspapers and periodicals

Alliance. A weekly journal of moral and social reform
Birmingham Mirror
Blue Budget
British Almanac
British Lion
British Temperance Advocate and Journal
Compositors' Chronicle
Conservative Magazine
England
Fleet Street Gazette
Illustrated Weekly Newspaper
John Bull
Journal of the Working Classes
Journalist and Newspaper Proprietor
Meliora
Monthly Censor or, General Review of Domestic and Foreign Literature
Moral Reformer
Mutual
Newspaper Press. The Press Organ: A Medium of Intercommunication Between All Parties Associated with Newspapers and a Record of Journalistic Lore
Pall Mall Gazette
Penny Magazine
Penny Protestant Operative
People's Phrenological Journal and the Compendium of Mental and

Moral Science
Press
Printer. A Quarterly Journal Devoted to the Interests of Printers and Printing
Printing Machine. A Review for the Many
Punch
Rambler
Reynolds's Newspaper
Saturday Review
The Times
Typographical Gazette
Weekly Dispatch
(All other periodicals consulted are listed separately by author under 'Articles' below)

Official Publications

Hansard's Parliamentary Debates

Printed sources

Books and pamphlets (All published in London, unless otherwise stated)

Altick, R.D., *The English Common Reader* (Chicago, 1957)

Amphlett, James, *The newspaper press, in part of the last century, and up to the present period of 1860* (1860)

Anderson, Patricia, *The Printed Image and the Transformation of Popular Culture 1790–1860* (Oxford, 1991)

Andrews, Alexander, *The History of British Journalism, from the foundation of the newspaper press in England, to the Repeal of the Stamp Act in 1855 with sketches of Press Celebrities* (1859)

Arnot, Sandford, *A Sketch of the History of the Indian Press during the last Ten Years, with a disclosure of the true causes of its present degredation ... with a biographical notice of the Indian Cobbett, alias 'Peter the Hermit'* (1829)

Aspinall, A., *Politics and the Press, c. 1780–1850* (1949)

Bain, Alexander, *On the Study of Character, including An Estimate of Phrenology* (1861)

———, *Mental and Moral Science: A Compendium of Psychology and Ethics* (1868)

Baines, Edward, *The Life of Edward Baines, late M.P. for the Borough of Leeds* (1851)

Ballaster, Ros, Beetham, Margaret, Frazer, Elizabeth and Hebron, Sandra, *Women's Worlds: Ideology, Femininity and the Woman's Magazine* (1991)

Banks, Elizabeth L., *The Autobiography of a 'Newspaper Girl'* (1902)

Black, Jeremy, *The English Press in the Eighteenth Century* (1987)

Blanc, Louis, *Letters on England*, vol. i, (1866)

Bourne, Henry Richard Fox, *English Newspapers: Chapters in the History of Journalism* (1887)

Boyce, G., Curran, J., and Wingate, P. (eds), *Newspaper History from the Seventeenth Century to the Present Day* (1978)

Brake, Laurel, *Subjugated Knowledges: Journalism, Gender and Literature in the Nineteenth Century* (1994)

Brown, Lucy, *Victorian News and Newspapers* (Oxford, 1985)

Campbell, Theophila Carlile, *The Battle of the Press, As Told in the Story of the Life of Richard Carlile* (1899)

Chartier, Roger, *The Culture of Print: Power and the Uses of Print in Early Modern Europe*, trans. Lydia G. Cochrane (Princeton, New Jersey, 1989)

Christian N. (ed.), *The Sociology of Journalism and the Press* (1980)

Collet, C.D, *History of the Taxes on Knowledge: Their origin and repeal* (1896)

Cooper, Charles A., *An Editor's Retrospect. Fifty Years of Newspaper Work* (1896)

Crawfurd, John, *The Taxes on Knowledge* (1836)

Croal, David, *Early Recollections of a Journalist, 1832–1859* (Edinburgh, 1898)

Curran J., Gurevitch, M. and Woollacott, J., *Mass Communication and Society* (1977)

Dahlgren, Peter and Sparks, Colin, *Communication and Citizenship: Journalism and the Public Sphere* (1993)

Davies, E.P., *The Reporter's Handbook* (1884)

Dawson, J., *Practical Journalism, how to enter thereon and succeed: A manual for beginners and amateurs* (1885)

Diblee, G.B., *The Newspaper* (1913)

Disraeli, Benjamin, *Coningsby* (1844)

——, *Sybil, or The Two Nations* (1845, 1950 edn)

'Distinguished Writer, A', *The Press and the Public Service* (1857)

Eliot, George, *Middlemarch* (1872, Harmondsworth 1994 edn)

Elliott, G., *Newspaper Libel and Registration Act, 1881* (1884)

Ellegard, A., *The Readership of the Periodical Press in Mid-Victorian England* (Göteborg, 1957)

Erskine May, Sir Thomas, *The Constitutional History of England since the accession of George the Third* (1861, 1912 edn)

Escott, T.H.S., *Masters of English Journalism* (1911)

Flint, Kate, *The Woman Reader 1837–1914* (Oxford, 1993)

Frankin, Bob and Murphy, David, *What News? The Market, Politics and the Local Press* (1991)

Fraser, W. Hamish, *The Coming of the Mass Market, 1850–1914* (1981)

Gagnier, Regenia, *Subjectivities: A History of Self-Representation in Britain, 1832–1920* (New York and Oxford, 1991)

Gissing, George, *In the Year of Jubilee* (1894, 1976 edn)

Grant, James, *The newspaper press: its origin – progress – and present position* (1871)

Gratton, Charles J., *The Gallery: a sketch of the history of parliamentary reporting and reporters* (1860)

Habermas, Jürgen, *Communication and the Evolution of Society*, trans. T. McCarthy (1979)

———, *The Structural Transformation of the Public Sphere*, trans. Thomas Burger (Cambridge, Mass., 1989)

Harrison, Brian, *Drink and the Victorians: The Temperance Question in England 1815–1872* (1971)

Harris, M. and Lee, A.J. (eds), *The Press in English Society from the Seventeenth to Nineteenth Centuries* (1986)

Haslam, James, *The Press and the People: An Estimate of Reading in Working Class Districts* (1906)

Hatton, Joseph, *Journalistic London: being a series of sketches of the famous pens and papers of the day* (1882)

Hildreth, Richard, *My Connection with the Atlas Newspaper: including a sketch of the history of the Amory Hall Party of 1838, etc.* (1839)

Hollis, Pat, *The Pauper Press: A Study in Working-Class Radicalism in the 1830s* (1970)

Houghton, T.S., *The Printers' Practical Every-Day-Book* (1841)

Hunt, Frederick Knight, *The Fourth Estate: contributions towards a history of newspapers, and the liberty of the press* (1850)

Hunt, William, *Then and Now, or Fifty Years of Newspaper Work* (Hull, 1887)

Hunt, Lynne, *The New Cultural History* (University of California, Berkley, 1989)

Institute of Journalists, *The Grey Book* (1898–)

Jackson, Mason, *The pictorial press: its origin and progress* (1885)

Jennings, Louis J. (ed.), *The Croker Papers: The Correspondence and Diaries of the Rt. Hon. John Wilson Croker*, vol. 2 (1884)

Joyce, Patrick, *Visions of the People: Industrial England and the Question of Class, 1840–1914* (Cambridge, 1991)

Knight, Charles, *Passages of a Working Life During Half a Century, with a Prelude of Early Reminiscences* (1864, 1865, Dublin 1971 edn)

Knightley, Phillip, *The First Casualty: the war correspondent as hero, propagandist, and myth maker from the Crimea to Vietnam* (1975)

Koss, S., *The Rise and Fall of the Political Press in Britain*, vol. i, The Nineteenth Century (University of North Carolina, Chapel Hill, 1981)

Leader, J.D., *Seventy-three Years of Progress: A History of the Sheffield Independent from 1819 to 1892* (Sheffield, 1892)

Lecky, William Edward Hartpole, *History of European Morals from Augustus to Charlemagne* (1869)

Lee, A.J., *The Origins of the Popular Press in England, 1855–1914* (1976)

Lemert, James B., *Does Mass Communication Change Public Opinion After All? A New Approach to Effects Analysis* (Chicago, 1981)

Lucy, Sir Henry, *The Diary of a Journalist* (1920)

Macdonagh, Michael, *The Reporter's Gallery* (1913)

Mackie, John B., *Modern Journalism: A handbook of instruction and counsel for the young journalist* (1894)

Mackintosh, Charles A., *Popular outlines of the press, ancient and modern ... with a notice of the newspaper press* (1859)

Meredith, George, *Beauchamp's Career* (1874, 1922 edn)

Marsden, G. (ed.), *Victorian Values: Personalities and Perspectives* (1990)

Mayne, F., *The Perilous Nature of the Penny Periodical Press* (1851, printed for private circulation)

Mitchell, Sally, *The Fallen Angel: Chastity, Class and Women's Reading, 1835–1880* (Bowling Green, Ohio, 1981)

Moran, James, *Printing Presses: History and Development From the Fifteenth Century to Modern Times* (1973)

National Political Union, *Taxes on Knowledge* (Southwark, 1832)

Nicholl, W. Robertson, *James Macdonnell, Journalist* (1890)

Oppenheim, Janet, *The Other World: Spiritualism and Psychical Research in England, 1850–1914* (Cambridge, 1985)

Pebody, Charles, *English Journalism and the men who have made it* (1882)

Perkin, Harold, *The Rise of Professional Society: England since 1880* (1989)

Phillips, Ernest, *How to Become a Journalist: A practical guide to newspaper work* (1895)

Reynolds, John Hamilton, *The Press, or Literary Chit-chat: A Satire* (1822)

Routledge, James, *Chapters on the History of Popular Progress, chiefly in relation to The Freedom of the Press and Trial by Jury 1660–1820, with an application to later years* (1876)

Saunders, Otley and Co., *The Newspaper Press Census for 1860 Showing the Newspaper population of the United Kingdom, and its Expansion since 1665, Including the Births and Deaths in 1860, Together with a Statistical and General Account of Its Present Politics and Position* (1860) (Also published by Arthur Hall and Co. in 1861)

Scott-James, R.A., *The Influence of the Press* (1913)

Searle, G.R., *Entrepreneurial Politics in mid-Victorian Britain* (Oxford, 1993)

Shattock, Joanne, *Politics and Reviewers: The Edinburgh and the Quarterly in the early Victorian age* (Leicester, 1989)

Shepherdson, William, *Starting a 'Daily' in the Provinces* (1876)

Stanhope, Leicester, *Sketch of the History and Influence of the Press in British India* (1823)

Stead, Estelle W., *My Father: Personal and Spiritual Reminiscences* (1913)

Stead, W.T., *A Journalist on Journalism*, ed. Edwin H. Stout (1892)

———, *Letters from Julia, or Light from the Borderland, Received by Automatic Writing from One Who Has Gone Before* (1897)

Taylor, Frank, *The Newspaper Press as a Power both in the Expression and Formation of Public Opinion: The Chancellor's Essay, 1898* (Oxford, 1898)

Timperley, C.H., *Songs of the Press and other poems relative to the art of printers and printing; also of authors, books, booksellers, bookbinders, editors, critics, newspapers etc.* (1845)

———, *A Dictionary of Printers and Printing, with the Progress of Literature, ancient and modern* (1839)

Thackeray, W.M., *The History of Pendennis* (1850, 1959 edn.)

Trollope, Anthony, *Phineas Finn: The Irish Member* (1869, 1944 edn)

———, *The Warden* (1855, 1859 edn)

———, *Phineas Redux* (1874, 1983 edn)

Vann, J.D. and VanArsdel, R.T. (eds), *Victorian Periodicals: A Guide to Research*, vols 1 (New York, 1978) and 2 (New York, 1989)

———, *Victorian Periodicals and Victorian Society* (Aldershot, 1994)

Vernon, James, *Politics and the People, a study in English political culture, c. 1815–1867* (Cambridge, 1993)

Vincent, David, *Literacy and Popular Culture: England 1750–1914* (Cambridge, 1989)

Wallace, Thomas, *Observations on the Discourse of Natural Theology by Henry Lord Brougham* (1835)

Walkowitz, Judith R., *City of Dreadful Delight: Narratives of Sexual Danger in Late-Victorian Britain* (1992)

Watts, W.H., *My Private Note-Book; or, recollections of an old reporter* (1862)

Webb, R.K., *The British Working Class Reader, 1790–1848* (1955)

Whyte, F., *The Life of W.T. Stead* (1925)

Wiener, J.H., *The War of the Unstamped; a History of the Movement to Repeal the British Newspaper Tax, 1830–1836* (Ithaca, New York, 1969)

——— (ed.), *Innovators and Preachers: The role of the editor in Victorian England* (Westport, CT, 1985)

——— (ed.), *Papers for the Millions: The New Journalism in Britain, 1850s to 1914* (Westport, CT, 1988)

Williams, Raymond, *The Long Revolution* (1961)

———, *Communications* (1968)

Articles

Alison, Sir Archibald, 'The Influence of the Press', *Blackwood's Edinburgh Magazine*, Sept. 1834

Bacon, Richard M., 'Journals of the provinces', *New Monthly Magazine*, Oct. 1836

Baylen, J.O., 'The Press and Public Opinion, W.T. Stead and the "New Journalism" ', *Journalism Studies Review*, 4, July 1979

Bennett, Scott, 'Revolutions in Thought: Serial Publications and the Mass Market for Reading', in Shattock, Joanne and Wolff, Michael (eds), *The Victorian Periodical Press: Samplings and Soundings* (Leicester and Toronto, 1982)

Bourne, H.R. Fox, 'London Newspapers', in *Progress of British Newspapers in the Nineteenth Century, Illustrated* (1901)

Brown, Lucy, 'The treatment of news in mid-Victorian newspapers', *Transactions of the Royal Historical Society*, 5th series, 27, 1977

———, 'The Growth of a National Press', in Brake, Laurel, Jones, Aled and Madden, Lionel (eds), *Investigating Victorian Journalism* (1990)

Colomb, P.H., 'The Patriotic Editor in War', *National Review*, Apr. 1897

Coulson, Walter (?), 'Newspapers', *Westminster Review*, July 1824

Cust, Henry, 'Tory press and Tory party', *National Review*, May 1893

Darling, J.J., 'The Liberal newspapers: effects of the reduction of Stamp Duty', *Tait's Edinburgh Magazine*, Nov. 1836

Elton, Charles Isaac, 'Early English newspapers', *Cornhill Magazine*, July 1868

Fox, W.J., 'On the duties of the press towards the people', *Lectures addressed chiefly to the Working Classes*, vol. iv (1846)

Fullerton, W.M., 'The significance of the newspaper in the United States', *New Review*, June 1893

Gilzean-Reid, Sir Hugh and Macdonell, P.J., 'The Press', in Samuelson, John (ed.), *The Civilisation of our Day: A series of original essays on some of its more important phases at the close of the nineteenth century, by expert writers* (1896)

Gleig, George Robert, 'The Government and the Press', *Blackwood's Edinburgh Magazine*, Dec. 1867

Gorham, Deborah, ' "The Maiden Tribute of Modern Babylon" Re-Visited', *Victorian Studies*, Spring 1976

Greenwood, Frederick, 'The Newspaper Press', *Nineteenth Century*, May 1890

———, 'The Press and Government', *Nineteenth Century*, July 1890

———, 'The Newspaper Press: Half a Century's Survey', *Blackwood's Edinburgh Journal*, May 1897

———, 'Forty Years of Journalism', *The English Illustrated Magazine*, vol. xvii, July 1897

Greenwood, James, 'Penny Awfuls', *St Paul's Magazine*, Feb. 1873

Greg, William Rathbone, 'The Newspaper Press', *Edinburgh Review*, Oct. 1855

Hall, S. Carter, 'The Penny Press', *New Monthly Magazine*, Feb. 1834

Hannay, James, 'Literature and Society', *Westminster Review*, Apr. 1857

Hope, A.J.B. Beresford, 'Newspapers and their Writers', *Cambridge Essays* (1858)

Humphery, George R., 'The Reading of the Working Classes', *Nineteenth Century*, Apr. 1893

Jerrold, William Blanchard, 'The Manufacture of Public Opinion', *Nineteenth Century*, June 1883

Johns, Bennett George, 'Literature of the streets', *Edinburgh Review*, Jan. 1887

Johnstone, Christian, 'Cheap Periodicals', *Tait's Edinburgh Magazine*, Sept. 1832

Katz, Elihu, 'Mass Communications Research and the Study of Popular Culture', *Studies in Public Communication*, vol. 2, 1959

Mackay, Charles, 'Periodical Literature of the North American Indians', *Bentley's Quarterly Review*, June 1837

March-Phillips, Evelyn, 'Women's Newspapers', *Fortnightly Review*, new ser., vol. 56, 1894

Massingham, H.W., 'The ethics of editing', *National Review*, Apr. 1900

Merle, Gibbons, 'The Provincial Newspaper Press', *Westminster Review*, Jan. 1830

———, 'Journalism', *Westminster Review,* Jan. 1833

Merriman, Josiah J., 'The English Newspaper', *The Popular Lecturer*, vol. ii, new series, 1857

Mitchell, Sally, 'The Forgotten Woman of the Period: Penny Weekly Family Magazines of the 1840s and 1850s', in Vicinus, Martha (ed.). *A Widening Sphere: Changing Roles of Victorian Women* (1977)

O'Connor, T.P., 'The New Journalism', *New Review*, Oct. 1889

'Popular Literature – the Periodical Press', *Blackwood's Edinburgh Journal*, Jan. 1859

Reid, T. Wemyss, 'Public Opinion and its Leaders', *Fortnightly Review*, Aug. 1880

Sala, George Augustus, 'The Press: what I have known of it – 1840–1890', in *Progress of British Newspapers in the Nineteenth Century, Illustrated* (1901)

Shadwell, A., 'Proprietors and Editors', *National Review*, June 1900

Stead, W.T., 'Government by Journalism', *Contemporary Review*, xlix, 1886

Stephen, Sir James Fitzjames, 'Journalism', *Cornhill Magazine*, July 1869

Stephen, Leslie, 'Anonymous Journalism', *St Paul's Magazine*, 63, May 1868

Stevenson, William, 'On the Reciprocal Influence of Periodical Publications', *Blackwood's Edinburgh Journal*, Nov. 1824

Strahan, Alexander, 'Our Very Cheap Literature', *Contemporary Review*, June 1870

Taylor, Whately Cooke, 'Educational Results of Cheap Fiction', *National Association for the Promotion of Social Science, Sessional Proceedings, 1867–68* (1868)

Traill, H.D., 'What is Public Opinion?', *National Review*, July 1885

Waters, Cyril Aubrey, 'Steadism in politics – a great danger', *Westminster Review*, June 1892

Wright, Thomas, 'On a Possible Popular Culture', *Contemporary Review*, July 1881

Unpublished theses

Berridge, Virginia S., 'Popular Journalism and Working-Class Attitudes 1854–1886: A Study of *Reynolds's Newspaper*, *Lloyd's Weekly Newspaper* and the *Weekly Times*', Ph.D. thesis, London University, 1976

McWilliam, Rohan Allan, 'The Tichborne Claimant and the People: Investigations into Popular Culture 1867–1886', Ph.D., University of Sussex, 1990

Vernon, James, 'Politics and the People: A Study in English Political Culture and Communication 1808–68', Ph.D. thesis, University of Manchester, 1991

Works of reference

Deacon, Samuel, *Deacon's Newspaper Handbook and Advertiser's*

Guide (1881–)

Griffiths, D. (ed.), *The Encyclopedia of the British Press* (1992)

Houghton, W.E. (ed.), *The Wellesley Index to Victorian Periodicals 1824– 1900*, v vols (Toronto, 1966–)

Linton, D. and Boston, R. (eds), *The Newspaper Press in Britain: An annotated bibliography* (1987)

May, Frederick, *May's London Press Directory and Advertiser's Handbook* (1871–)

Mitchell, Charles, *The Newspaper Press Directory* (1846–)

Poole, William F. (ed.), *Index to Periodical Literature* (Boston, Mass., 1882)

Sell, Henry, *Sell's Directory of the World's Press ('The Fourth Estate'), including a Register of British Periodical Literature, and the 'Philosophy of Advertising'* (1883–)

Index